"As schools continue to recognize the need for financial education, Kobliner delivers a master class for the most important teachers of all—parents. No question: *Make Your Kid a Money Genius* is required reading for families from every background."

—Arne Duncan, former U.S. Secretary of Education

"Many of us don't have a clue about money management and, therefore, chances are good that our kids won't either. Beth Kobliner throws a lifeline into that abyss with her frank, factual, and funny how-to manual. A must-have whether your kid is in preschool or grad school."

—Julie Lythcott-Haims, author of the *New York Times*
bestseller *How to Raise an Adult*

"How should parents handle allowance? Should your child work while in school? Are credit cards a good idea in college? Kobliner helps us think through these small, yet important, questions that lead to a life of financial literacy for both parent and child."

—Susan Fuhrman, president of Teachers College, Columbia University

"Beth Kobliner understands that children should begin to learn money skills early, and gain new ones as they grow. This guide is designed to help parents put their kids on sound financial footing by untangling a difficult but critically important topic."

—John W. Rogers, Jr., chairman and CEO, Ariel Investments,
and chair, President's Advisory Council on Financial
Capability for Young Americans

"With a keen sense of what is appropriate at each age, from allowance to math games to giving children independence, Kobliner introduces parents to money talk as part of daily interactions."

—Tovah P. Klein, director of the Center for Toddler Development
at Barnard College and author of *How Toddlers Thrive*

Also by Beth Kobliner

*Get a Financial Life: Personal Finance
in Your Twenties and Thirties*

MAKE YOUR KID A MONEY GENIUS

(even if you're not)

A PARENTS' GUIDE FOR KIDS 3 TO 23

BETH KOBLINER

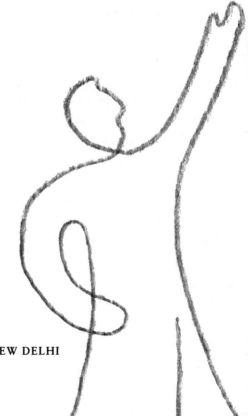

Simon & Schuster

NEW YORK   LONDON   TORONTO   SYDNEY   NEW DELHI

Simon & Schuster
1230 Avenue of the Americas
New York, NY 10020

This publication contains the opinions and the ideas of the author. It is sold with the understanding that neither the author nor the publisher is engaged in rendering legal, tax, investment, insurance, financial, accounting, or other professional advice or services. If the reader requires such advice or services, a competent professional should be consulted. Relevant laws vary from state to state. The strategies outlined in this book might not be suitable for every individual and are not guaranteed or warranted to produce any particular results.

No warranty is made with respect to the accuracy or completeness of the information contained herein, and both the author and publisher specifically disclaim any responsibility for any liability, loss, or risk, personal or otherwise, incurred as a consequence, directly or indirectly, of the use and application of any of the contents of this book.

First Simon & Schuster hardcover edition February 2017

SIMON & SCHUSTER and colophon are registered trademarks of Simon & Schuster, Inc.

For information about special discounts for bulk purchases,
please contact Simon & Schuster Special Sales at 1-866-506-1949
or business@simonandschuster.com.

The Simon & Schuster Speakers Bureau can bring authors to your
live event. For more information or to book an event, contact the
Simon & Schuster Speakers Bureau at 1-866-248-3049
or visit our website at www.simonspeakers.com.

Cover and interior design by Pentagram

Line drawings by Felix Sockwell

Manufactured in the United States of America

10   9   8

Library of Congress Cataloging-in-Publication Data is available.

ISBN 978-1-4767-6681-2
ISBN 978-1-4767-6682-9 (ebook)

To my parents, Shirley and Harold Kobliner,
who instilled money values in my brothers
and me when we were kids in Bayside, Queens,
once upon a time.

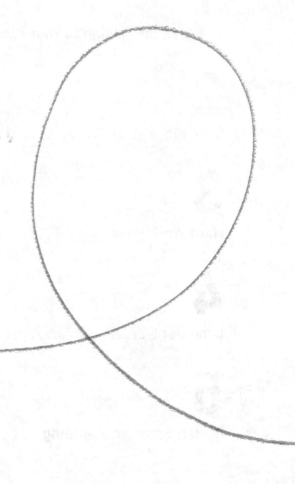

Contents

MAKE YOUR KID A MONEY GENIUS

(even if you're not)

Introduction

My friend Karen, now in her forties, loves to tell the story of the time she asked her mom where babies come from. Her usually chatty mother got up from her chair, muttered something about a pot roast in crisis, and hightailed it out of the room. The next day, Karen found a book about the birds and the bees on her pillow. Her mother never mentioned the subject again.

What cracks me up about this story is that today Karen, a mother of three, wouldn't dream of letting "the talk" play out like that.

She, like most other parents I know, is comfortable telling it like it is to her kids, and feels it's her job to do so. Whether discussing sex, the dangers of drugs and alcohol, the necessity of seat belts, or the benefits of whole grains, we make sure we've got our facts straight, and we choose our words carefully. Unlike *our* parents, we try to confront these squirm-inducing questions head-on, and pride ourselves on being honest and forthcoming.

Except when it comes to money.

When our kids raise the subject, most of us go into panic mode: We lie. ("Sorry, honey, I can't buy that for you because I didn't bring my wallet.") We worry. ("How will my kid be able to pay off his student loans?") We procrastinate. ("We're *totally* coming up with a consistent system for allowance! Next month.") In short, we avoid teaching our kids the financial facts of life—whether it's the ins and outs of budgeting, how to cope with credit and debt, or the basics of saving and investing. And for parents, it's only getting more difficult. Anyone who's ever watched a toddler navigate an iPad knows that our kids interact with the world in an entirely different way than we did. Can you remember the last time your child actually went into a bank? Exactly.

Having spent most of my adult life writing about personal finance, I have theories about why we're so mum about money. Most parents feel they don't know enough themselves. The mere mention of the topic causes anxiety, if not outright terror, in many of us because, well, what if we answer wrong and send our kids careening into a life of debt? Some parents are mortified by how badly they've handled their own financial lives and are afraid to let their kids see what a hot mess they are when it comes to money. Even parents who are in decent financial shape find it tricky to talk about money—if they talk about it at all.

And that's a problem, since research shows that parents are the number one influence on our children's financial behavior. So having these conversations before our children start school is important. A report out of England's University of Cambridge concluded that by age seven, many of the habits that will help kids manage their money are already set.

Over the last three decades, I've done a lot of talking about kids and money—and even more listening. I've visited Sesame Street to teach Elmo about saving, and I've spent time on Wall Street, where I've picked the brains of some of the top experts in the field. I've advised President Barack Obama as a member of the President's Advisory Council on Financial Capability for Young Americans and headed up an initiative, Money as You Grow, to teach parents what their kids need to know about money at every age. Along the way, I've pored over reports and studies in the fields of behavioral economics, social psychology, and, of course, finance to keep up with a subject that grows more complicated every day.

At the same time, I've spoken with or heard from dozens of families—both parents and kids—and their stories are woven throughout this book. Some were already friends, and others were people I came to know while researching. (In most cases, the names and identifying details have been changed to protect the innocent—and sometimes the guilty.) The insights I've received from these families about how they interact with money have been as valuable as any academic study.

The result is this book. In it, I lay out the lessons you need to teach your kid, whether that child is 3 or 23. I've broken the chapters into six age groups: Preschool, Elementary School, Middle School, High School, College, and Young Adulthood. Along with financial basics, you'll get the inside scoop on a range of money-related topics. You'll learn why allowance isn't the Holy Grail when teaching your kid to handle money, and why after-school jobs aren't always the answer, either. You'll learn why giving in to your preschooler's demands at the checkout line could make him more likely to misuse credit cards as an adult. You'll find out why opening a brokerage account to teach your teen about the stock market is a straight-up bad idea. You'll discover the right age to give your kid a credit card, and see why doling out a wad of cash can actually be a good parenting move. I'll show you concrete steps to take to help your kid develop a strong work ethic and save more of what she earns. And you'll get a jargon-free guide to talking about paying for college, and learn why you have to start these talks no later than ninth grade.

Because here's the thing: The stakes have never been higher. The country's increasingly "you're on your own" approach to managing our personal finances—everything from health care coverage to planning for retirement—makes giving your kid money skills now more important than ever before. More concerning is that parents are no longer optimistic about the next generation's chances. The expectation that our children will be better off than we are has long been a cornerstone of the American dream, yet the majority of parents now tell pollsters the opposite: They don't believe their kids will do better. Instilling good financial practices now can mean the difference between a life of economic stability and one fraught with financial worry.

Okay, you're thinking, you can give me smart advice, Beth. I get it. But make my kid a money genius? C'mon.

Yes, reader! I do mean genius. Let me explain.

One of the best-kept secrets in the world of personal finance is that there are really only a few concepts that matter. The smartest, most financially successful people understand this. The problem is that there are entire industries devoted to getting the average Joe and Joanna (and their kids) to ignore them. Whether they're marketers who persuade kids that they "need" the latest sneakers or video game, or companies dangling credit card offers in front of cash-poor college students, these hucksters distract us from the commonsense rules that help us keep more of our money. Remember: They're all about lining *their* wallets, not yours.

But there is good news.

See, you don't need to *be* a money genius to make your kid a money genius. Regardless of your comfort level with finance—or your family's income—this book is your guide for passing along enduring financial principles. It's a playbook of tips and, yes, even some tricks that will stay with your kids for life, making them wise beyond their years—and peers—when it comes to money.

One thing this book is not: something that you can leave on your kids' beds, hoping that they read it and absorb the lessons on their own. It's a conversation starter, but it's up to you to actually start the conversation. What are you waiting for?

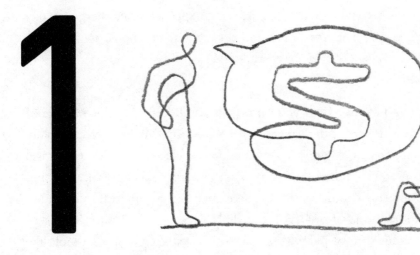

14 Rules for Talking to Your Kids About Money

The fact that you're reading this means you know you should talk money with your kid. Whether the subject terrifies you or intrigues you, or you're simply looking for ways to broach the topic, the good news is that you're plunging in. Go, you!

A few quick words about this chapter. Though its title might make it sound like I'm expecting you to be a financial drill sergeant (*"Now drop and give me twenty compound-interest calculations!"*), I'm not. This chapter is the gentle one, meant to ease you into some overall concepts—and context—that'll help you engage with your child about money. Some points will apply, others might not, depending on your kid's age, interest level, and even gender. So don't think that you need to commit everything to memory or take furious notes. The idea here is to put down your highlighter and just read.

One final thought before we begin: Money conversations don't happen in a vacuum. Instead, they pop up at various times throughout the messy business of living. Though it's become a cliché, most learning happens during these everyday "teachable moments." The tips below and throughout this book are meant to help you take advantage of these opportunities.

So here we go.

1 **Start even earlier than you think you should.** By the ripe old age of three, researchers at the University of Wisconsin–Madison report, many children are able to grasp economic ideas such as value and exchange, albeit in a very rudimentary way. They can also delay gratification and make choices. Though basic, all these concepts are important in understanding the role of money in our daily lives. Although there's no economic equivalent of Baby Mozart videos, no stuffed dolls that look like Warren Buffett to tell your kid to "buy low and sell high" when you squeeze them, that doesn't mean you shouldn't pay attention to this stuff when your child is small.

Your toddler is eager, and able, to understand a lot. When you notice your little one "swiping" a pretend credit card, asking to push the buttons at the ATM, or looking through your wallet, instead of chuckling indulgently in a "kids say the darndest things" way, start teaching him some of the basic lessons in this book about where money comes from and how to pay for things. Even if your preschooler doesn't absorb it all, he will still notice that you're talking to him about something that matters— something grown-ups care about. And odds are, he's already soaking up more than you think.

2 **Keep it age appropriate.** Sticking to the truth is good when it comes to money, but so is adapting your message to your kid's level. If you lose your job, it's fine to say to your elementary schooler, "We're going to cook at home more, since that costs less than eating out." Skip the part about being in such dire straits that you're dipping into your 401(k) to make ends meet. Given the same scenario but with a kid in high school, talking about how the loss of an income will affect college financing would be not only acceptable but also wise. You can discuss the reality that your family might not be able to put as much toward college expenses, but at the same time explain that she might qualify for more financial aid. In general, when it comes to having any hard money talk with your kid, it's good to tell it like it is, but also offer reassurance that she—and you—will be okay.

3 **Use anecdotes.** More often than not, when we launch into lecture mode, our kids tune out. Or, worse, our pontificate-y good intentions backfire and push our children to do the opposite of what we're trying to get them to do. Instead, use stories to illustrate a point. When my friend couldn't get a decent rate on a car loan because she'd run up too much debt on her credit card on a monthlong, over-the-top European trip the year before, I told my kids the details (without mentioning her name). Anecdotes such as these, which highlight how financial blunders lead to consequences, tend to stick in kids' minds. Same is true of positive lessons, like an example of the neighbor who saved religiously for ten years, putting aside 1% of every paycheck, so that he could finally buy his dream fishing boat. You get the idea.

4 **Use numbers, even if you're mathphobic.** People understand money concepts better when a point is made with specific numbers. Saying to your kid, "It's so important to put money into your 401(k) even when you're young," is much less effective than offering an example. "If you put $315 every month into a 401(k) starting at age twenty-two, by the time you reach age sixty-five, you could have more than a million dollars." (The very words *million dollars* invariably make kids take notice.) If you have no idea where to get the numbers to show your kid, use some of the examples from this book or, if you're feeling ambitious, check out the simple online financial calculators on a website such as Moneychimp .com. (I used a compound-interest calculator to crunch the numbers for the example above, and I promise it's easy. Really.)

5 **Don't lie about your money past—but don't overshare, either.** Most of us have had a flirtation with bad money management at some point, whether we ran up too much on a credit card or bounced a check or two (or ten). But resist the urge to come clean about your money mistakes to purge your own feelings of guilt or irresponsibility: Your kid isn't your financial advisor—or your priest. Take a page from the latest research on talking to kids about drugs, which shows that parents who have themselves indulged in the past should not go into details with their kids. If you're answering a direct question, definitely pick and choose which financial sins you disclose; tales of emptying your bank account for a road trip with an old boyfriend or blowing through your 401(k) savings to fund a wacky business scheme may glamorize what were actually regrettable decisions that took you many years to overcome.

6 **Never fib about how much money you have on you.** This is something that nearly all harried parents do at some point. Whether our wallets are full or empty, in the heat of the parenting moment, it is natural to want to lie a little to avoid tantrums when passing our kid's favorite stores or during difficult checkout-line discussions. Try not to. Although it might seem harmless to tell a young child, "I don't have any money with me, so I can't buy you that bag of gummy bears," it's better to say something like, "No, I don't think we need to spend money on that now. Besides, the dentist told us to avoid chewy sweets." Straight talk is a good example to set, and if there are real reasons behind your decisions, it's actually helpful to share them with your child. If what your kid wants simply isn't in your budget, say so and explain why. Or if you oppose the purchase for some other reason (say, you don't want your kid toting a bazooka water gun around the neighborhood), then explain that, too. Remember that children are smart and won't just settle for "We can't afford it," which, surveys show, kids mostly don't believe anyway. No matter what your reasons, saying that you don't have cash won't work, since kids know there are lots of ways to pay for things. If you swipe your credit card a few minutes after pleading poverty, you'll be busted. Once you get caught in a lie, your child will always wonder if you can be trusted. It's just not worth it. Bite the bullet at the point of purchase now, and it won't bite you in the backside later.

7 **Identify your financial baggage—then leave it behind.** Nina, now in her midthirties, used to tell anyone who'd listen, including her kids, that her "inability to do money," as she put it, is due to her parents' financial ineptitude. "They knew nothing about budgeting, never saved, and lived life in a completely irresponsible way," she'd say. I also know people who tell me the opposite: They're bad with money because their parents were so controlling and frugal, and they promised themselves that they wouldn't live that way when they were parents. Here's the point: It's good to be aware of how your parents handled money and the ways that has affected your behavior, but don't use it as an excuse to explain away your money foibles or, worse, to avoid teaching your kids about the subject. Approach money in a positive way—you might need to fake it, at least at first—instead of passing on that negativity.

8 **Keep the money fights behind closed doors—and don't let your kids get caught in the middle.** Researchers have found that college kids whose parents regularly fought about money when they were younger were nearly three times more likely to owe $500 or more on their credit cards than kids whose parents kept the financial peace. You and your spouse aren't always going to see eye to eye on family finances, but it's important to shield your children from your big money disagreements whenever possible. Try your best to present a united front to your children. It's perfectly fine to call a money "time-out" for parents only and tell your teenager, "We're not sure what we think about paying for you to go to that music festival with your friends, so we'll discuss it and get back to you."

If you and your spouse or ex are often at odds over money, you will need to figure out in private how you are going to work out a compromise. One study found that children of divorced parents who are drawn into the details of child support and parental salaries, for instance, tend to equate financial support with love, and make one of their parents the bad guy. Telling your son he can't play in the local soccer league because your ex is late on child support and you can't afford the uniform fees yourself can mess him up about money. Even though parents who are no longer together might find it hard, speaking with "one voice" on financial matters is usually the best thing for your child. And when kids try to play the two of you—divorced or not—against each other, as they invariably do, resist the temptation to act the hero. Try your hardest to reach an agreement, and present the decision as coming from both of you.

9 **Don't expect your child to have money skills if all you've given him is money.** Daniel and Mindy were devoted parents. They checked over their three sons' homework each night when the boys were in elementary school, excused them from basic chores in middle school so that they could do homework instead, and, before the kids went away to college, handed each a credit card to cover all bills. When their oldest son graduated, he moved back home and proceeded to binge-watch every HBO series since *The Sopranos*. One day, after he'd asked his mom if she'd mind throwing his T-shirt in the wash, Mindy snapped. "I'm done! You're a man, and you need to move out next month," she yelled. Though Mindy felt awful for losing her cool, Daniel reassured her it was just the "tough love" approach that their son needed.

As a parent, you might sympathize with Mindy and Daniel, but here's the thing: They are just as much at fault as their son. Cutting a kid off financially after years of support without laying the groundwork is akin to abandoning him in a foreign country where he doesn't know the language, customs, or laws. With money, as with most other aspects of parenting, it's important to introduce expectations gradually rather than go from zero to sixty.

10 **Share the talking.** Research shows that most of the time, kids ask their moms their financial questions. That said, I've personally observed supersmart women who are extremely successful in the business world pull the old "Ask your father" routine when the subject of money comes up. It's possible they've just had a long day or are preoccupied with thoughts of work or sick pets or the malfunctioning range hood, but when this deferral to Dad becomes a pattern, it sends the message that money is a man's turf. Um, I don't think so.

No matter your family configuration—mom and dad, single parent, two moms, two dads, or two parents *plus* two stepparents—make it everyone's business to participate actively in the money talk with your kid. Avoid phrases such as "Mom is better with money" or "Dad is the financial brain around here." It's completely fine to say, "You know, I'm not sure about that, but I'll get back to you." And then go find out the answer. Just make sure to actually follow up and relay it to your kid.

11 **Avoid creating a money gap.** Though the "math gap" between boys and girls has been well documented, there's also a definite "money gap." And parents are part of the problem. In numerous studies and surveys, kids say that Mom and Dad talk to boys more than they talk to girls about money—particularly subjects like investing. The result? Boys express more confidence about money—and *parents* think their sons understand the value of a dollar better than their daughters do. Given that your daughter will very likely be paddling upstream to keep pace with the boys financially anyway—women still earn less than men and have less money socked away in retirement accounts—they really need to hear the facts early and often. Bottom line: Boys and girls alike should know this stuff.

12 **Don't try to keep up with the Joneses (let alone the Kardashians), because you will teach your kids to do the same.** It's natural to make comparisons with other people; it's just something we do. Living in a consumerist, instant-gratification, media-driven culture doesn't help. Nevertheless, fight the urge to compare your family's money choices with anyone else's. Sounds easy, but there are times we all feel that annoying tug to judge others or second-guess our decisions when sizing up our friends and neighbors. You might feel that saving for a family trip to Nepal trumps renovating your old kitchen—you can live for another year with a retro countertop and chipped floor tiles. Your neighbors might prefer to splurge on a basement game room and travel no farther than the town pool. Hey, different strokes.

Resist making assumptions or drawing conclusions about another family's spending habits or values—especially within hearing range of your offspring. Not only are you setting a bad example, but also research shows that comparing various aspects of our finances with those of our friends makes us less happy overall. The ways that people choose to spend money are very personal. If you want to teach your kid to avoid the trap of keeping up with—or looking down on—their friends and neighbors, steer clear of that behavior yourself.

13 **Choose your moment—and your place.** Kids, especially teenagers, are hard to corral for anything—especially lectures. That's why it's important to weave the money lessons in this book into day-to-day life. Did your son get a check from Grandma? It's a great time to finally take him to the bank, open that savings account you've been talking about, and help him deposit the money. That also leads to discussions of interest rates and choices between, say, certificates of deposit (CDs) and regular savings accounts. Are you about to buy a new family laptop? Have your kid help you shop around for it (and, if you can, allow him to keep a portion of the difference between the price at the local electronics store and any better deal he can find you online). And when making a big purchase—say, a car—take your kid with you to the lot and discuss negotiation techniques.

14 **Don't flaunt bad money behavior in front of your kids.** It's easy to fall into the "Do as I say not as I do" camp when it comes to money. But try to police yourself. You might not need to be a money genius to raise one, but there's no need to rub your bad money habits in your kid's face. If you're talking to her about the hazards of credit card debt while holding a fistful of Macy's bags, she *won't* find it cute, and she *will* find it hypocritical. So take whatever baby steps you can. Trying your best to get your own financial life in order sends a powerful message.

7 Things You Don't Need to Tell Your Kids About Money

Some people believe it's wise to tell all to their children. I don't. When it comes to money, I think there are some things that kids—particularly young kids—aren't ready to process and, frankly, don't need to know. In some cases, it's simply a pragmatic decision. If you tell your kid your salary, for example, be prepared to be hounded about why he can't go on that beach vacation or get that $8 bag of popcorn at the movies. Or just as likely, be prepared for him to tell his friends.

The point is, as a parent, you have a right—and, arguably, an obligation—to sometimes say, "This is something for Mom and Dad to keep private. It's not that we're trying to keep a big secret from you; it's just that there is some information that parents do not share with children until they are much older." Here are a few things your kid probably doesn't need to know:

1. **Your salary.** Whether you earn $50,000, $150,000, or $500,000, there's no need to share numbers. That doesn't mean you can't give your kid context. For instance, you can tell him that the median (meaning exactly in the middle) income in the United States for a family is about $65,000, then let him know where you stand in relation to that number. These amounts might sound like a lot or a little to your child depending on his age and his awareness of what things cost. This can be a starting point for many of the discussions about spending and saving described in this book.

2. **Which parent makes more.** If you and your spouse both work full-time, avoid discussing who earns more. Putting dollar figures on what Mom and Dad earn can send the message, especially to young children, that one parent's contribution is more important than the other's. If the disparity weren't important, why would you have shared it with them? Of course, many teens will know, for example, that corporate lawyers tend to make more money than schoolteachers. If your child brings up the topic and wants to know why your job as a social worker pays less than your spouse's banking job, this is a great chance to talk about the psychic rewards and trade-offs that one or both of you make in order to

have the lives you choose. If one spouse takes care of the kids full-time and the other works for a salary, it's a good idea to discuss the value of stay-at-home parenting, making it clear that this is a job, too. In general, regardless of the details, it's best to display a unified front: We're a team, we work together, and it doesn't matter who earns what.

3 **The amount in your 401(k).** When I was about 10, my neighbor Susan told me that her parents had a million dollars saved in their retirement accounts. My first instinct was to think she was a liar. After all, I didn't know anyone who had a million dollars. Whether it was true or not, no good came from my knowing this information—or misinformation, as the case might have been. Your 401(k), pension plans, savings, and investment accounts are your business. Your kid doesn't have the perspective to understand that this isn't money you should tap now, and that even when you do start drawing it down, it has to (hopefully) last a very long time.

4 **Your belief that Cousin John or Aunt Louise is cheap/rich/a deadbeat.** All families have their eccentric characters. And truth be told, a great deal of family dysfunction centers on money. But this type of talk is to be had out of the earshot of children. Sure, you're irritated that your loveable but irresponsible younger brother owes you $1,000 but is going to Aruba before paying you back as promised. But if you mention this around your child, he'll not only hold it against his uncle but also remember it long after your brother has paid you back—an update you might be less likely to mention. If you're looking to teach a lesson about the hazards of lending to family members or friends, go with a story that's not about people they know (or simply change the names).

5 **How much you pay the babysitter/nanny/tutor.** Jana likes to tell the story of how shocked her kids were when they learned that their beloved babysitter Jennifer—who was always a joy—was actually paid. They believed that, if anything, Jennifer was paying *their mom* to hang out with them. It's fine to tell kids early on that babysitting is a job like any other (albeit the most important one I have ever hired someone to do). But definitely do not tell your kids *how much* you pay. Doing so gives your children an informational upper hand that you don't want them to have when it comes to their caregivers, whose job it is to be the boss when the parents aren't around. The last thing you want to do is strip that person of his or her authority.

6 **What you spent on a gift.** The joys of giving and receiving will be lost on your kid if you mention the price each time you give a present—whether it's for your son or daughter or for someone else. First and foremost, the value of a gift is not always reflected in its price. After all, some of the best gifts, like making pizza with Dad or building a couch fort with Mom, are basically free. But during gift-giving occasions, you might encounter upset kids, and that's an opportunity to talk about money as well as the spirit of giving. Remember that sometimes kids aren't so much entitled as clueless and need to know the facts. The 10-year-old nephew of a friend was in tears at his birthday party when he noticed that he had gotten fewer presents than in previous years. His mom had to explain that now that he was older, the things he wanted cost more money. So a few of his relatives had pitched in to get him the pricey iPad he really wanted, rather than a bunch of smaller gifts.

7 **How much you worry about paying for college.** If you're like most parents, the idea of paying for college one day is nothing short of terrifying. Though you will learn in Chapter 9 why it's great to talk about college when your kid hits high school, there's a difference between having purposeful conversations and radiating anxiety. Avoid overly negative talk about how expensive college is or how stressed out you are about affording it. Even if we are talking in general terms, our rants and raves can easily be misinterpreted by our offspring, and they might conclude that college is a major burden that they don't want you to have to shoulder. Of course, you shouldn't make a blanket promise that you'll foot the bill no matter where your kid gets in if you aren't sure you can do that. But you can and should say that college—or any sort of higher education—is a priority, and you are truly glad to be saving for your child's future.

2

Save More

Even the most relaxed parents get stressed out by the famous Marshmallow Test. You probably know the one: Young children were each given a marshmallow and told that if they didn't eat it right away, they'd get a second one. As researchers watched behind a two-way mirror, some kids gobbled it up immediately; others showed amazing restraint and waited. The crazy part is that researchers tracked the group for decades and found that the kids who waited for the second marshmallow ended up as significantly more successful adults. They had better relationships, achieved higher levels of education, and even scored a whopping 210 more points, on average, on the SAT.

Just reading this might be enough to make you want to (a) run to your local Safeway to buy a bag of marshmallows and test your kid yourself, or (b) curl up into a ball with that bag, pull the covers over your head, and stuff your face while worrying that your (mildly) impulsive child is doomed for life.

But seriously. So what if a five-year-old can't wait for a pillowy, sugary treat? And even more important (at least to readers of this book): What does any of this have to do with saving?

A lot, actually. Research has shown that people who rate highly on the self-control spectrum save more money. A study out of the University of Pennsylvania found that couples over 50 who took a personality test and demonstrated a strong ability to stick to long-term goals had saved nearly $200,000 more than the average American household.

Of course, it isn't all that surprising that people who are good at waiting are also good at saving. The ability to set aside money, avoid impulse purchases, and work toward building a nest egg is not all that different from the ability to resist eating those oh-so-tempting marshmallows in the first place.

So while there's no sugarcoating the results, there is some solace here for those who feel their blood pressure (and maybe blood sugar) rising: You can actually *teach* your kids to wait. Though this fact doesn't get the same play as the hilarious YouTube videos of kids jamming marshmallows into their mouths, it's true. You just need to know some simple techniques.

Fortunately, being good at waiting doesn't mean your kid has to excel at self-denial. The fact is, most kids want stuff. That's really, really normal—whether it's a second marshmallow, an iPhone, or a car. Your job as a parent is to resist buying these things for them—since, let's be honest, sometimes that's the path of least resistance—and, instead, help them wait, save, and get some of those things with their own money. This chapter will help you do that.

Teaching your kid to focus on the long-term payoff doesn't take nearly as much effort as it might sound. I will give you some age-appropriate ways to encourage your kid to save, whether it's his natural bent or not. I will also give you the details about where and how he can save smart.

As a parent, you'll need to do some waiting too, at least in terms of your expectations. Kids grow and change. Just because your first-grader is more of a live-for-the-moment type—frankly, a charming quality in a child or even a college boyfriend—doesn't mean you can't gently help him become better at waiting as he gets older. Scientists estimate that only a third of our ability to save money can be attributed to genetics. The good news here is that since a third of your kid's saving behavior is embedded in his DNA, an even bigger chunk can be influenced by what you teach him. So be a force for good.

6 Tricks to Teach Your Kids to Help Them Wait, Save, and Get What They Want

Your child doesn't have to be a monk, shunning all material goods. He doesn't even have to be superdisciplined. He's just got to know the tricks to help him avoid frittering away his money and instead save those dollars for something he really wants. Here are six smart strategies, inspired by the research of Walter Mischel, the brilliant psychology professor who created the Marshmallow Test decades ago, among other experts.

1 **Inoculate yourself.** Before you enter a place with temptations, have a game plan. For little kids, you can keep it simple. As you prepare to walk into a store, you can say, "Today we are buying underwear for your brother, and that's it. So if you see something you want, remind yourself that we are not going to buy it today." You can add that you will do the same. Letting a child know what to expect and how to react prepares him to resist the urge to make impulse purchases (or throw tantrums about them). By rehearsing his response to the lure of a candy bar or a toy, your kid is (slowly) training his mind to ignore temptation.

2 **Think about tomorrow.** It's hard to remember how cool the thing you're saving for is when you're staring at a bag of cheesy chips at the checkout line. But focusing on the long-term negative outcome has been shown to be surprisingly effective. "If I spend money on a bag of chips today, then it'll take me longer to get those Legos that I really want." When your kid is wavering, commiserate about how tough it can be to wait for something *you* really want, and give an example of a situation where *you* had to wait for something. Then praise her after you see her resist an impulse purchase.

3 **Distract yourself.** When your child throws a fit at the checkout line in a store because he will "*die* if I don't have gum you have to get me gum buy me gum you don't love me buy me gum gum gum," be ready with a story, a joke, an awesome funny-cat or crazy roller-coaster video on your phone, or a special secret that you want him to hear but must swear him to secrecy first. Once you're out of the store, point out how you really admire that he was able to get it together even though he wanted the candy so badly. Even if he is still a little mad at you, he will realize that the distraction did help make the feeling pass.

4 **Use your imagination.** This is a quirky one, but it's been shown to work. Encourage your child to think of whatever temptation she is encountering as not real but just a photo or a picture that she can put a "frame" around in her mind. Turns out, some of the most successful waiters in the Marshmallow Test did this naturally. It's a little abstract for young kids, but some can get into it. Another strategy is to pretend that a treat she wants is covered in ants or worms. In a store, if a kid tells herself that a tempting toy is broken or junky or that a candy is spicy or booger covered, it can work.

5 **Habits can help.** Make saving automatic. Be consistent with this message: "The minute we get any cash—whether we earn it or get it as a gift—it goes right into our savings jar or piggy bank." Don't just rely on willpower; that's the hard way. Instead, make it routine. But build fun splurges into that routine, too. ("We get ice cream after school on Fridays, so no need to ask to buy candy on Wednesday, because the answer is no. We buy special treats only on Fridays. That way we can save the rest of our money for the bigger stuff we want.")

6 **Ask "What would a smart kid do?"** Sometimes it helps your kid to remove herself emotionally from a tempting situation by "stepping outside" it and asking what someone else would do. Let her decide who that person might be—perhaps a classmate, or her favorite cartoon hero, or just a hypothetical kid who's smart. Kids like to give advice, and this technique allows them to think more coolly about their choices rather than act on impulse.

PRESCHOOL

Research shows that even some six-month-olds can develop strategies that help them exert basic self-control and calm themselves down: for instance, sucking their thumb. By the age of three, children are even able to quash impulses that might throw them off course. Emphasize the points below to help your id-driven toddler develop the precursors to the habit of saving.

- **It's good to wait.** We all know that waiting is an inconvenient time suck, whether it's sitting in traffic, killing time in the pediatrician's waiting room, or standing in line at the store. And it's particularly annoying for kids. But they have to do it. That said, it's good to let your kid know that there's light at the end of the car ride. Often, when we are waiting, it's for something we really want: to arrive someplace we want to be, or to buy something we've had our eyes on. So when you can, point out the benefits of waiting. At the playground, when your kid is standing in line for the swings, you can discuss how democratic the system is: "You have to wait for your turn, but that little boy will have to wait for you to finish *your* time on the swing." Show your kid how the two of you can make the time go by faster if you distract yourselves. ("I'm thinking of a number between one and ten" is always a favorite.) It's also good to talk about waiting for far-off goals such as a birthday or a holiday, and how great it is when the day finally arrives. To help pass the time, you can discuss what will happen at the birthday party, who will attend, what games you'll play, and what the theme will be. When the day arrives, make sure to mention how it was worth the wait.

- **Save your money in a safe place.** For very young kids, coins are choking hazards, and dollar bills are just paper that's fun to rip. Still, by about age three, kids are able to latch on to the basic idea that money has value. The parents of one precocious kid I know reported that their daughter began requesting "green money" instead of "metal money" long before she started school, because she knew it was worth more.

    Start making sure that your kid doesn't leave his coins—and even bills—all over the house. One tried-and-true technique is to find three jars and have your child label one to save up for things to buy in the future, one to buy stuff right now, and one to share with other people who need help. An opaque container is even better, since it reduces the temptation for your kid to pilfer from his stash. Think a piggy bank, a coffee can, a special envelope in a drawer, or even a safe. (Kids love safes!) It doesn't matter exactly how your kid's money gets divvied up—a third in each category or some other formula—because at this age, the allocation is more symbolic than anything else. The real trick is to ensure that your kid is consistent about saving and always stashes away a set amount of money—whether it's cash from Grandpa, a few coins found on the floor, or birthday money from you.

- **Pitch in to the family savings pot.** Starting a family savings pot will allow you to have a communal project with your kid—and it lets you teach by example rather than just lecturing on the value of savings. It's best to set up a shoe box or cookie jar in the living room or kitchen or somewhere else where it's plainly visible and then tell everyone to chip in. Start with a goal that's easily attainable and attractive to a little kid, such as pizza night or a trip to the water park. Your preschooler, of course, might be able to contribute only a small amount of his allowance (see the allowance box on p. 28) or quarters discovered between the sofa cushions. The amount doesn't really matter. What does help is when you point out creative ways to come up with money, and keep the savings pot a topic of frequent conversation: "Hey, I have all this change from my trip to the grocery store, and I'm going to dump it into the pot!" When it's time to redeem the family's reward, have your child help you count up how much is there and figure out if you have enough for deluxe toppings on the pizza or ice cream at the water park.

- **Parents: Don't help your kid skip the line.** Once, as I was in line at an airport bathroom, I overheard a mom tell her very small child, "This is part of life. Sometimes you just have to wait." It was a simple message but quite profound. If you want your kid to learn to wait, you have to be patient yourself. Circumventing the rules so that your kid doesn't have to cool his heels sometimes is not good—whether you're allowing him to linger on the seesaw while you hold his spot on a swing or taking him with you as you cut the line at the grocery store. Winner of the Most Outrageous Parenting award? The moms and dads who reportedly hired physically disabled "guides" to usher their able-bodied kids to the head of the lines for rides at Disney theme parks. Eventually the folks at Disney found out and had to change the way they accommodated disabled riders. Of course, this was over-the-top behavior. But even the most upstanding parents can be blinded by devotion to their kids and feel tempted to bend the rules in little ways. Doing so not only shows your kid that it's okay to cheat but also ensures that you'll end up with a kid who doesn't have self-control.

- **Parents: Teach your kid about numbers and coins.** When my son was in preschool and we had a playdate with twins who lived nearby, I was impressed that they knew the difference between a penny, a nickel, a dime, and a quarter. And I felt sort of embarrassed—me, the money writer—that I hadn't taught my little guy. Experiments with babies as young as five months show that they already have an intuitive number sense, which will help them understand money. If you show that you are putting two dolls behind a screen, but take it down to reveal only one doll, the baby will act surprised, just like an adult would.

    When you think about it, number games are everywhere. Sorting socks after you do the laundry, counting the number of bananas you put in the shopping cart, and noting each duck on the pond at the park are examples. For older preschoolers, you can even try playing a version of "store," using coins or paper money to have your kid "buy" items. You may have to help your kid count the money at first, but don't be too quick to jump in and do the math for him. It's good to give him the time to work it out himself. Also, make sure to repeat counting activities; although you might get bored, repetition is a primary component of learning.

- **Parents: Follow-through is everything.** There are all kinds of creative ways to spur your kid to be an excellent saver, but none of them will work if you, as a parent, don't keep your word. Of course, no one is perfect. But when you promise something, you have to do it—not only because that's what's right, but also because it will build the trust necessary for a child to feel confident that if she saves today, she can get what she wants tomorrow.

    A striking study conducted at the University of Rochester shows how important this is. Kids were divided into two groups of 14 each. Both groups received used, broken crayons, and an adult informed the children that she was going to leave for a few minutes to get better art supplies. In group one, the adult returned promptly with fancier pens and crayons; in group two, she returned empty-handed, offering nothing but excuses. Next, the adult repeated this exercise, this time saying that she was going to get a selection of bigger, better stickers. The first group got the goods; the second, one lame little sticker. Finally, the children were given a version of the Marshmallow Test. Interestingly, a clear pattern emerged: Kids in group one, with a "reliable" grown-up, were much better at waiting. In fact, while 9 out of 14 kids in group one waited 15 minutes for that second marshmallow, just *1* kid in the broken-promises group waited that long. You get it: Broken promises can crush a kid's incentive.

The Man Who Didn't Eat the Candy: An Inspirational Tale of Saving and Making a Lot Out of Very Little

Harold was brought up in the 1930s, a time when money was tight for many families, though his had it particularly rough. During the Great Depression, Harold's father lost the grocery store he owned and sank into his own deep depression, while Harold's mother tried to provide for four young children by working for a seamstress.

Though only ten years old, Harold decided to generate some income by filling a need, if not an actual job, that existed in the local candy shop. Every day after school, he'd sit by the pay phone and wait for a call to come in for one of the neighbors in the nearby tenement building. Since few people had phones of their own, this pay phone served the entire community, and Harold would get a tip of a few pennies or a nickel each time he alerted someone of an incoming call. At the end of each week, he'd proudly hand the money over to his mother to help make ends meet.

Despite the fact that he spent long hours in that candy store, Harold never used the money he earned to buy candy. Not even once. He knew that the extra money would alleviate some of the tension at home, and that in itself was a reward.

A few years later, Harold, just 17, met the love of his life, Shirley, 16, and a few years after that, they married. Shirley was a chemistry teacher, and Harold, who started off as a history teacher, rose quickly through the ranks and became a junior high school principal. Before they knew it, they had two boys, a girl, and a mortgage, and Shirley decided to give up teaching to stay at home full-time.

One day Harold heard about a brand-new retirement plan that would allow him to set aside up to half of his income—then about $30,000 a year—in a tax-free account.

When he told his wife, she panicked. "Harold, that's insane. We can't afford to raise three kids on $15,000 a year."

Harold's response? "Shirley, we can't afford not to."

Harold won the argument. Today the couple, both now in their eighties, are happily living off that retirement savings.

How do I know all this? Harold and Shirley are my parents. The trait that my father had innately—and my mom quickly came to adopt—was the ability to delay gratification. He knew that by living a financially lean life, he was building a healthy retirement nest egg for himself and his wife down the road. This didn't benefit just them. By starting to save early, he ensured that he and my mom would not have to rely on their own kids—my brothers and me—in their old age.

ELEMENTARY SCHOOL

Research shows that by age seven, kids are able to focus on goals—and are receptive to what they need to do to reach them. And most of these kids are not only aware of money, they're earning (okay, "earning") it, whether through allowances or odd jobs. Here's what to tell them to keep them on the savings path.

- **Pick a rule of thumb and stick with it.** "Save a quarter for every dollar you get" is my favorite because it's easy. If your kid is into math, you can get a little creative talking about ratios ($1 saved for every $4 earned) or percentages (25% means 25 cents for each dollar). Rules of thumb can be more useful than complicated explanations or mathematic formulas. Just as you strive to teach your kid necessary habits such as brushing her teeth and putting on her seat belt, you want her to make the savings habit automatic too.

- **Think about "opportunity cost."** One mom I know would spend about a dollar to buy her son a snack, usually a small bag of Doritos, at the local bodega each day after school. He really wanted a $15 set of toy airplanes, so they agreed that for the next two weeks, he would forgo the purchased snacks and instead eat rice cakes with peanut butter that his mom made at home. Although she didn't realize it at the time, she was teaching her kid a great lesson on the concept of opportunity cost, which is basically the thing we give up by doing something else. Teach your kid the term. You can use my Doritos example and say, "If I'm spending a dollar a day on Doritos, I can't spend that money on something better. That's the opportunity cost."

- **A bank or credit union account is the safest place for money.** When your kid was a preschooler, she might have stashed her savings in a jar, but now that she's a little older, it's time to put some of that money into a kid-friendly bank. Savings accounts at federally insured banks are still the most secure place for your child to start accumulating her dollars. Most banks and credit unions offer federal insurance—either through the Federal Deposit Insurance Corporation (FDIC) or the National Credit Union Association (NCUA). By law they must display a sign declaring this in every teller's window. When you go to the bank, point it out and explain that this means your kid's money will be there when she needs it.

  This is also a great time to give her a quick history lesson: The FDIC was created in 1933, during a period called the Great Depression, when many people were losing their jobs and many companies were going out of business. Banks were closing, and many customers lost the savings they had deposited. So that even more people wouldn't lose their savings, the U.S. government created the FDIC, which we still have today. This agency guarantees that if your bank goes out of business, the government will give you back up to $250,000 of your money. (Not that your kid will come close to saving that much anytime soon, unless you have spawned a tiny, tiny Silicon Valley entrepreneur.)

  Before you go to the bank, call ahead to see if someone's available who is especially good at talking to kids. The one time I didn't do that, my eight-year-old son was making a deposit at the counter. When he asked the bank teller where his $43 was going, the man pointed silently at the account number on the deposit slip. That, of course, made no sense to a second-grader. Only after I cajoled the bank rep to show my son the vault did he feel satisfied that his money was safe.

- **Interest is "free" money.** To entice your child to deposit his money in a bank, explain that banks have two advantages: They keep your money safe (remember the vault?), and they pay interest, which means that a bank gives you a little extra money to get you to deposit your savings there. Of course, in recent years, bank savings accounts have paid a pathetically low fraction of 1%. (Back in the early 1980s, savings accounts paid double-digit interest and, though that's not likely to happen again anytime soon, interest rates will creep back up at some point.) Even so, it pays to teach these concepts now. After all, earning 1% on $100 is $1 a year, and $1 for free still sounds pretty great to almost every kid in elementary school.

- **Parents: Set up a matching program.** Given the small amount of interest that banks pay on savings accounts these days, if you can afford it, you might want to give your child matching funds to encourage her to save. Matching is a big incentive for adults to put money in 401(k) plans, and it works for kids too. Consider pitching in 50 cents for each dollar your kid saves—or even match dollar for dollar, if you can swing it. But be sure to set a cap on the arrangement if you don't want to contribute more than a given amount in a month. One man I know told me about his friend, a well-intentioned dad, who set up his son with a savings account. But the bank's 0.3% interest rate was so pitiful that his kid didn't see the point of saving. So the dad made a deal: "For every dollar you save, I'll pay you five percent interest." A few months later, my friend saw the dad and asked him how it was going. "Terrible!" the dad said. "My son hoards every dollar he gets, and I can barely afford to keep up the interest!"

- **Parents: Don't rip off your kid's piggy bank.** This might sound obvious, but it's worth mentioning. A friend's spouse used to sneak into his kids' bedrooms when he was running low on cash and pilfer their savings stash. Then he'd replace the funds a day or two later, before the children knew it was gone. Once he forgot to, and when his daughter went to get some ice cream money, she started screaming like a banshee that she'd been robbed. Of course, many of us have been tempted to tiptoe into our little one's room to grab a ten when we've forgotten to withdraw cash from the ATM. In fact, in one poll, nearly a third of parents said they raid their kids' piggy banks. The problem is that if you're caught, you're undermining lessons you want your children to embrace: It pays to save, and a piggy bank is a safe place to keep your money. Parents get to make all the calls about what the family spends money on, so it's important for your kid to feel that her money is truly hers. It makes her feel independent and grown up. Don't take that away from her. Of course, every now and then, the pizza delivery guy shows up and the only cash around for a tip is your kid's stash. It's okay to ask your child for a loan, but make sure to pay her back the next day—and give her a dollar for "interest."

The 5 Cs of Allowance

"We suck at allowance."

That's the gist of what most moms and dads tell me sheepishly when I ask about the subject. They admit that they don't have a system that works effectively and fret about being horrible parents. "We started in the New Year and were really good for the first four weeks," Kathy, a mother of three, told me. "But after that, we forgot to give it regularly, and then suddenly it was June, and no one could remember who was owed what."

I'm here to let you off the hook: It doesn't really matter whether you give your kids allowance or not. That's what I concluded after combing through more than two dozen academic studies on the subject. The findings are all over the map. One Canadian study, for instance, showed that kids who get allowance understand credit cards and prices better than those who don't. Yet according to research from the United Kingdom, kids who were paid allowance were actually *worse* at saving than kids who earned their spending money by working odd jobs. My takeaway: Follow the advice on teaching money smarts in this book, and do what feels right to you personally when it comes to allowance.

That said, I do believe that allowance is a fine, practical way to dole out money to your kids. That is, as long as you follow my rules below. If you do give allowance, it's not necessary to sign up for one of the growing number of allowance apps and websites that offer to help—sometimes for free, but often for a fee. Some have gimmicks such as issuing "currency" in the form of beans, credits, or IOUs, which sometimes can be used only to buy certain items or in certain online stores. I'm less a fan of these because your child isn't dealing with real money. If you find one that works for you, that's great, but just make sure that using the site doesn't take the place of the all-important money conversations that should come with allowance.

1 **Be clear.** Keep it simple, and be realistic. The key is letting kids know from the start what this money is to be used for. Every family is different, and you'll have to make these calls, but here are some general guidelines. With young kids, keep it really basic: You cover food, necessary clothes, and things like birthday gifts for friends' parties and the occasional movie. For extras such as trendy hair barrettes, Milk Duds at the movies, and iTunes, it's on them. Once they hit middle school, you will probably still pay for most of the basics, although you'll have to define what that means. For example, you might pay for a couple pairs of $50 jeans for school, but if they're hankering for a $100 pair, then they can make up the difference. By high school, the balance shifts some more, with you giving your kid a higher allowance but also more responsibility. Maybe now she has to cover presents for friends and meals out with her crew. College is a paradigm shift—for specifics, see Chapter 9. Whatever you do decide, make it clear to your kid that these decisions aren't arbitrary: His allowance is part of the larger family budget.

2 **Be consistent.** It's actually less important to make the "right" rules than it is to stick to whatever you decide. Of course, it would be awesome if you could blow a whistle and have your kids line up like the von Trapp family to get allowance at the same time each week. But realistically, you'll occasionally forget to give—and they will forget to ask, believe it or not. When that happens, don't worry that you've screwed up allowance for all time. Get back on track, pay your kids what's owed, and start using a spreadsheet or worksheet to keep on top of things.

3 **Give control.** It's fine to have some spending rules, such as limited candy, no toy guns, and a ban on lipstick for little ones. But in general, let your kid have the freedom to buy what she wants, particularly as she enters middle school. The big area that you do control, however, is how much to give. It's good to know social norms, so ask other parents about the "going rate." There's a rule of thumb floating around that says you should give a dollar amount equal to your kid's age per week. Some parents hear $10 a week for a 10-year-old, do the math, and decide that giving $520 a year to a prepubescent son or daughter is ridiculous. And if that's out of your budget, I get it. But if it is in your budget, there's a good chance that you are spending this sum anyway on the array of little items you buy your kid all the time. By giving allowance, you are empowering him to make the decisions about how that money gets spent. You might decide that this is too much discretion for your 10-year-old. But for some kids, it's a perfect way to see what it's like to run out of money and not be able to buy what he wants. And that's where rule number 2, consistency, becomes really important.

4 **Use cash.** Studies show that all of us spend more when we use credit or some other form of online payment, since the pain of paying is put off to the future. That's why it's important to give your kid paper money. (Of course, you need to be willing to launder some of this cash for her into iTunes and other online retailers.) Debit cards are all the rage, but I don't like them before college. (To find out why, see Chapter 4.) While you're at it, talk to your kid about the importance of saving some of it instead of spending it all. One point that the findings from many allowance studies seem to agree on is that the conversations we engage in with our kids about money are even more important than handing them the money in the first place.

5 **No chores.** Research shows that chores are good for kids because they teach responsibility and the importance of chipping in to help others. But it's a mistake to link those chores to money. Unless you're willing to negotiate each time you want your kid to empty the dishwasher or put his clothes in the hamper, steer clear of systems that pay per chore. Chores should simply be part of everyday family life. You can pay your kid for jobs above and beyond his usual responsibilities—but that's work, not allowance. (For more on this, see p. 43.) Also, linking allowance to chores or other desired behaviors can backfire. I've seen too many parents in the heat of the moment use allowance as leverage and sometimes payback. "You didn't make your bed?" Bam! "No money for you." What if your kid thinks it's worth it to, say, leave his bed unmade or miss curfew and lose $10? You see the problem. Discipline your kid in some other way, and keep the allowance issue separate.

MIDDLE SCHOOL

The middle school years are a great time to get kids hooked on the habit of saving. They can understand the concept better at this age than when they were little, and they haven't yet hit high school, when they'll be more likely to roll their eyes at your lecturing and just want you to hand over the money already. Not only that, but they'll be coveting big-ticket items that will require saving to purchase. Offering these tips can make that happen.

- **It's never good to have no money.** I know this phrasing is a bit odd, but here's my reasoning: While it's great to save up for a concrete item—after all, that is one of the key points of this chapter—your kid shouldn't spend her last penny on it. If a purchase would wipe out her bank account entirely, then she needs to wait and save more before buying. Put another way, it's good to have savings for saving's sake, too. This isn't meant to be a buzzkill. The reality is that you never know when you'll need cash—sometimes for something that's truly a need or sometimes for something that you just really want, like a concert ticket when your favorite band is coming to town. If you spend all your money, you aren't left with any choices. Not to mention that it's good to have some money set aside for an emergency.

- **Get the highest interest on the safest accounts.** Take a trip to the bank or credit union with your middle schooler and ask to see a list of the various supersafe accounts that your kid can consider. (See the box on p. 33 for a rundown.) Although in recent years the interest rates paid by these accounts have been extremely low, that's okay. The goal here is to preserve your kid's money, which is what these accounts do.

  You can also shop around with your child at sites such as Bankrate.com or DepositAccounts.com, or pop into a couple neighborhood banks with him to see which offers the highest interest rates. Even if the difference between two banks is tiny, you're teaching your child to comparison shop. Just be supercareful of fees, since most banks will slap your kid with one if his balance falls below a minimum. Nothing worse for a kid than depositing $10 and finding out that, instead of earning interest, he's lost half his savings to a $5 monthly fee. Local and regional banks, as well as credit unions (you may find one you can join at ASmarterChoice .org or MyCreditUnion.gov), tend to have the lowest balance requirements, and some offer special accounts for kids or waive the monthly fee if your child's account is linked to yours. Sadly, passbook savings accounts have mostly gone the way of the landline, so your kid won't have tangible evidence of her banking activity, but once the money is deposited, you can show your kid her balance online or on your smartphone.

- **Parents: Skip online banks—unless your kid is really interested.** Online banks tend to pay higher rates, which you may notice if you consult comparison sites, but for your middle schooler, transacting with a physical bank is probably still important. My advice is to have her stick with a brick-and-mortar bank for now, so that she gets to hand her cash to the teller or use an ATM and feel that she is a participant in the financial world. When she's older, she can open an account with an Internet-only bank if she finds a higher rate. This is something that you have to feel out with your kid. If she's ready for the abstract experience of an exclusively cyber savings account now, feel free to skip ahead to the high school section and read about online banks.

3 Supersafe Accounts for Saving Money

1 **Savings account.** This is the simplest way to keep money in the bank and earn a little interest on it. You usually need to maintain a minimum balance in order to avoid a monthly fee, but some banks offer youth savings accounts that waive the fees and minimums. Your kid should know that withdrawals from savings accounts are limited by federal law to six per month.

2 **Money market account (MMA).** Very similar to savings accounts, MMAs historically have tended to pay slightly higher interest, but they usually have higher minimum balance requirements. No need to go with one of these unless it's really a better deal than a plain old savings account.

3 **Certificate of deposit (CD).** These accounts require you to keep your money in them for a set period, and offer a fixed interest rate. Because you can't withdraw your money before that period is up without a penalty, you get a somewhat higher rate than for a savings account. Most kids won't have the $500 or so minimum necessary to open a CD, but hearing that the more savings you have, the higher the rate you'll be paid is a great motivator for them.

HIGH SCHOOL

Come high school, your kid will have a lot more discretion about how she spends her money. But parents need to make sure that kids are saving with a post–high school goal in mind.

- **Save for college.** Research shows that kids whose parents carry the full burden of college costs score lower GPAs than kids who chip in. Although it's not exactly clear why that is the case, my guess is that when a child knows he has some skin in the higher-ed game, he is that much more motivated to make the most of the experience. And that's one reason it's good for your child to help at least a little with college costs. Though many parents say they expect their kids to kick in for college, few actually let their kids know until it's too late for them to save much. One survey found that although 85% of parents feel their children should contribute, only 34% have asked their kids to start saving for it. Starting in ninth grade, make it clear that you expect your child to set aside for college a portion of any money earned at a job or received from relatives.

There are a variety of ways to do this. Your child will want to save in the place that will be least likely to reduce your family's financial aid eligibility. When colleges determine how much federal financial aid to give a family, they look at the student's savings and expect her to contribute 20% of that amount. Parents are expected to contribute a lower portion—only 5.6%—of their savings because schools realize that they have many other expenses, including mortgages and car payments, not to mention other kids. (Colleges do require you to pitch in a much larger share of your current income, but I'll get to that later.) However, there are some ways around this rule, like having your child save in a special college savings account called a 529 plan. (For much more on these accounts, see Chapter 9.)

No matter what, make sure not to fall into the trap of thinking that there's no point in your kid's saving for college, since the financial aid office is just going to penalize her because she's got money in the bank. While I'm sympathetic to that argument, there are several reasons that it's wrong. First and foremost, having *some* money is better than having *no* money. Even if your kid does get financial aid, it will probably include loans, and any money saved can help reduce that debt. Plus, because financial aid formulas change all the time, it's good not to bet that having nothing in the bank will leave your kid in the best shape at college time.

- **Consider putting your savings in an Internet-only bank.** Your kid's goal at this point is to preserve her money, not earn outsize returns. That said, now is a good time to have her look for the best interest rate on a supersafe savings account—perhaps at an Internet-only bank, many of which offer higher rates than banks with physical branches. Your kid is old enough now to understand the concept of Internet-only banks in a way that she wasn't when she was younger. Tell her to check Bankrate.com or DepositAccounts.com to find the highest rate. In recent years, interest rates on savings accounts have been so low that the best you could probably do is the difference between 0.05% and 1%. Although that doesn't really mean much in dollars, it's good for your kid to get in the habit of finding the best interest rates. It's likely that they will rise in the future, and at that point, shopping around will make a significant difference. The main thing about money in savings is that it's safe. This is why it's important to make sure that any Internet-only bank your kid uses is FDIC insured by looking for the familiar FDIC logo or the words "Member FDIC" or "FDIC Insured" on the bank's website.

- **Save up for the "extras."** Some parents worry—and even express a sense of shame—about not being able to afford to dole out money for all the stuff that their kid desires. If you're that parent, get over it. It's actually really good to say no to your kid sometimes, and to make it clear that if he really wants something, he might need to chip in or even pay for it himself. That's true whether you actually have the money to buy it for him or not. Kids who typically get whatever they want without having to save and wait are missing out on acquiring key life skills. The next time he asks for something extra, have a conversation about what you'll cover and what he needs to pay for from his own savings. You might be surprised at how creative he suddenly gets about scrounging up the money to pitch in for that Fender electric guitar. Don't apologize to your kid for not being able to get him everything; he is lucky that you're giving him the opportunity to learn to save up for what he wants himself.

If Your Kid Comes into Big Bucks

Sweet 16. First communion. Bar or bat mitzvah. Quinceañera. Confirmation. Dastar Bandi. Graduation. All of these huge coming-of-age rituals include friends and family—and perhaps big cash gifts. (And if you have relatives who didn't give generously, you'll remember. Oh, you *will* remember.)

If your family celebrates an event like this, you should set the expectations for where the money goes *before* your kid is holding a wad of cash or a handful of checks. Later, when your postparty kid is rolling around on his bedroom floor covered in twenties like a lottery player who's hit the jackpot, is *not* the time to make a rational plan for his windfall. Does it belong in your kid's college savings account? Will some of it be donated to charity? Will your kid get to blow it on stuff he wants (a drum set or an expensive spring break trip)? Or will your family need to use it to pay for the expense of the celebration party? (That's what my folks had to do.) Or (most likely) will the money be divided up and used for more than one purpose?

Of course, what you choose to do will depend on your own family's finances and the sum involved. I say that if you're allowing your child to consider the money "his," then you should require that he set aside a significant portion of it for long-term savings, especially college. If you are so inclined, having him donate a portion of it to a meaningful project or charitable organization of his choice is great too. While it may be "his" money, he's still your kid, and you can help him come up with a wise plan. It'll be good practice for when he's older and gets a cash bonus at work or a fat tax refund.

COLLEGE

These are not the years a kid will build up a big nest egg. Much of what he has saved will go toward education costs, as well as the basic expenses of college life. Saving beyond that? It'll have to wait until after graduation. Still, the following advice holds.

- **Use some savings to chip in for college costs.** As mentioned earlier, research shows that if your kid contributes a bit of money toward college, he's likely to do better in school because he feels more engaged and invested. Whether he's covering the cost of books, his dorm room decorations, or a portion of tuition, having him dip into his savings to chip in is smart. And if you took my advice in the high school section and had your kid save for college, he should have at least a small amount that he can pitch in.

- **Save during the summer if you can.** Summers are a prime time to earn. Money saved will give your kid breathing room during the school year, when he really needs to study and wants to work less, or it can allow him to take on less student-loan debt. If your kid ends up doing something over the summer that doesn't make money (like an unpaid internship), be sure to remind him of the opportunity cost of that decision. It likely means that he will be working while in school, instead of relying on money he saved from his summer paychecks. (For more on jobs, see Chapter 3.)

YOUNG ADULTHOOD

No way around it: Your grown child needs to save in order to achieve financial freedom. The ability to delay gratification is more important than ever, and here's what you need to tell her.

- **Set up an emergency savings cushion.** When you broach the topic of emergency savings with your grown-up child, you might well be greeted with a rant about high rents and low-paying jobs, and how saving is virtually impossible for his generation. That's your cue to explain why it's time to start saving now, even a tiny bit, regularly. An emergency cushion can mean the difference between an inconvenience and financial disaster—so he won't lose his job because he can't afford to fix his car, and then get evicted because he can't pay the rent. Now that he's an adult, he'll have to create his own safety net rather than count on one held up at the corners by his parents. The rule of thumb has been to save a cushion of six months' worth of living expenses—enough to tide him over until he finds work. That said, I recommend telling your child initially to shoot for a three-month cushion so that the goal doesn't seem so unattainable. For an online worksheet to help your kid figure out how much to set aside for living expenses, go to BethKobliner.com.

- **Paying off high-rate debt can be the smartest way to save.** Granted, this is another idea that might seem laughable to a recent college graduate with zero in the bank. But it's an important concept for your kid to get now—and one that even many adults don't understand. Here's the gist: Before long, your kid will build up some savings—particularly if he is living at home—and he should use it to rid himself of expensive debt.

    Start with this example. Say that your kid owed $1,000 on a credit card with an 18% interest rate, and also had $1,000 in savings in an account earning 1%.

By the end of the year, he'd have paid out $180 in interest to the credit card company and earned just $10 in interest on the savings account. Even though he technically had money in the bank, he'd actually have had a net loss of $170. If he instead used that $1,000 to pay off the credit card, he wouldn't have earned any interest, but he wouldn't have paid any, either; it'd be a draw. And that's much better than losing $170.

But, you might be thinking, shouldn't my kid have the emergency savings cushion mentioned above? The answer: It depends. If your kid is living with you, he should rid himself of high-rate debt first and then save up his first month's rent and security deposit for his own place. That is one of the supreme financial benefits of moving back home. This approach requires his firm commitment not to charge any more on his credit card than he is able to pay off in full the following month. Even if he's out on his own, I say devote at least half of his savings to whacking away at that high-rate debt, and deposit the other half into a savings account for true emergencies only. Once he has one month's worth of living expenses in his savings cushion, he can start putting even more toward getting rid of that credit card debt. Only when it's gone does it make sense for him to turn back to building up his emergency cushion to the minimal three months' worth of expenses.

- **Make saving automatic.** Behavioral economists know that getting someone to save voluntarily is a bit like getting someone to cheerfully sign up for a root canal. As your trusty Magic 8 Ball would say, "Outlook not so good." That's why your kid needs to set up her finances so she doesn't have to think about saving every time she gets paid. It's a neat mental trick: Because we never see the money in our checking account in the first place, we don't experience the pain of "losing" the money had we transferred it to savings. Your kid's employer might be able to automatically deposit part of her paycheck into a separate savings account—or she can arrange to have her bank make regular transfers from checking to savings on every payday. Taking this small onetime step can literally pay off for years to come.

- **Don't buy until you have the savings to do so.** Once your kid gets out of school, there are a million things that she'll feel she just *has* to spend money on. These can be dangerous years for your kid, especially if she's newly in possession of a credit card. But hear this, perhaps one of the most important messages in this entire book for you to convey to your kid: She needs to wait to buy big-ticket items until she has saved the money for them. Period. In this day and age, it feels almost old-fashioned to write that purchases should be made with money that's already saved. You might be imagining me wearing a shirtwaist and bustle and typing this on a Teletype machine. But it's true, and it's the best advice you can give your child. For much more on the dangers of debt, see Chapter 4.

- **Parents: Let your kid move back home—if she saves.** Moving back into her old room after college can be a smart move for your kid, and it's not surprising that a record number of young people are doing just that. But if your child moves back home, you need to lay down some ground rules, one of which is that she needs to be saving—not just for an apartment but also for emergencies. Otherwise you could find her right back under your roof soon after she moves out. Start with a basic contract that sets out in writing your general expectations. (And yes, I'm serious.) Will you charge a modest amount in rent (while leaving her enough to save)? What are the other expectations (chores, money for groceries, and so on)? If you're loaning your kid money, will you charge interest? (For the IRS rules on charging interest to relatives— yes, they exist!—see p. 96.)

- **Parents: Talk to your kid about saving for a home down payment.** In the early years after college, your kid's buying a home might seem as likely as her indie band's headlining Coachella. But saving will bring it within the realm of possibility. Don't lead the conversation with, "Hey, when I was your age, I owned my own home and had three kids!" This does not add to your authority; it only makes you sound out of touch and a bit mean. Besides, speaking statistically, this generation is waiting longer than previous ones to buy a home. Still, once your kid has an ample emergency fund and is contributing to her 401(k) at work, suggest that she consider putting a small amount each month into an account for a home down payment. (For info about your kid's first mortgage, see p. 93.)

She should shoot to have a down payment of at least 10%—but preferably 20%—of the total purchase price. The typical first-time home costs around $170,000, which means she'll need to save between $17,000 and $34,000, plus at least another $3,000 for closing costs. That money belongs in a safe place such as a savings account or CD, I bond, or money market fund. (For more about those investments, see Chapter 7.) You shouldn't feel at all obliged to give your kid money to buy a home. Most parents don't. But about 25% of first-time home buyers do get a gift from relatives to help with the down payment. (Guess who that generally is, Mom and Dad!) A final bit of advice: Chipping in doesn't give you the right to dictate what kind of neighborhood your kid lives in or what kind of house or apartment she should buy. Your intentions might be good—safety, resale value, and so forth—but your kid is the person who has to live there.

3

Hard Work Pays

Ask parents their greatest wish for their kids, and the answer is usually the same: "We just want them to be happy."

Well, sure, that sounds great.

But here's the problem: Often the way we try to help our children achieve happiness is by giving them stuff and fun experiences they want. But research tells us that the secret-sauce ingredients to a happy life are hard work, achieving personal goals, and enjoying the satisfaction that comes with the effort.

Here's an example of what I mean. When I was growing up, my father's favorite refrain was, "In our family, we do what we have to do before we do what we want to do."

Clearly, there wasn't lots of wild partying in the Kobliner household.

Though my brothers, mom, and I still laugh about my dad's motto, in retrospect, it's clear that it really was a great way to be brought up. There was plenty of joy and fun but also a strong emphasis on the feeling of pride from a job well done—whether that job was completing your homework, doing the dishes, or, in my dad's case, being the best school principal he could be.

Intuitively, my father knew that the authentic sense of accomplishment that comes from working hard is the key to a successful, happy life.

Turns out that Harold wasn't alone in his thinking. A few decades later, at the University of Pennsylvania, psychology professor Angela Duckworth was researching the same thing. Duckworth, a MacArthur Foundation "genius" award recipient who knows her stuff, found that people with stick-to-itiveness (or *grit*, the education buzzword she helped popularize) not only do better in school but also earn higher incomes, save more money over their lifetimes, and are more satisfied with their lives overall.

Her most startling finding: Grit matters even more than intelligence to your kid's success.

Her most heartening: It's possible to teach your kids to be gritty.

Instilling grittiness in your kid is doable no matter what his default level of determination is. We know that some children are born superconscientious, while others are more laid-back and carefree. And that's great. Still, our job as parents is to make sure our kids know how to persevere when doing their work—whether it's household chores, schoolwork, extracurricular activities, or paying jobs.

This chapter will not only help you teach your kid to dig deep but also help you guide her to prioritize, so that she knows when to give her all and when a mellower approach is just as good, if not better. In the end, teaching your kid the following lessons will mean less work for *you*, since it will produce a more financially secure, more independent, and, yes, happier adult.

PRESCHOOL

At this stage, you might assume that the only grit your little one will have is the playground sand in her shoes. After all, how much work can a three-year-old really do, anyway? But keep reading. Now is the easiest time to start instilling a work ethic in your kid.

- **Doing chores is part of life.** Back in the days when most families lived on farms, chores weren't negotiable—the work had to get done, and there was no one else to do it. But today, research shows, most American kids aren't expected to do much housework. Blame technology, fast-food culture, longer school days, overindulged children in tiaras—pick your theory. Before you decide it's not worth your kid's time to have him bring his plate to the sink, consider this: A University of Minnesota study that tracked kids from pre-school age through their midtwenties showed that one predictor of achieving important milestones, including getting a degree and starting a career, was whether they participated in household chores when they were small.

  The good news: It's easy to get kids as young as 18 months to do simple chores. If you've ever washed the dishes or dusted in front of a toddler, you've no doubt seen him try to join in on the "fun." Take advantage of this (sadly) fleeting attitude. Assign him a simple task like putting away his shoes or hanging up his coat (place the hooks low enough), make sure he sticks to it every day, and praise him when he does it without prompting. When possible, invite him to help you with harder tasks, such as drying a few (plastic) dishes or helping to sort the recycling. Be okay with imperfection. The goal here is to make the chores part of his routine, not to have a spotless house.

- **You make money by working.** When my friend Melinda was little, she thought her dad's job was to read the newspaper, since he left for work every morning carrying one under his arm. (He was a middle school guidance counselor.) Small children don't understand intuitively what a job is, or the connection between going to work and earning money. And though you might tell your kid that you are paid to work—and say that your job brings home the bacon to buy all the stuff he has—it's more effective if you can *show* him.

  If possible, take your child to work one day, or even just swing by your workplace over the weekend and show your kid your office/desk/workroom. Let him play with the tape dispenser and twirl in a swivel chair. Give him a clear, simple explanation of your job, tell him that you receive money to do it, and repeat the message that your work allows you to pay for his home, food, and toys. Most very young children can understand complicated jobs if you explain them at the proper level. I know a mom who's an online community manager for big companies, helping to ensure that customer talk on message boards is civil and that representatives reach out to customers with support issues. When asked what his mother does for a living, her four-year-old son says, "My mom takes bad words off the Internet!"

- **It's good to have a job and even better to have a job you love.** One of the best pieces of advice I got when my son was really little was from his nursery school teacher, who told parents to pretend that we liked bugs and worms. The reason: My son's class was doing an earth science unit, and she had found that almost all kids love to dig and play with the dirt. That is, until, at pickup time, their parents scream, "Ewwwww, worms are gross!"—which often squashes their interest in biology.

    Kids get many of their early ideas and prejudices from us. So how you feel about your own work—and how you talk about it in front of your kid—affects how she views work in general. If you enjoy your job, say so. Even if you don't love your job, you can probably say that you love *having* one. It's important to relay the idea that a job is something to take pride in.

- **Parents: Point out real jobs of real people you know.** Talking about the kinds of jobs that you and your kid see every day—the restaurant owner, the doctor, the teacher—exposes him to the range of choices out there, and not just what he sees on TV. It also makes clear that everybody around him works to earn money, and plants the idea that one day he will too. If you're a stay-at-home parent or are married to one, talk about the fact that this job involves many tasks, including doing laundry, cooking meals, and managing the logistics and budgets of kids' activities—but it does not draw a salary. My point: Work takes many forms. Your kid will get it.

- **Parents: Praise effort, not smarts.** Stanford University psychologist Carol Dweck has conducted several studies showing that parents who repeatedly tell their children they're smart or talented might unwittingly be squelching their work ethic. Shower a young child with praise for her innate gifts, and you're likely to create a person who will frustrate easily when, perhaps for the first time, the work becomes a bit harder. Once she no longer finds it a breeze, she might quickly give up, assuming her natural talents have reached their limit. Instead, give meaningful, specific praise about the hard work that goes into her accomplishments. So for instance, when she shows you a picture she has drawn, don't say, "You're so artistic," but rather, "I like the way you worked so hard on this picture, and I love the blue you chose for that line that connects the two circles." That specificity shows you're paying attention to the work your child put into the drawing rather than sending the message that she's the next Basquiat. The ability to stick with something is what will help your kid recognize that having a job (whether a part-time stint at Chipotle or a full-time gig as a student) isn't always easy, but overcoming the challenges and setbacks is part of everyone's life.

- **Parents: Tell your child to pretend to be Batman.** Fascinating research shows that young children can learn to stick with a task longer if they imagine that they are someone else who is a hard worker. Some researchers refer to this rather cutely as the "Batman effect." In one study, groups of four- and six-year-olds were asked to be good helpers and given a boring task to do for 10 minutes. They were also given an iPad with a fun game on it and told that they could take breaks whenever they wanted. Some kids were told to ask themselves periodically, "Am I working hard?" Other kids were told to refer to themselves by name (for example, "Is Samantha working hard?"), and still others were invited to pick a character such as Batman or Dora the Explorer, given a cape or some other costume or prop, and told to ask themselves, "Is Batman working hard?" The kids in the "I" group spent the least amount of time on the task, while the Batman/Dora group spent the most. (Psychologists call this technique "self-distancing.") It's fairly easy to adapt this approach to your child by encouraging him to choose a figure he admires and to "get in character" when he has work to do. (If this sounds familiar, that's because this technique also helps kids to delay gratification so they can save money. See the box on p. 19.)

ELEMENTARY SCHOOL

Kids this age are fascinated by earning money—whether they're hawking lemonade or selling duct tape wallets to their friends. Here's what to tell them to harness that willingness to work.

- **Doing household chores is part of being in our family.** As I've mentioned, research demonstrates that kids who do chores become more successful adults, possibly because of the sense of mastery that they get from a job well done or the feeling of harmony that comes from chipping in as a team player.

  The tasks you assign shouldn't be overwhelming, and your expectations need to be made clear. One way to get your kid's buy-in is to work out a schedule *with* him. Discuss the consequences if the task doesn't get done. You'll probably be surprised by just how draconian your child's proposed penalties can be. ("If I don't walk the dog without being reminded, I have to eat dog food!") Still, that's a good launching point for a conversation in which you suggest a punishment that's a bit more reasonable: "No screen time for a month for not making your bed is too harsh, but what if we decide you lose an hour of weekend screen time instead?" Hammering out a mutually agreed-upon chore system (some families use a chart) will give everyone a sense of being in this together. You might want to make the last "chore" on your kid's list asking the question, "What else can I do to help the family?" This emphasizes to him that he is part of a larger unit, and that just doing the minimum isn't always enough. And no matter what, don't pay your kid for doing his chores. (For details on why that isn't the way to go, see p. 31.)

- **But you can get paid for doing extra jobs.** Okay, so you hear me loud and clear that paying for regular chores is out. But you *can* pay for jobs that fall outside of everyday tasks, particularly if they're tasks that you might hire someone else to do if your kid didn't do them. I'm thinking about things such as cleaning out the garage or organizing online photos. When Rachel, now a writer, was nine, her dad told her that she could earn a few dollars a week if she kept the yard on their family farm spick-and-span. "I developed a sense of pride in it," she says. "Honestly, I became a bit of a tyrant, getting on the case of my three brothers and sisters when they left their toys lying around." In fact, if you're clever, you can use your kid's desire for cash as a force for good. Put her in charge of saving energy around the house (turning off lights, unplugging chargers, monitoring the thermostat), and offer her a portion of the difference between your fat and lean utility bills. Is your attic overflowing with stuff that needs sorting through? Have your kid take a first crack at it, and allow her to take what she finds and sell it on eBay (after you look it over). My kids were excited to learn they could make a bit of cash on some old comic books that Grandma had saved. (Nothing amazing, but $20 isn't bad.)

- **Work isn't always fun, but it's great to have a job.** Now that your child is a bit older, it is fine (actually, better) to tell him that you don't always love your job. It's okay to admit that you have a boss you don't always agree with—just like your kid might have a teacher he isn't wild about—because that's a reality everyone has to deal with at some point in life. This is also a good time to talk about the need to always be respectful and even to just suck it up to be a good worker or student. At the same time, you can still express gratitude that you have a way to make enough money for the family to afford food, clothes, and a place to live. And you can mention the things you can do to make your job better, such as working hard to get a promotion or investigating other divisions in your company where you might be able to transfer. You can also share your plans to get additional education or a specific certification that might enable you to take on more responsibility at your current job or to switch to a totally new career. The message should be consistent: A job isn't always perfect, but you're happy to have a way to earn money.

- **Money isn't everything.** This idea is a cliché to you, but not to your little kid. Yes, you want your child to grow up to be financially comfortable (that's why you're reading this book, after all), but choosing a field or a job just because it might command a high salary can be a big mistake. This is the time to get the message across that it's important to choose work that he enjoys, and that money doesn't always equate to value. Having discussions about trade-offs is a good idea. If you've made choices about the kind of work you do versus the salary you earn, talk to your kid about those decisions. No need to use dollar amounts. Do you work in the arts because you love it despite the modest paycheck? Or are you in a job that gives you satisfaction because you are able to give back—as a teacher, a social worker, or a lawyer who gets to do pro bono work? Or if you run a business, talk about why you like it. Do you enjoy managing people, or is it the idea of being an entrepreneur that excites you? Make sure your kid knows what you love about your job besides the paycheck.

- **Be respectful to people in all jobs.** Not long ago, I observed a kid and his dad at a baseball game. The kid, who was probably 11 or so, was attempting to take a picture of the field from a spot that was roped off for employees only. When an usher asked him to stop, he ignored the man and rudely continued to take photos with his phone. All the while, his dad stood by and didn't say a word. This seemingly small episode transmitted the message to that kid that being obnoxious is okay—and, worse, that being disrespectful to someone who is just doing his job is acceptable.

    Most parents tell kids to say "please" and "thank you." But it is also important to set a good example for your kid and be friendly to the people who do the jobs that make your life easier. Do this even when you're having a bad day—or when, say, the waiter accidentally brings you the wrong order. Whether dealing with a babysitter, a bus driver, or a store clerk, it's easy—and free—to be kind, and to show appreciation for work in all its forms.

- **Parents: Don't turn your kid's lemonade stand into a Whole Foods.** A friend told me recently about a fancy roadside lemonade stand she saw during a weekend trip to the beach. The fresh-squeezed lemonade was in an elegant glass pitcher, the hazelnut truffle ganache cupcakes were iced to perfection, and the sign looked as though a professional calligrapher had worked on it for days. Unsurprisingly, two hyperalert parents hovered over a couple of bored-looking kids who were supposedly running the stand. The problem? Those well-intentioned parents had commandeered the venture, sapping any pleasure their kids might have gotten from it and undermining their desire and drive. If your kid wants to earn some money, it's good to be supportive. But by taking over completely, you will rob him not only of the fun but also of the chance to learn by making mistakes. It's best to let your kid take the lead, even if that means serving lemonade from a packet and cookies from a box.

    Taking over also detracts from a real lesson you can talk about: profit margins. You don't want to be a lemonade-stand Debbie Downer, but after the day is over, it's good to sit with your child as he is counting his cash haul and review the cost of the ingredients—lemons, sugar, paper cups—versus the dollars that came in. You can talk about the trade-offs. "I wonder how much you could save by using a Betty Crocker brownie mix rather than raw ingredients like organic cocoa powder." "Is it worth the time to squeeze real lemons versus using a mix if that means less time to spend actually selling at the stand? On the other hand, can you charge enough for fresh-squeezed lemonade to make it worth it—or even more profitable?" These behind-the-scenes lessons matter more than having a Martha Stewartesque lemonade stand.

- **"Getting rich" is not a career goal.** When Andy visited his kid's fifth-grade class, he was somewhat horrified to read his son's essay on what he wanted to be when he grew up. "He wrote in all sincerity that his goal was to 'get rich and famous by playing professional basketball,' " Andy told me. "Considering that his dad's a short dude with asthma and no jump shot, that's just not happening." At some point it became common wisdom that it's the parents' job to tell their kids that all they have to do is "follow their dreams" to achieve greatness. But if your kid is buying into some unattainable dream not only because he loves to play ball or sing ballads but also because he thinks these pursuits will show him the big bucks, a few gentle words from you are in order. You'll want to choose your moment, of course, and gauge your kid's maturity before you speak. But it's fine to tell your son that he's much likelier to get an MBA than to make it to the NBA—while still encouraging him to shoot hoops. Who knows? Your kid could grow to be six foot eight, with slam-dunk talent. But helping to open his mind to alternatives will only benefit him in the future. Meanwhile, don't freak out if he seems maniacally mercenary at times; it's natural, and that doesn't mean he'll grow up to be the next Wolf of Wall Street.

MIDDLE SCHOOL

At this age, kids can begin to take on more responsibility and even earn money doing it. At the same time, though, you need to continue to stress the many unpaid responsibilities your child should focus on, the most important job being school. Here's what to say to strike that balance.

- **It's time for more advanced chores.** Middle schoolers are more capable now than when they were little, and they have less homework and academic pressure than they will in high school. Plus, a middle schooler can experience a great deal of satisfaction, at least initially, from doing what seems to be an adult job such as raking leaves or doing his own laundry. Once you show your kid the ropes, be hands off. This isn't about achieving excellence in the domestic arts; it's about raising a self-reliant kid. I get that it can be faster and less hassle to sweep the kitchen floor or scrub the bathtub yourself rather than nag your kid continually to do it. But these are the life skills that children should know.

    I know high school seniors who are genuinely more stressed out about the prospect of doing their laundry than managing their coursework at college. Cleaning the toilet, scouring a frying pan well (my personal obsession), and knowing how to mop the floor without making a mess are all good ones. If you time it right, you might be able to get a sixth-grader mildly interested in learning a new skill. It's up to you as a parent to decide whether these new chores are part of the essential pitching-in that you've talked about doing as members of a family, or extra paid jobs.

- **Ask for the going rate when you take a job.** My friend's niece still remembers the bum advice I gave her in seventh grade when she got her first babysitting gig. I suggested that when the mom asks what you charge, tell her, "Whatever you think is fair. Honestly, being with your cute kids is reward enough." I thought it was the polite approach and assured the girl that there was no chance the woman would stiff her. My bad. When the time came to pay up, her neighbor simply said, "Oh, if you're sure you don't want me to, thanks! That's great!" And then didn't give her a cent. Lesson learned: While it's good for your kid to be gracious, it's wrong to discount the value of her real work just because she's a kid.

    Help her come up with a fair rate—whether it's for babysitting, yard work, or spending a couple hours showing an elderly neighbor how to master social media or do genealogical research online. Suggest she consult her friends about what they charge and then be ready with a polite but forthright answer when she's asked what she's owed. This can also be an opportunity to explain some basic labor market concepts: If you charge more than all the other kids for babysitting—say,

$20 an hour when most other kids charge only $10—you're likely to lose customers to your competition. But if you charge too little (say, $5 an hour), you're selling yourself short.

- **If you signed up, stick with it.** It's important for us to make sure our kids live up to their obligations, whether they're job-like commitments such as manning a booth at the school book fair or activities like piano lessons or the soccer team. When you've made a commitment, you don't get to decide midway through the year or the season that you don't want to do it anymore. Take piano lessons until the end of the year. Finish the soccer season. Then you and your kid can figure out together—with some distance—whether she was in a temporary slump (and perhaps it's time for her to switch to rock climbing or hip-hop dancing) or you simply need to enroll her in fewer activities because she's stretched too thin.

  Now, of course, you have to use your judgment. I've cut the cord midway through a class when an instructor was much too harsh or the other kids in the group were truly obnoxious. But in general, it's good to make sure your kid knows that you expect her to stay the course. You can also make the point that the rest of the team, cast, or volunteers are relying on her, and leaving them in the lurch isn't fair. It's certainly not something she'd want someone else to do to her. Bring up a story from your own life—a time when you wanted to drop Girl Scouts or track, but in retrospect you're glad that you didn't because you felt a sense of accomplishment by getting through the year. (It's okay, by the way, if you haven't looked at your merit badges or gone on a run in two decades. The point is that it was something that felt good to complete at that time, long ago.)

- **Understand the minimum wage.** Quick quiz: Do you know the federal minimum wage? As of this writing, it's $7.25 an hour. (Some states set a higher one—in Massachusetts, for example, it's $11.) Now, why should we care? First, it's good for your kid to know that our country introduced the concept of a minimum wage in 1938 (when it was 25 cents an hour!), with the goal of keeping people out of poverty. (Adjusted for inflation, that's about $4.25 an hour today.) It's also good to point out that today about 3 million Americans earn $7.25 an hour or less. So let's do the math: If a person works the typical

40-hour workweek at minimum wage, that comes to about $14,500 a year—less than the amount the government says a parent with a child needs to stay out of poverty.

This fact alone is a good way to introduce your kid to the current debates. What are the arguments for increasing the minimum wage? What are the reasons that some employers oppose raising it? What solutions seem right? This doesn't need to be an AP civics class discussion, but the issue is worth addressing, especially because it could affect your child directly. Minimum wage doesn't apply to everyone or every job. Students, kids, and people in jobs where they receive regular tips, like waiting tables, don't always get $7.25 an hour. In fact, the minimum wage for waiters is $2.13 (which is why it's important to tip generously for first-rate service). And your kid should know that if he's under 20, his boss can pay him only $4.25 for the first three months on the job; after that, he has to be paid at least the full minimum wage. For more info about the minimum wage in your state, visit the U.S. Department of Labor at dol.gov/whd/minwage/america.htm.

- **Parents: Take your kid's entrepreneurial urges seriously—to a point.** Since kids this age seem to be obsessed with making money, they'll probably come up with some questionable schemes. ("Joey and I are gonna pretend we found a rat in our fast-food order so the restaurant will give us money to shut up!") Or they might have amazing business ideas that are, in some way, utterly flawed. ("I bet a skateboard company will totally pay me to get their logo tattooed *on my face*!") You need to listen and resist rolling your eyes. Kids take these projects seriously, so don't be condescending. Encourage the good, gently steer them away from the bad, and stay firm with an unequivocal no to anything that compromises virtual—or actual—safety or ethics.

HIGH SCHOOL

Your kid's main job is school, since working hard at it is the best way to increase his chances of getting into the college of his choice and perhaps scoring some scholarship money. But there are so many distractions. Your job as the parent of a high schooler is helping your child prioritize, using these pointers.

The Money Genius Guide to Understanding Your Paycheck

When your kid gets her first paycheck, she may be confused about why it's so small. Here's a chance to explain the basics—and to refresh yourself—using this handy cheat sheet. Not everything here will appear on your kid's statement, but as she gets older, it's good for her to know what to expect.

1 Pay Schedule
Paychecks are often doled out biweekly (every two weeks).

2 Deductions
These are subtracted from your paycheck before the government takes any taxes out. (That's a good thing.) They go toward things like your 401(k), health insurance (medical, dental, and vision), an HSA (Health Savings Account) or FSA (Flexible Spending Account), etc.

3 401(k)
If you have access to this retirement savings account, contribute at least as much as your company is willing to match. Both your contribution and any employer match will appear on your paycheck.

4 Taxes
There are generally three types of taxes subtracted from your paycheck: There's income tax (federal, state, and local), which helps the government fund schools, highways, and more. You'll also pay into Social Security and Medicare.

5 Gross vs. Net Pay
Gross pay is the amount you earn before taxes are taken out. Net pay is the amount you receive after taxes and other deductions are subtracted.

- **Work in the summers instead of during the school year.** For man having their kid get a paying job during high school can take som off the family budget. A job can also give a student invaluable real perience. Besides, when a kid earns money, it feels like "his" in a w amount of allowance or birthday money does. According to som working a few hours a week might even boost GPA slightly. In the er your kid works will be determined by your family's values and yo situation. I look back with fondness on the jobs I had in high school: Pharmacy, Springfield Diner, and Prestige Caterers (whiskey sour, ar I'm sympathetic to parents who decide that an after-school job [of their kid's academic burdens may simply be too much. And so suggests that parents have reason to be cautious. In a U.S. Bure Statistics study, high school students spent less time—49 fewer mir homework on the days they worked at part-time jobs. Given that have found that kids who put in more time cracking the books e higher grades, why take a chance? My advice: If it's feasible, have the after-school job and focus on making money over the summ course, if he wants to pick up occasional odd jobs such as babysi ing, that's great, as long as they don't eat into homework time.

- **You're going to pay taxes.** When your kid gets her first real pa probably seem tiny. She'll also have no idea what it means, esp been paid off the books for odd jobs up until now. (A recent int found that three out of four American 15-year-olds lack the sk a pay stub.) Time for a quick income-tax lesson. In a nutshe income taxes to the government to fund everything from highw to air traffic control, to the military, to health care for the poo picture. But on an individual level, there are a couple impo your kid to grasp. One is the difference between gross pay (earn before taxes are subtracted) and net pay (the amount yo your paycheck, which is lower, since taxes are removed).

    When your kid started her job, she probably filled out a ` determines how much is taken out of each paycheck and sent to

Your Employer				**Pay Statement**		
123 45th Street				**Period Start Date**	01/04/2017	
Anytown, NY 00000				**Period End Date**	01/17/2017	
				Pay Date	01/20/2017	
				Document	6090452	
				Net Pay	$1,110.24	

Pay Details

Your Name				**Pay Group**	PRN/Sales	**Federal Income Tax**	S2
247 Working Road					Non-exempt	**NY State Income Tax**	S0
Anytown, NY 00000		**Employee No.** 341637		**Location**	123 45th St.	**(Residence)**	
		SSN xxx-xx-xxxx		**Division**	Publishing	**NY State Income Tax**	S0
		Pay Rate $20.18		**Department**	131033 -	**(Work)**	
		Pay Frequency Biweekly			EMPLOYER		
		Annual Rate $36,734.00			EDITORIAL		

Earnings

Pay Type	Hours	Pay Rate	Current	YTD
Overtime .5	0.0000	$0.0000	$0.00	$19.60
Regular	35.0000	$20.1835	$706.42	$0.00
Regular	35.0000	$20.1835	$706.42	$2,475.12
Straight OT 1.0	5.0000	$20.1835	$100.92	$0.00
Straight OT 1.0	5.0000	$20.1835	$100.92	$299.82
Vacation	0.0000	$0.0000	$0.00	$352.72
Total Hours	80.0000			

Deductions

Deduction	Pre-Tax	Employee Current	YTD
401(k)	Yes	$98.88	$188.83
Critical Illness	No	$1.04	$2.08
Delta Std	Yes	$7.23	$14.46
Group Accident	No	$4.85	$9.70
Anthem BCBS CDH	Yes	$16.88	$33.76
HSA Single	Yes	$1.16	$2.32
Life Ins 50K	No	$0.00	$0.00
LTD 50	No	$0.00	$0.00
Vision	Yes	$3.00	$6.00

Taxes

Taxes	Current	YTD
Employee Medicare	$23.01	$44.82
Federal Income Tax	$145.88	$280.19
New York R	$41.40	$79.79
NY State Income Tax	$64.76	$124.54
Social Security Employee Tax	$98.35	$191.62

Paid Time Off

Plan	Current	Balance
Personal Time	0.0000	28.0000
Sick Pay	0.0000	70.0000
Vac Carryover	0.0000	31.9026
Vacation	5.3851	10.7702

Net Pay Distribution

Account Number	Account Type	Amount
xxxxx5437	Checking	$1,110.24
Total		$1,110.24

Pay Summary

	Gross	FIT Taxable Wages	Taxes	Deductions	Net Pay
Current	$1,614.68	$1,489.53	$373.40	$131.04	$1,110.24
YTD	$3,147.26	$2,901.89	$720.96	$257.15	$2,169.15

enue Service. At the end of the tax year, she might need to fill out a tax return and send it to the IRS to make sure she paid enough taxes, and perhaps to get money back if she ended up paying too much. (To see if you do need to file, take the IRS quiz "Do I Need to File a Tax Return?" at IRS.gov.) Other categories withdrawn from her paychecks include state and local taxes, and contributions to FICA, which stands for Federal Insurance Contributions Act. This money pays for Social Security (which primarily goes to your child's grandparents) and Medicare (which helps pay her grandparents' medical bills). For a paycheck primer, see p. 54.

- **Put some earnings in a Roth IRA—no joke.** Most kids who have a part-time or summer job use their income for gas, clothes, and other personal expenses— and, if you read Chapter 2, savings for college. But if it's at all possible, your child should put some money in a Roth IRA. This might sound like an idea that only a financial journalist would float, but it actually can be a smart move if your kid can swing it. Although the IRA in Roth IRA stands for individual retirement account, that's a bit of a misnomer. It should be called a super-smart-place-to-see-your-money-grow account, since it allows your dollars to earn interest free from tax forever (as opposed to a bank savings account, for which you have to pay taxes each year). Another nice thing about a Roth IRA is that your kid can withdraw the money he puts in at any time, without taxes or penalties. The tricky part is that he can put only earned income into this account, so he can't use money from Grandma or cash he got for babysitting but didn't report to the IRS at tax time.

  Now it's time to seduce your kid with the math. When he's 16, say he socks away $500 from a summer job in a Roth IRA that earns 7% interest. Then he leaves it alone, not tapping it during high school or college or beyond. When he turns 65 (yes, he'll really be that old someday), that $500 would have grown to nearly $14,000. What's more, if he were able to add an additional $500 a year, every year, to that IRA, he would have roughly $200,000. Of course, socking away $500 every year—or even once—isn't realistic for some families. But there are ways to open an IRA with about $100. (For more on how to start an IRA, see Chapter 7.)

  An added bonus: If your family applies for federal financial aid for college, the form does not ask whether your child (or you, for that matter) has money in IRAs. And while students will be expected under this formula to contribute 20% of their savings toward the cost of college, the IRA money is out of bounds and therefore won't reduce the federal financial aid your child is eligible for. (Note: Some selective schools *do* ask about IRAs. For more about IRAs and financial aid, see Chapter 9.)

- **Parents: Ease up on the chores a bit.** I know that I've been preaching the gospel of chores for junior high schoolers, so why the sudden change? Here's why: The high school experience is more intense than it used to be. You can blame it on a range of factors: overzealous parents, increased competition for spots at top colleges, superambitious kids. Whatever the reason, the pressure is real: We know from research that teens are more stressed out in high school than ever before. With AP classes, SATs, sports, music lessons, and countless other commitments—not to mention all that homework—piling on loads of laundry and vacuuming duties seems excessive. But letting your child off the hook from all household duties isn't the answer, either. Insist on the basics, such as clearing the table (or at least bringing his plate to the sink) and making his bed (though not necessarily with hospital corners). If your kid has a good routine and does simple household chores without much drama, stick with that schedule. But if you've been somewhat lax about requiring your child to do household duties in the past, now isn't the time to pick this battle.

4 Rules for Kids Working Part-Time Jobs in High School

If your kid is going to work while in high school, there are a few ironclad rules for him to follow.

1 **Don't work more than 15 hours a week during school, including weekends.** More than that, and your kid's grades will likely start to suffer. Research shows that students who work long hours are much less likely to obtain a college degree—and more likely to drop out of high school. If your kid wants to work more, there's always the summer.

2 **Put school first.** This might sound obvious, but when, say, your kid's supervisor at the supermarket insists he work crazy hours during finals week just to make sure all the shifts get covered, he isn't factoring in your kid's academic future. Kids sometimes aren't used to advocating for themselves with adults, so it's up to you to check in with your kid and make sure that work isn't interfering with important tests or school activities.

3 **Save for college.** If your kid is earning enough to buy clothes, electronics, video games—you name it—he's making enough to save some money for college, too. And that's what he needs to do. Besides, spending all that money now results in what University of Michigan researcher Jerald G. Bachman has dubbed "premature affluence." Kids can get an inflated view of the lifestyle they'll be able to afford when they're older and paying for everything (not just the extras) themselves. (See Chapter 9 for specifics on how kids can contribute to college expenses.)

4 **Use your job as a credential.** Encourage your kid to consider asking his boss for a college recommendation if he thinks he has made a significant contribution on the job. Some colleges value real-world experience, and a reference that includes specifics—say, your kid completely automated the shoe store's inventory or developed a new customer service survey that led to increased sales—can be a boon.

COLLEGE

While your kid is in school, the main focus should be on his studies and probably a paying job. At the same time, he needs to prepare for work after college, so help him get launched with this advice.

- **Get a part-time job while in school.** Studies have found that college students who work in on-campus jobs up to about 20 hours a week actually get higher grades than those who don't work at all. One explanation: These students feel more engaged in campus life as active community members, and that attitude extends to their academics. (Interestingly, this trend didn't hold for students with off-campus jobs.) Another reason, suggested by a nationwide study out of the University of California, Merced: Kids who help pay for their college costs, whether they need to or not, feel more invested in their education because they *are* more invested financially. What's more, unlike high school classes, college courses typically take up just a few hours a day. Many students feel that having a job helps them structure their time better. Whether he works in a cafeteria, the student union, or the lab of a favorite professor, having a campus job could boost your kid's grades as well as his earnings, as long as the hours aren't too long.

- **Weigh the pros and cons of unpaid internships.** A student who wants to work at a nonprofit, in the arts, or even in business might have to settle for an unpaid gig to get a foot in the door. The law says an employer can offer an unpaid internship only if it has a significant educational component. Obviously, that's subjective, and the question of what exactly an employer can justifiably ask an unpaid intern to do has received a great deal of attention in recent years. In one highly publicized case, young college graduates who were interning on the 2010 film *Black Swan* from Fox Searchlight Pictures objected to having not been paid. They felt the grunt work they were doing, including keeping track of takeout menus and finding a nonallergenic pillow for the movie's director, didn't meet the educational value standard. (After a five-year court battle, the case was settled.) As similar cases make their way through the courts, the question continues to hang in the air.

  Whatever the legal outcomes, in the end, it's up to your kid to figure out whether a particular internship will be a career jump-starter or a waste of time. Even if she's emptying the trash, will she be able to observe, learn, and make some valuable contacts at a PR firm, hospital, or nonprofit organization? Discuss the practical details with your kid early on. Who will pay for her room and board if it's an unpaid internship over the summer and she lives away from home? (It's more than okay to explain to her that although some of her friends and classmates might be able to take on unpaid internships while their parents support them financially, that's not something you can afford or are choosing to do.) How will she earn money so she can chip in for college expenses? She might have to wait tables nights and weekends or pick up other part-time work, as nearly 40% of unpaid interns do. She should check with her college to see if the internships she is interested in will earn course credit—or perhaps qualify her for a stipend to cover living expenses. Of course, there's no guarantee the experience won't end up being a bust. But remember, it'll be over at the end of the summer and will add another notch to her résumé—and her life.

- **Consider public service—even if you have lots of student loans.** Hefty college debt doesn't mean you can't take a job that gives back. Service programs including AmeriCorps, Teach for America, and the Peace Corps might make you eligible for loan forgiveness. Full-time AmeriCorps members, for instance, are eligible for an education award of close to $6,000 after a year of service, which can be used to pay off outstanding student loans, and a two-year stint with Teach for America can net a participant more than $11,000 to put toward existing student loans. Separately, college grads who go into teaching and other public service jobs might qualify for federal loan forgiveness after working a certain number of years. See p. 90 for more details about this last repayment program.

How to Conduct a Smart Job Search

If your kid is about to graduate from college without a job lined up, he's not alone. Although most schools offer extensive career services, the majority of students don't take advantage of them as they should. As long as you follow these steps, you will almost certainly find something. As my mom told me when I was in college, "Keep your eyes open, and the job will find you."

- **Tap any and all contacts.** Almost every parent belongs to some club or organization, or has a coworker with a nephew in finance or a second cousin who works in fashion. If you don't have contacts, help your kid figure out who his are. Encourage him to be creative and follow even the most far-fetched leads. And tell him that although it's natural to feel shy about asking, the fact is that many professionals get a kick out of the chance to offer advice to someone genuinely interested in their field. The worst that can happen when your kid asks is that the person simply says no.

- **Use that alumni network creatively.** When I was in college, my dad and I combed through a couple years' worth of back issues of my college's alumni magazine and found names of alums working in fields that sounded interesting. I sent out letters (no email in those days, kids) to each, met with a half dozen alums, and ended up landing a wonderful summer job in New York City at a management consulting firm, and another gig right out of school as an editorial assistant at Simon & Schuster. (Thanks, Suzanne Rosencrans!)

- **Think outside the box.** Sometimes an offbeat experience—say, staffing a concession stand at Yellowstone National Park or working as an office assistant at an affordable housing nonprofit—can open doors to future jobs and also look appealing to grad schools seeking students with varied experiences and a bit of gumption. I'm also a firm believer in encouraging kids to work at a restaurant, supermarket, or clothing store at the mall. There's no better way to learn about customer service and business in general—not to mention human nature, warts and all. Once you've been screamed at by a disgruntled shopper attempting to use a long-expired coupon while everyone behind him groans in unison, you're a lot harder to fluster.

- **Pick up the phone.** I know, it's so retro. But a well-timed call can lead to an interview, or at least a note by your kid's name that this is an applicant who's serious. (Of course, if a job listing makes a point of saying "No phone calls," don't make the call. Not rocket science here, people.)

- **Go to every interview you get.** If your kid is offered an interview, he should go, even if he thinks he's not interested in the job. It's great practice, and he might learn something useful if, for instance, the interviewer points out a discrepancy on his résumé or, worse, a typo. Plus, your kid will get a chance to ask questions about the industry and then take that intel to other interviews.

Who knows? He might even discover that a job he'd totally written off is much cooler than it sounded. One last thing. Whatever you do, don't talk trash about former employers. You never know who the interviewer knows, and in general it doesn't reflect well on you.

YOUNG ADULTHOOD

Of course, work can provide us with a sense of purpose and meaning. It's not just about a paycheck. But let's be realistic: The paycheck is important! Now that your kid is out of college, here's how to help him get paid.

- **Just take a job, damn it.** So your college grad expected to work at Google, but his only offer is from the Gap. Here's where you need to give the best parental pep talk of your life, which goes something like this: Be the best T-shirt folder/Starbucks barista/office assistant you can be. Your job performance not only affects what your boss, coworkers, and customers think of you but also has karmic repercussions that can pay it forward. A friend's nephew, Jay, wants to be a zoologist and is planning to go to grad school. But for now, he needs to work for a couple years to save money for tuition. So after college he moved home and took a job at Petco, since it meant he was working around animals and helping people take care of their pets. He threw himself into the job, and that experience helped land him an internship at the San Francisco Zoo. Lastly, just because you take a job doesn't mean you have to feel locked in. The conventional wisdom has been that you need to stay in a job for at least two years or risk looking like you move around too much. But the majority of recent grads today don't stay in their jobs for more than a year. Briefer stints have become the norm.

- **Get paid or move on.** While your kid is in college, an unpaid internship can be a great way to sample some interesting fields and gain valuable experience. Once he graduates, though, remaining in internship limbo can be problematic. Internships are great for employers but can be a dead end for a kid who needs a real job. (In fact, as I mentioned on p. 59, a number of interns have sued employers on the grounds that they are being exploited for the free labor they provide.) Unless you're willing to subsidize your college graduate indefinitely, make clear just how long you'll pay his way—if you can afford to do so at all. It's also fair for you to chime in if you think an internship isn't leading to a real job or helping him build a résumé in a meaningful way. My advice? After six to nine months in an internship, your kid should ask that the position be made full-time at the end of the year or look for a new gig that pays. Discourage your kid from becoming a serial unpaid intern.

- **Negotiate—but do it wisely.** I received my first real job offer over the phone, and I accepted the quoted salary on the spot. Minutes later, my new boss called back to say that he felt guilty about the low offer. My dopey response? "No, no! I'm thrilled." Not surprisingly, he said, "Okay," and I was locked into a low starting salary. I'm not proud of this story. But it does illustrate how unnerving salary discussions can be, particularly for young people and women, who, research shows, typically are more hesitant to negotiate. Getting that initial number right is important; studies find that most wage growth occurs during a person's first decade in the workforce, and increases are calculated off that original amount. Unfortunately, much of the advice out there isn't very good, since it coaches people to negotiate no matter the offer—a tactic that can easily backfire. You'll need to combat that with the real scoop.

  Salary often isn't discussed at a first meeting, so tell your kid not to bring it up on his own. But he *should* go in knowing what the salary norms are for that industry. Have him check out Salary.com, Glassdoor.com, and PayScale.com. If he knows people who work at the company, he can ask them tactfully what salary range they think he should expect; studies show that people are much more willing than you'd think to give you an idea of what they make. Women in particular need to do this, since recent female college grads earn, on average, 7% less than male peers with the same degrees, jobs, and hours. That common advice about never being the first to name a number isn't always practical—so if your kid is asked point-blank what salary he's looking for, he should be prepared to give a range. Once a formal offer is made, if your child is being lowballed, he should politely provide a specific rationale for getting more—perhaps citing the data he's collected on industry norms or his experience in the field. If he's unsure, it's okay to ask for 24 hours to think it over and then do some quick research. But if he knows that the offer is generous, he should take it. It's a mistake to negotiate simply because he thinks he'll look like a chump if he doesn't. Being pushy in the face of an attractive offer can color the way a new boss views you. And being likeable actually makes you *more* likely to get what you want. Finally, in any negotiations, your kid should be sure to ask about benefits, which are the equivalent of roughly 30% of the average person's salary. If vacation time, education stipends, or other benefits matter to your kid, now is the time to make sure he's getting what he wants, or is at least asking for it. And clue him in to the importance of a good 401(k) with a company match. (See p. 153 for details on retirement saving.)

- **Being your own boss can be great, but it's also risky and a ton of work.** Entrepreneurial fever has swept the nation with the rise of shows like *Shark Tank* as well as a burgeoning number of institutes and incubators that promote entrepreneurship. It's no wonder that a survey by the consulting firm Deloitte found that roughly 70% of millennials picture themselves working independently at some point. What's often lost in the romance of the entrepreneurial dream is how difficult it is to attain. One in three new businesses closes within two years of opening its doors. A full 50% close within five years.

  It's important for your kid to understand the long odds, and to approach being an entrepreneur as a job, not a lifestyle. I'm not saying your kid can't be successful, but I *am* saying that it takes more than a spiffy PowerPoint and a workshopped business plan to make it happen. While a kid just out of school might have the energy (and, most likely, no family responsibilities or mortgage) to work long hours for low pay to get her idea off the ground, according to a study published in the *Harvard Business Review,* the average tech entrepreneur in the New York City area isn't an Ivy League dropout wunderkind but was 31 years old when she founded her company, and had gotten her degree and spent several years working in her industry before setting out on her own.

- **Work the job you have, not the job you think you deserve.** Your kid might have already snapped up a URL for his own tech start-up, but for now, he should also make sure he knows how to use the office copier. Encourage him to try to make himself indispensable in general. Lisa, now president of a major New York college, reflects, "At one of my first jobs, I was in a room with a bunch of guys, and someone needed to take the minutes of the meeting. They all found it degrading, but I volunteered. When the boss got my notes, he said they were so good that he asked me to be the author of the report. I never turn up my nose at anything." Bottom line: Even if your kid's throwing herself into the job doesn't make a difference to anyone else (and odds are that it will), at the end of the day, it will mean something to her.

4

Drop Debt

Just a few years after Sienna graduated from college, she thought she had it made. She'd earned an Ivy League degree, and after working at a small newspaper for a couple years, she was accepted to a top writing program. Sure, she had student debt and would have to take on more in grad school, but none of that fazed her. She relied on a couple credit cards to fill in the gaps when she needed cash—whether for a trip during a school break, books for a course, or gas for her car. "I kept telling myself throughout my twenties, 'I'll catch up at some point,'" Sienna recalls.

Then she graduated with just over $10,000 in credit card debt—plus $25,000 in student loans. Reality set in. Sienna spent her nights lying in bed worrying about money, dreading each credit card and student loan statement, and generally stressing out. Though she was lucky to land a position at a literary website, the only way she could afford to accept the job and its modest salary was to sell her car, get a roommate, and waitress nights and weekends. Even then, she could barely keep up with the minimum payments on her debt.

"I was past thirty before I was finally able to turn the ship around," Sienna says. "I spent years regretting each pair of shoes and jeans I'd gotten and every restaurant dinner and movie ticket I'd charged to my card. It felt like my hands were tied by decisions I'd made in the past."

If this story sounds familiar, you're not alone.

Maybe you were a Sienna. Or maybe your kid is, or is on her way to being, someone just like her.

In a recent survey, parents were asked to name their biggest financial regret. The number one answer was that they wished they'd taken on less debt. What is most striking (and, frankly, depressing) about this finding is that most of us have no idea how to prevent our kids from making the very same mistake.

There's no doubt that debt in all its forms is an integral part of life. Our little ones watch from their strollers as we swipe cards and magically get what we want. Our middle schoolers see some of their friends receive debit cards from their parents, and ask for their own. And though recent rules have made it tougher for college students to obtain credit cards, they're digging themselves out from more student loan debt than young people have ever had.

The recession of 2007 to 2010 had at least one upside: Many young people are more skittish about taking on debt. But there are times when borrowing makes sense, and avoiding debt completely can be problematic too. For instance, taking out reasonable federal student loans to afford college is smart, since grads, on average, earn much more than those who don't go to college. And borrowing to buy a home, when done wisely, is generally a good investment over the long run. But in just about every other aspect of your financial life, it's better not to borrow. Period.

Helping our kids to be truly smart about debt means more than warning them of the horrors of outrageous interest rates and calls from persistent debt collectors. The job we have as parents is trickier than that: It's teaching them that living beyond their means—despite the fact that using debt in all its forms to do so has become the American way—isn't really okay. Obviously, it's even harder to get this across if you are mired in debt yourself. This chapter will help you teach your child a healthy way to handle credit.

PRESCHOOL

This is the perfect time to start teaching basic debt concepts: We have to pay for the things we buy, a credit card is one way to do this, and we can't have everything, no matter how much we want it. Here are some simple lessons to pass on.

- **Buying stuff costs money—whether you use cash or credit.** The acquisition of things is both mysterious and ridiculously simple in the eyes of a child. When Jessica took her four-year-old son to Target and pulled out a $20 bill at the register, she was horrified to hear him say, "Don't pay for it, Mommy. Use your card instead." She hadn't realized he even noticed how she paid for things, much less that he was learning to think that a credit card was a way to avoid payment. So try this: The next time you're in the grocery store, tell your child to pick out something that costs a dollar. Then take out four quarters, a dollar bill, and a credit card, and explain that you could use any of these to buy it. Let him choose and see you pay for it.

- **You can't always get what you want.** Amanda's parents were hardworking people who always had trouble making ends meet. So when she had her own daughter, Ella, she loved that she could afford to give her kid all the things she'd wanted but couldn't have as a little girl: Barbie dolls, Burberry dresses, Dr. Martens shoes. Since Ella was just four, Amanda figured that she had plenty of time to learn about waiting for what she wants. The problem was that Amanda was doing her girl harm by not letting her experience limits early, and instead acting like a human credit card. Researchers led by Duke University psychologist Terrie Moffitt followed a thousand children from birth to age 32 and found that the ones who had trouble exercising self-control as little kids had accumulated more credit problems in adulthood, which makes sense, no?

  To help your child flex that muscle early on, make it standard practice when you're running errands or grocery shopping not to buy little extras whenever she asks for them. This will reinforce the message that being in a store does not mean that you are going to indulge every whim. Setting the precedent that there are limits will not only stop the constant nagging but also will help her when she has her own credit card one day. (See the box on p. 19 for tricks to teach your kid in tempting situations.)

ELEMENTARY SCHOOL

Starting in kindergarten, your kid's consumerism kicks into high gear: "I want it" leads to "I need it," which turns into "I'm the only one who doesn't have it." It can be maddening to hear your kid prattle on about brands, logos, and what's cool and what's not. This is your big opportunity to lovingly but firmly teach your kid about limits. As for what's actually cool? Good luck.

- **Using a credit card to buy something can cost you more.** Starting around second grade, your kid will be able to understand most of this explanation: "When I use my credit card, I'm borrowing money from a lending company. That lending company pays the store for me, then sends me a bill. If I don't have enough money to pay it all back right away, they will charge me extra money, called interest." That's where an example might be useful: Say you bought a chocolate bar for $1 using a credit card. If you weren't able to pay it back immediately, you'd end up paying interest, and that chocolate bar could cost you closer to $1.25 or even more. The point: A credit card should be used for convenience; it's a way to buy stuff without having to carry lots of cash. If you use it and pay it in full as soon as you get the bill, you don't have to pay extra. But if you use it to buy stuff you can't really afford, you will end up wasting money.

- **Never give out personal information online.** You need to repeat this to your kid early and often. Make it clear that he should never enter the following information online: your name or his, your family's address, his birth date, his school, his phone number, his email address, photos of him or your family, online passwords if someone asks for them, his Social Security number, and, of course, your credit card number. He shouldn't email any of that info to anyone, either, without checking with you first. These details can be gold to cybercriminals looking to steal your financial info or your kid's identity.

  Identity-safeguarding rules are easier to enforce for younger kids if you limit the websites they can be on—and here's where the law is on your side. Websites that have users under 13 must have special policies in place to protect kids and their personal information, which is why many—including most major social media sites like Facebook and Instagram—do not allow kids under that age to have accounts. If you want to go to the next level, read the privacy policy of a website your kid is begging to sign up for—you might find the level of data collection that many sites describe shocking. Also, these policies often will specify that children under 13 can't have an account. You can then say, "Let's check the company's website and follow whatever is spelled out in the rules."

- **Parents: Don't give your kid your credit card number—ever.** Natalie told me about the time her six-year-old son was playing a computer game and she was nearby doing some work. "He started asking a string of innocuous questions, like whether our address was 220 Riverpark Road," she recalled. After about five minutes of queries that she answered absently, he asked for her credit card number, which, of course, stopped her cold. Turned out he was trying to order an action figure online. "It was the first time we talked about what you can and cannot do on the computer," she said.

  Most kids this age like to shop or at least browse online. Whether your kid is buying a computer game, a movie, an app, or a song, he'll need your credit or debit card info. Although the easiest thing is for you to enter and save your credit card information on a variety of sites your family uses so that you don't have to type it in each time, don't. Be aware that even if you type in your credit card number for a onetime purchase, on apps and websites there's often a window of time after that when additional purchases can be made without a separate authorization. (See p. 105 for more on this issue.) And make a rule for yourself that you won't give your kid your card info so that he can type it in, either; the temptation is too great for him to use it in a moment of weakness. (Tell him that it's not that you don't trust him, but your policy is that you're the only one who gets to use your credit card, without exception. Definitely a good message for when he has his own card in the future.) Separately, if you're buying something for him online that you probably would not buy for him in a store, tell him he needs to pay *you* back. Don't feel weird or petty about this. It's no different from being in a store and buying him something that he wants; reimbursement is part of the deal.

MIDDLE SCHOOL

Kids this age are intrigued with the idea of credit cards and can understand the details of how they work. Exploit their curiosity—and their desire for stuff—to teach them these important lessons about debt.

- **Use cash.** When Lynn's thirteen-year-old, Maya, asked to go shopping with her friends, she mentioned to her mom that several of her classmates' parents were giving their daughters their credit cards so that the girls didn't have to walk around the mall with wads of cash. Lynn knew these weren't particularly overindulgent parents. In fact, each girl was given a strict limit on how much she could spend. Still, Lynn gave Maya cash instead: "I knew that if Maya got to the register and the bill was even just a dollar more than the fifty dollars I gave her, she'd have to make a hard decision and put something back. That's not the case with a card."

  Lynn's gut was good. A famous MIT study found that people are willing to spend twice as much to buy the same item when using a credit card rather than cash. And it's not just credit cards but all plastic that can trick us into spending more. Debit cards and prepaid cards don't necessarily allow kids to feel the weight of their spending choices, either. Studies show that parting with actual dollars when you make a purchase can be more "painful" than simply flashing a plastic card. In a nationwide study, kids who paid for lunches with debit cards spent more than those who used cash. (Interestingly, the debit card users also seemed to spend recklessly, opting for more French fries and candy over fruits and veggies.) Although lots of people recommend prepaid cards for kids and teens as a cash alternative, since there's a limited amount loaded on these cards, I prefer the mindfulness that comes with handing over dollar bills. (See the "Parenting and Plastic" box on p. 79.) Of course, the downside of cash is that if your kid loses it, it's lost. But that's a lesson worth learning, too.

- **Understand what "net worth" is.** In school, usually around the sixth grade, your kid will learn about negative numbers. This is a good time to explain that debt, in a sense, is "negative money." Here's what I mean: Say that you owe someone $10. Even if you have $6 in your pocket, you basically don't have any money at all. You will soon have to give that $6 to the person from whom you borrowed. So, technically speaking, you have negative $4. And that's the concept of net worth: It's the money you have minus the money you owe to everyone else. And it's a concept that many, many adults don't get.

- **Credit card interest can kill you.** Okay, so maybe not *kill* you, but it certainly can be painful. This is the perfect age at which to deliver the message that it's a complete waste of money to ever pay interest on a credit card. To review: If you owe money on a credit card and don't pay it back right away, you get charged interest on the original amount you borrowed. That amount is called the principal. If you still don't pay it all off the next month, you'll not only be charged interest on the principal but you'll also be charged interest on your interest (which is known as compounding). When interest compounds like this, your debt grows very quickly. Or, put another way: If you don't pay your credit card bill in full each month, you're charged really high interest payments that can add up to hundreds, if not thousands, of dollars over time.

  Here's where numbers help. Show your kid how much more expensive an item is when you make only the minimum payment the credit card company requires each month. (The way the companies calculate minimum payments varies, so check with your credit card company.) When your child asks for an iPad, tell him this: If we buy it in cash, it costs $500. But if I put it on a credit card with a 19% interest rate and make just the minimum monthly payments, it would take almost four years to pay it off, and that iPad would end up costing $716. Take a look at the chart on p. 74 with your kid to see other examples. He will get the message.

- **"Just say no" to a store credit card.** It's just about impossible to purchase something at a clothing or department store without the person at the register trying to lure you into opening a store credit card—usually dangling 10% or even 20% off your purchase. The next time you're shopping with your kid, use that sales pitch to make a point. Ask the clerk, with your kid right there, what the interest rate is. Half the time, the clerk doesn't even know. Regardless, say no, and then once you are out of the store, tell your kid why. Generally, the interest rate is ridiculously high: usually 20% or more. If you don't pay the bill in full every month, the interest will end up costing you much more over time than any initial discount you get. Tell your child how much higher that interest rate is than the interest rate on the credit card you usually carry. (If that's not the case, get a new credit card!) The one exception: If you pay your bill in full every month, and you shop frequently at a particular store that offers discounts, coupons, and other rewards on stuff you would buy anyway, it's possible that a store card could save you money.

The True Cost of Paying the Minimum on Your Credit Card

Carrying a balance on your credit card is an incredibly expensive way to buy stuff. Use the examples below to start a conversation with your kid. All were calculated using a 19% APR (annual percentage rate).*

Item	Initial Purchase Price	Months to Pay It Off	True Cost, Including Interest
Back-to-school wardrobe	$300	25	$364
Laptop computer	$829	96	$1,548
Family trip to the Grand Canyon (airfare and hotel for 4)	$2,400	202	$5,606

* All minimum monthly payments were calculated on CreditCards.com using the formula of accrued interest plus 1% of the current balance, with an absolute lowest payment of $15.

- **Bad spending behavior ruins your credit cred—and can cost a lot of money.** Kids this age are obsessed with their reputations and how they're viewed by other kids. You can tell your child that adults also worry about how they are looked upon by others—including lenders. People who pay their bills on time build up a good credit history, are viewed favorably by lenders, and get good deals on loans. And to get even more fine-tuned than that, adults are actually rated with a number, known as a credit score, which represents a person's potential ability to pay her bills. (Be prepared for your kid to ask you yours. If you're brave, go to CreditKarma.com and show her. For more about your own credit score, see p. 215.) The next time your family makes an expensive purchase, like a car or house, it can be particularly powerful to point out how the interest rate you got on a loan or a mortgage was affected by your credit score.

- **Parents: Take your kid when you go shopping for a big-ticket item and explain how you're paying for it.** Of course, teaching your kid about debt isn't only about telling him what he can't have; it's about showing him how to plan to get what he wants. That means showing him what it takes to commit to a financial goal. Around this age, your kid may start to ask about how you pay for stuff like a home and a car. And if he has older siblings, he might also become more aware of college and start thinking about how much it costs. What's more likely is that he'll want an expensive pair of jeans or headphones and wish he could have a credit card of his own to swipe. When you buy a car, for instance, take your kid along. Explain that borrowing money is a serious commitment, and you should do it only when it's absolutely necessary.

- **Parents: Know the signs of foul play in your kid's credit report.** Child identity theft is shockingly common. If your child is receiving credit card offers in the mail, notices from the IRS about overdue income-tax payments, or calls from bill collectors, don't blow them off as bizarre mistakes. They could be red flags that someone is tampering with your kid's financial record. One problem is that creditors and employers don't have a way to verify the age attached to a Social Security number. If a thief uses your 12-year-old's Social Security number and says he's 24 (the most common form of child identity theft is to pair a kid's Social Security number with a different age), that's what will go into your kid's credit file until you dispute it. One thing to note: It's often someone your child knows who's using her Social Security number.

  If you suspect that someone has stolen your kid's identity, you'll need to check your kid's credit report. If your kid is 14 or older, you can do this for free at AnnualCreditReport.com. (There are several similarly named sites that imply they're free but aren't, so don't get snookered.) If your kid is younger than that, you will have to go directly to the bureaus themselves: Experian, TransUnion, and Equifax. Since you're checking for fraud, this process is free. For more on how to do this and what to do if you discover fraud, see the U.S. Federal Trade Commission's primer on child identity theft at consumer.ftc.gov/articles /0040-child-identity-theft. I'm going to be honest: This can be a bit of a nightmare.

HIGH SCHOOL

These are the years when kids will want to know about car loans and even more about credit cards. Your job is to fill them in, and also to start talking about the realities of student loans and what they will mean for the future. Here's what to say to keep your kid grounded about borrowing.

- **Stick with cash until 12th grade.** In most states, your child can't get a credit card of her own until she's 18—and even then there are plenty of restrictions until she's 21. But she might ask you to let her use *your* credit card or to make her an authorized user on your account. Don't give in. You also should not give her a debit card linked to your checking account. Sure, it's a hassle to go to the ATM to get cash for your kid. And yes, it's a pain for her to be the only 11th- or 12th-grader with cash if all of her friends have debit cards or are using their folks' credit cards. But this is a good one to hold out on as long as you can. Cash runs out. That means your kid will see when she has no dollars left. And remember, studies show that people spend up to twice as much on the same item when using plastic as when paying with cash, which also makes debit and prepaid cards less useful for making your kid aware of her spending. If your kid has her own checking account, during senior year she can apply for a debit card that draws against it. Make sure that the bulk of her savings is in a separate account that can't be tapped with the card and also that she opts out of overdraft protection. That way, she'll figure out that her spending has limits when her card gets declined, instead of getting hit with overdraft fees.

- **Buy only what you can afford to pay for now.** It's great if you taught your kid this lesson when he was younger, but if not, don't beat yourself up. Better late than never, and reading this book means you're taking action now. So explain it like this: If you can't afford to buy something and you put it on a credit card, when you get the bill, you won't be able to pay it in full. Then you'll be charged high interest payments that can add up to hundreds, if not thousands, of dollars. Talk about, say, the college friend who charged a pizza out almost every night on a credit card. Though the pizza vanished within minutes, because the monthly bill was more than the friend could afford to pay, the debt was still there on graduation day. This kind of story is particularly useful at this age, since kids often think it's the big purchases that can get you into serious debt and don't consider how the little things can add up.

- **Check your credit report once a year.** The Federal Trade Commission advises all families to check a child's credit report once they turn 16. You can sit with your kid and together go to AnnualCreditReport.com to check with each of the three credit bureaus for free. Of course, most teens don't have a credit report, since they don't have loans or credit cards, so you probably won't find anything. If you do, it could be a sign of fraud, and you'll need to follow the steps outlined at consumer.ftc.gov/articles/0040-child-identity-theft.

  Use this opportunity to talk to your high schooler about credit reports and why he will want to keep his clean. Discuss the need to check his reports once a year. Explain to him that one in four credit reports contains errors. Some of these are minor mistakes, such as a wrong address. But 5% have something really wrong—like being confused for someone else with bad credit—that could materially affect your kid's ability to get credit.

- **Be wary of lending to or borrowing from friends.** Jake, my friend Lisa's son, learned this lesson the hard way. He and his buddy Gus took an after-school weight-training class and got obsessed. Gus wanted to buy a weight bench but couldn't afford to, so Jake offered to pay for it, with the understanding that they would share it and he'd be paid back. When the school year ended, Gus wouldn't pay up. Jake didn't want to take the bench away from him, so he left it behind—along with the friendship. Kids can be really generous when it comes to their friends, but, sadly, friends can wind up betraying and disappointing them. A good rule of thumb: There's no such thing as a loan to someone close to you. If you do want to help a friend out of a tight spot, think of it as a gift and don't count on getting back the money. (If you do, consider it a bonus.) The lesson is that if you can't afford to lose money, don't lend it. And if you can help it, don't borrow from friends if you can't pay them back immediately (say, within 24 hours). Otherwise, there can be hard feelings—and even lost friendships.

- **Memorize your Social Security number and never share your bank password or debit card PIN, even with friends.** My friend's daughter Clara was in Los Angeles and lost her wallet with her ID and her plane ticket in it. She had nothing except her suitcase full of swimsuits and sundresses. At the airport, she had to explain her predicament to security. In order to get on the plane, she was asked a battery of questions, including her Social Security number. Fortunately, she had memorized it recently and was able to board. Even if something that dramatic doesn't happen to your kid, at some point during high school she will probably be asked for her Social Security number—whether while filling out paperwork at a new job or applying for financial aid—and it's good to have it stored in her mind.

  Although it seems that there's little reason to memorize anything anymore—you can simply look it up on your phone, right?—personal info can be dangerous if it falls into the wrong hands. For instance, someone can use your Social Security number to apply for credit in your name, or use your bank password or PIN to access your bank account. Your kid is better off simply memorizing this info.

  At this age, kids tend to be unconditionally trusting of their friends. That's why it's important to emphasize the necessity of keeping this kind of financial data private, even (or maybe especially) from those they are closest to. Explain to your kid that he shouldn't give out his Social Security number if someone calls and asks for it, even if that person claims to be from your kid's bank or school. Instead, your kid can end the call and then phone his bank or school directly to see if the information is legitimately needed.

- **Parents: Don't buy your kid a car—and don't cosign her car loan, either.** Believe me, I understand the instinct to buy your kid a safe car to get around in, if you can afford it. Yet I don't think it's a good idea financially. First, big college expenses are looming, and they should be the priority. If your child really wants a car, encourage her to save her money from summer jobs for a couple years so she can buy an inexpensive used one, which should cost much less than a new model. If you want, you can offer to match part of what she saves. If your child says, "But I'll pay for it with a loan," you will almost certainly need to cosign—a bad idea, since your credit will be affected if your kid can't make the payments. Adding a kid to your auto insurance will also jack up your premiums. For tips on how to lower that cost and get your kid to share the burden, see p. 126.

- **Parents: Tackle the topic of student loans.** Most families need to borrow to pay for college. Explain this to your kid at the beginning of high school and let her know that she will probably have to take out student loans. Reassure her that you'll help her do it the smart way, and explain that this is one of the few times when debt might be necessary—and if so, it can be a good investment. For everything you need to know about financial aid and taking out student loans, see Chapter 9.

Parenting and Plastic: Which Cards Are Right for Your Kid?

The problem with cards is that they can feel like Monopoly money, and result in kids spending more than they would if they had to part with cold, hard cash. That said, here's a list of your options. For more information on how these cards affect your and your kid's credit, see p. 83.

Prepaid Debit Cards. You can buy these at many retail stores or online, and they work a lot like store gift cards, except that you can use prepaid cards anywhere. You decide how much money you want to load onto the card—and many cards are reloadable. However, charges ranging from monthly "maintenance" fees to card activation fees to ATM fees make them expensive.

Bottom Line: Although there is a trend among parents to give these to their kids instead of cash, I say skip 'em. Give cash instead so that your child feels the pain of parting with his dollars.

Debit Cards. These cards, which you get from your bank, allow you to make purchases or withdraw money from ATMs by drawing on the cash in your checking or savings account. If your child is underage—younger than 18 or 21, depending on your state—he might not be allowed to get a debit card, or the bank might require that he share an account with you. Policies vary, so check with your bank. Another sticking point: Most banks offer overdraft protection, meaning that they'll lend you money if you overdraw your checking account with your debit card, but they may also charge interest and a "courtesy" fee, which can add up in a very big way.

Bottom Line: Never give your kid a debit card linked to *your* checking account, since that would mean unfettered access to your money. The first choice is to have him get his own checking account that comes with a debit card. If he is not old enough for a debit card of his own and needs to access money for a specific reason (for example, travel abroad), you can open a separate account, linked to yours, that gives him access with a debit card.

Authorized User Credit Cards. These are credit cards issued to someone else (such as your child) from your own credit card account. While you still pay all the bills, your kid has access to your full credit limit. (As of this writing, only one major card issuer, American Express, allows you to limit how much an authorized user can charge on your account.) Many parents make their kid an authorized user with the idea that doing so will allow their child to build a credit history, but this isn't always the case, since some lenders don't report authorized users to the credit bureaus that track such things. Also, your credit score will take a hit if you can't pay off your kid's charges, which is why it's a good idea to monitor the account's activity closely.

Bottom Line: These cards can be convenient to give to your kid, say, while she's in college in case of emergency or for other specific expenses. But think very, very hard about whether you want to do this. Then establish clear rules for the card's use and make it known that this is only a temporary arrangement.

Cosigned Credit Cards. These cards are for people who don't qualify for a credit card on their own—because they don't make enough money, don't have a long enough credit history, or don't have good enough credit—and therefore need a responsible person (like a parent) to cosign. In this case, your kid is the one who gets the bills and builds up a credit history. But there's a huge downside for parents: Unlike when you make your kid an authorized user and you are in charge of paying the bills, with a cosigned card, your kid is in control of making the payments. If he messes up, you're still responsible for paying the bill, and it will hurt your credit score as well as his.

Bottom Line: Just don't do it. Nope, no, nah, *nyet*. If your kid can't get a credit card on his own because he's too young or financially irresponsible, don't cosign for him.

Secured Credit Cards. These cards are used by people (maybe like your kid) who want to build good credit but can't get a "regular" credit card because of a thin credit history or money mistakes in the past. They work like regular credit cards but with one big difference: With secured cards, you deposit money with the issuer in a special savings account, as collateral. So, for example, for a card with a $300 credit limit, you'd need to put $300 in that special account. The card issuer holds on to the money and doesn't apply it to your bill, which you still must pay every month. Sometimes, after a few months of on-time payments, the issuer may raise a cardholder's credit limit without asking for a bigger deposit. Most secured cards report to the major credit bureaus, but not all do, so if your kid is shopping for one, he'll need to check. Also, secured cards tend to charge higher interest rates and have annual fees that typically range from $25 to $49.

Bottom Line: This is a good option only if your young adult child is having trouble getting a "regular" credit card.

Regular Credit Cards in Your Kid's Name. Unlike a decade or so ago, when college campuses were flooded with credit card companies hawking cards to anyone who wanted one, today it's much harder for college students to get their own plastic. Federal law prohibits students under 21 years old from obtaining a card unless they have an adult cosign or they have enough income to pay the bills. What qualifies as income can vary from company to company;

some lenders require a job, but others will count parental support and even scholarships and student loans as money that can be tapped to cover the credit card bills. (Scary, when you think about it.) Plenty of kids circumvent the rules and find an older sibling or friend to cosign for them—obviously, a horrible idea.

Bottom Line: Although your kid will probably want a credit card at some point, a first card can wait until he's a junior or senior in college.

COLLEGE

Chances are, your kid will need to borrow to help pay for college. This may also be the point at which she wants a credit card in her name. As she heads off on her own, here's advice she should take with her.

- **Bank smart at school.** Perhaps your child has a checking account at a bank close to home. If it's a regional or national bank, she should check to see if there's a branch near campus. If so, she can simply stick with this bank while at school. That keeps it simple. She can use her debit card to spend, make free withdrawals from convenient ATMs, and deposit paychecks into her account. If her home bank doesn't have branches near her school, it might make sense to find a local bank or credit union with free checking, a good mobile app, and ATMs near campus (to avoid fees). Credit unions tend to have low balance requirements to avoid monthly fees and also pay higher interest on savings. To find one, your kid should check ASmarterChoice.org and MyCreditUnion.gov.

  When it comes to banking, don't assume anything is too basic to explain. For example, my friend Ellen deposited $1,000 into her daughter Jade's checking account before she left to begin her freshman year and told her that she could use the money for books, supplies, and emergencies. Just a couple of months later, Jade called home in a panic. She said that someone had hacked into her account and drained it of most of the money. When Ellen asked Jade if it was possible she'd unwittingly spent it, Jade was adamant that she had hardly used her debit card at all. Then they began to review the charges over the phone. Suddenly Jade remembered the dinners, gifts, and Uber rides she had paid for. My friend wondered aloud, "How can my honors math student not get the fact that each little purchase she made on the card added up?"

Building Credit with Cards

Paying with plastic is just one of many factors that go into your credit history. Here's a rundown of the types of cards your kid may have, and what effects they could have on his credit and yours. For more details about these cards, see the box on p. 79.

Kind of Plastic	Does It Help Your Child Build a Credit History?	Could It Ruin Your Child's Credit Score?	Could It Ruin Your Credit Score?
Prepaid Card	No	No	No
Debit Card	No	No	No
Authorized User Credit Card	Usually. Not all issuers report activity of authorized users to the credit agencies. Check with the card issuer.	Sometimes. Negative activity is not always recorded on the credit report.	Yes. Whoever is the primary account owner (a parent, presumably) is on the hook for activity on the card.
Cosigned Credit Card	Yes	Yes	Yes
Secured Credit Card	Usually. Check with the card issuer.	Yes. Could negatively impact score if the child doesn't make payments on time.	No. Card is in the child's name only.
Regular Credit Card in Your Kid's Name	Yes	Yes	No

- **Be wary of school-sponsored debit cards.** Many colleges are partnering with banks to offer debit cards with the school logo. These cards also function as student IDs, meal cards, and even dorm room keys. The terms of these cards can be worse than those offered by a competing credit union or bank, so your kid shouldn't feel obliged to use one as his default debit card. Instead, he should follow my advice to shop around for the bank that offers the best terms rather than simply go with one suggested to him at freshman orientation. Warning: Some schools even put students' financial aid money on these cards. If that is the case, tell your child to request that his financial aid funds be deposited directly into his own bank account to avoid the card's bad terms—and to prevent him from "accidentally" spending his college money.

- **Your credit score rules your financial life.** Now that your child is grown, it's time to introduce him to his credit score: the number that determines a huge part of his financial life. The type of credit score used by most lenders, known as a FICO score, ranges from 300 (poor) to a perfect 850. (The national average hovers around 700.) Your FICO score is determined by the following five factors:
  - your track record in paying your bills (35%);
  - the utilization ratio, which is the current amount you're borrowing versus the total amount you have access to (30%);
  - the number of years you've been using credit (15%);
  - your credit mix, which looks at the type of credit you use—from student loans to credit cards (10%); and
  - your number of credit applications in the last 12 months (10%).

  Generally speaking, the lower your kid's score, the higher the interest rate he'll have to pay on loans. (One big exception is federal student loans, because one interest rate applies to everyone when the original loan is issued.) Lower credit scores can also make it harder for him to rent an apartment, since landlords will often ask for authorization to look at an applicant's credit report and score.

- **Pay *all* your bills on time.** Maybe your busy college kid thinks the only cost of making a tardy payment is the late fee. But that is not the case. A single late payment can mess up her credit score, so it's critical for her to get in the habit of paying all her bills on time. What's more, even bills that don't show up regularly on her credit report—such as her rent or cell phone—can wreck her score if she is late enough that they get turned over to a bill collector—basically, a company hired by your kid's creditor to track her down. Convey this to your kid: She absolutely must pay on time.

  Numbers can help prove the point. Take the case of a young woman who has a FICO score of 750. Let's say she has two credit cards, $8,000 in student loans, and a two-year credit history. If she misses one credit card payment, her FICO score could plummet by 100 points or more. The fewer years you've had a credit history, the more dramatically one late payment can affect your score. So in this woman's case, she had only two years of experience, and her credit file was deemed "thin." That meant any negative mark had a relatively large impact. The resulting lower credit score could end up costing her big-time on the interest rate for a car loan or a new credit card.

- **Don't get a credit card of your own until junior year.** The current rules can make it tough for a new college student to get a credit card (see the box on p. 79 for details), but even if she qualifies for one, I recommend waiting until junior year. Despite what credit card companies say, your kid doesn't need to start building up a credit record the moment she sets foot on campus. Besides, if she has student loans, she will be establishing a good credit history once she starts paying them off. Your kid is going through all kinds of adjustments freshman year—and even sophomore year—and the last thing she needs is to run up big credit card debts and deal with the stress of getting in over her head. Another danger of getting a credit card while in college: If your kid runs up a balance, she might be tempted to use her student loans to pay it off—in violation of her loan agreement. This kind of creative financing scheme is a onetime fix that doesn't address the problem of overspending. In many cases, kids simply run up a new credit card balance after paying off the old one with the student loan, creating a snowball effect of debt.

7 Rules for Doing Credit Cards Right

When choosing a credit card, your kid should ignore chirpy ads promising perks and "rewards" points. And once he gets one, there are some key rules to follow. Here's what matters.

1 Comparison shop to get the best deal. Odds are, the credit offers that come to you in the mail or pop up on websites you're browsing aren't pitching the best deal you qualify for. Instead, look for options on CreditCards.com or CardHub.com.

2 **Choose the card with the lowest APR you can get.** The annual percentage rate generally includes both interest and any fixed fees (such as an annual fee) charged over a year. Even if you're determined to pay off your balance every month, if you do slip up, having a low APR can save you real money. Beware of "affinity" cards (the ones that give a small percentage of your purchase amount to a charity or other cause, such as your alma mater), because they often have higher APRs.

3 **Skip cards with annual fees.** If you shop around, you can easily find a card without one. Some rewards cards have high annual fees that may exceed the value of any reward you receive. The one exception: If you are extremely diligent about paying your bill, and the card offers a reward you really could use—with a value that exceeds the annual fee—fine, consider it. You can find a list of the best rewards cards at NerdWallet.com.

4 **If you apply for a card and get declined, wait before applying for another.** If you get turned down by a credit card company, don't apply for a number of other cards right away, since each time you do, an inquiry will show up on your credit report. A few of those bunched together will lower your credit score temporarily. Instead, call the company to find out why you were rejected; then wait about six months if you can before reapplying. Spend that time trying to improve your chances by, for example, paying bills on time or paying down debt.

5 **Pay off your balance in full each month. Period.** I'll say it again: When you carry a balance, you pay interest, which makes whatever you bought with your card much more expensive. Check out the box on p. 74 to see just how much making the minimum payment on your credit card can cost you, and use the minimum payment calculator on CreditCards.com to see for yourself. One option is to set up an automatic-payment plan with your credit card company that pays off the balance every month. Just be sure you have enough money in your bank account to cover the bill, or you'll be hit with fees from the card company or overdraft charges from your bank.

6 **Never max out your card—even if you pay the bill right away.** It can hurt your credit score. That's because credit card companies often report monthly balances to the credit bureaus—which determine your score—before you pay the bill. So that high balance will be included in the calculation of your score that month even if you pay it off a few days later.

7 **Don't use more than about 20% of your available credit.** Even if you have a few cards and don't max out any of them, if the total amount you owe exceeds 20% of your available credit (which is all your credit limits added together), your credit score could go down.

YOUNG ADULTHOOD

Once your kid has graduated from college or is otherwise launched into the world, the debt tutorial is over. Now comes real life. From paying back student loans to getting out of credit card debt to perhaps taking out a car loan, your kid will need some practical guidance from you.

- **Take control of your student loans.** I hear this a lot: A kid is about to graduate from college—or *has* graduated—and has no idea how many loans he has, what his monthly bill will be or when it's due, or even where to send his payments. That's a disaster waiting to happen. Most federal student loans go into repayment six months after graduation. Your kid will be enrolled automatically into a standard repayment plan, which requires him to make the same payment every month for 10 years until the whole loan is paid off. But your kid has options about how and when to pay back that loan. The box on p. 88 will tell your graduate everything he needs to know about his federal student loans but was too terrified (or disengaged) to ask.

    If your child has had to take out private student loans, make sure he gets in touch with his lender to find out the repayment details ASAP. (If he's not sure who his private lender is or if there are multiple lenders, he can find them listed on his credit reports, which he can access once a year for free at AnnualCreditReport .com or by checking with his school's financial aid office.) Not only will missed payments hurt his credit score, but also, since you probably cosigned the loan, you're on the hook for repayment as well—and your credit score will suffer if the debt doesn't get paid. Unfortunately, most private lenders do not offer the range of repayment options that federal loans do.

A surprising number of college grads miss their first student loan payment, whether because they don't have the money or they're just straight-up clueless. Make sure your kid isn't one of them.

The 4 Steps to Repaying Federal Student Loans

The average college grad with debt owes about $37,000 in student loans. But while your kid might have left school with a stunning understanding of chemical engineering, metaphysics, or onomastic genesis in the works of Edna St. Vincent Millay (no, I don't know what that means, either), he probably is baffled by how to pay back those loans. Make sure he's ready by passing along these four important steps.

1 **Confirm how much you owe and to whom, and make sure the loan servicer has your current contact info.** Visit the National Student Loan Data System (NSLDS) at nslds.ed.gov. Click on "Financial Aid Review," register, and log in. You'll see what you owe and find out the company to whom you will be making your monthly payments—known as the loan servicer. (Remember, this is just for federal loans; if you have private loans, you'll need to dig up who your lender is and contact it directly. See p. 94.)

2 **Postpone your payments if you don't have a job yet.** There are few things more nerve-racking than not being able to make your loan payments. If you can't afford the payments because you can't find a job, you've gone back to school, or, say, you're serving in the Peace Corps, you might qualify for a deferment. This basically means that you are off the hook from paying back your loans for months or even years, depending on your circumstances. (Added benefit: If you have what are called "subsidized loans," interest won't accrue during the deferment.) If you don't qualify for a deferment, you might still be able to get a forbearance, which allows you to reduce or stop making payments for up to 12 months. The downside is that interest continues to accrue on both subsidized and unsubsidized loans. For more information, check out studentaid.gov/deferment-forbearance.

3   **Choose a repayment plan.** You're enrolled automatically in the Standard Repayment Plan, which requires making the same payment every month for 10 years until the whole loan is paid off. But if you can't afford that payment, there are other options. Of course, you might feel like you need a PhD in applied math just to sort through them. The great news is that the government's Federal Student Aid website includes a handy tool called the Repayment Estimator (studentaid.gov /repayment-estimator). A good rule of thumb: Choose the repayment plan with the highest payment you can afford. That way, you'll minimize the total interest paid over the life of the loan. The one exception is if you have credit card debt with a higher interest rate than the rates on your student loans. In that case, pay the least you can on your loans until you've paid off your card, and then raise your monthly loan payment. One final point: If you qualify for a repayment plan that forgives your remaining debt after a certain number of years, you may be required to pay tax on the forgiven amount. Make sure to check. Here's a brief rundown of the options.

- **Graduated Repayment.** Payments start really low but then step up a notch every two years until your loan is paid off in 10 years. The downside? You'll pay more in interest over time—sometimes thousands of dollars more—than under the standard plan.

- **Extended Repayment.** This plan, which is available only to borrowers who owe more than $30,000, stretches out the repayment period up to 25 years. You get a lower monthly payment than with the 10-year standard plan, but you'll pay more interest overall—in some cases tens of thousands of dollars.

- **Income-Driven Repayment Plans.** These are plans based on how much you *earn*, as well as how much you owe. They are temporary options to help you while you're young and not making much money. One rule of thumb: If your debt is more than your annual income, chances are these plans won't be a good deal for you. As your salary grows, you should switch back to Standard Repayment.
    - **Pay as You Earn.** The PAYE plan offers the lowest monthly payment, and your remaining debt is forgiven after 20 years. But it also has the strictest eligibility requirements.
    - **Revised Pay as You Earn.** REPAYE is easier to qualify for and forgives your remaining debt after 20 years, but it generally has higher monthly payments than PAYE.
    - **Income-Based Repayment.** IBR, another program that's easier to qualify for than PAYE, forgives remaining debt after 25 years.
- **Public Service Loan Forgiveness Program.** PSLF completely wipes away your remaining federal student debt after 10 years of on-time monthly payments if you choose a service career in areas such as teaching, public health, law enforcement, or the military. If you're in it for the long haul, combine this program with a repayment plan with the lowest possible monthly payments and the longest repayment period. That way you'll still have a lot left to pay back after 10 years, but instead it will be forgiven. Unlike the other loan forgiveness programs mentioned above, this one rewards you with not having to pay any tax on that forgiven amount. For more info, go to studentaid.gov/public service. (There are additional loan forgiveness programs for teachers who work in underserved areas, so if you're in education, be sure to check those out too.)

4 **Make sure you're set up to make on-time payments every month.** No matter what, pay on time! (Does it seem as though I say this a lot? Well, I have good reason to!) If you don't, you will be hit with late fees—and you'll hurt your credit score. If you miss payments for nine months, you'll be in default, which means the government can take money out of your paycheck or tax refunds. Sign up for automatic payments so that you never get into a messy situation like that. An added benefit: If you do this, some servicers will reduce your loan's interest rate by 0.25%. (And if you have a little extra cash, send in a separate payment directing that it be applied to the principal on the loan with the highest interest rate.)

- **If you take out a car loan, be smart about it.** Sometimes your kid absolutely needs a car and doesn't have the cash for one. Here are four tips for taking out a car loan. And my advice from the high school section still stands: Go with a used car! (For more about how to actually shop for the car, see p. 111.)

  - **Go with the shortest-term loan you can afford.** Some lenders offer terms of eight or nine years to help people buy cars that are a stretch for their budget. That's too long. Ideally, get a three-year loan. Though your monthly payments are cheaper if you extend the term, you'll end up paying more interest overall, and you could owe more than the car is worth by the time you trade it in or sell it.

  - **Do your research before going to a dealership.** Make sure you have a sense of current auto loan rates and car pricing information. Helpful sites include Bankrate.com (auto loan interest rates) and automotive resource Edmunds.com (auto loan payment calculators).

  - **Never settle for financing through a dealership without shopping around.** Bankrate.com will tell you the national average on car loan rates, and, using your zip code, it can also tell you where to look locally—but it won't produce an exhaustive list. So be sure to check with your local bank or credit union, as it might offer a more competitive rate. If your credit score is especially low—around 640 or below—you may be offered a subprime loan. Steer clear. Subprime loans carry interest rates that can be three times what you'd pay if you had good credit. If you can hold off on the purchase and bump up your credit score, you will qualify for a better rate. If you absolutely need a car, look for a low-cost used model so that your monthly payments will be lower.

– **Don't tell the dealer how much you can spend on monthly payments.** Instead, get him to agree on a price first and then discuss financing. That way he won't be able to adjust the price around your monthly payment amount.

• **Don't live off credit cards—regardless of how little you earn.** You've said it before to your kid (I hope), but it's worth repeating: She should use plastic only if she can pay the bill in full each month. Of course, when she's earning a low starting salary, she might think it's okay to put basics such as gas or food on a credit card. Sounds reasonable, right? Wrong. It's a slippery slope, which is why you should urge your kid to adopt a zero-tolerance, zero-balance policy. In fact, the less your kid makes, the worse an idea it is to charge living expenses to a credit card, since the prospect of paying it off is so very far in the future. Avoiding this trap will mean some bare-bones living at first, but the best time to do that is when you're young, single, and unencumbered. Whether that means getting a roommate, taking public transit to work, or getting a second or even third job, staying out of debt should be your kid's goal.

• **Refinancing can save you money.** If your kid does have high-interest-rate debt, she should try to refinance, which means switching from an existing loan to a new loan with a lower interest rate. At this point in your kid's life, the concept of refinancing applies probably to her credit card debt only. But down the line, refinancing could save your kid tens of thousands of dollars when she has a mortgage. This option is generally open only to people with very good credit, which is yet another reason your kid should pay her bills on time.

Let's say your child got a credit card in college with a rate of 18% and has been good about paying the bills. Ideally, she isn't carrying a balance from month to month, but if she is, she should call up the credit card company and say that she's shopping around for a lower rate and is wondering what it can give her. Surveys reveal that this tried-and-true tactic is still surprisingly effective, especially for those with good credit. If your kid's current credit card company is playing hardball, she might want to consider getting a new card with a lower interest rate or an attractive introductory offer and transferring her balance to that card. But before she does, she needs to check the transfer fee (3% or 4% is typical) to make sure that she'll end up ahead. Bankrate.com has a balance-transfer calculator that'll help your kid figure out if the transfer makes sense. (Another way to deal with credit card debt is to use any savings you have to pay it down. For more on this strategy, see p. 37.)

- **Don't ignore your bills, even if you can't pay them.** There might come a time when your grown child loses his job or makes some poor decisions and ends up in a situation where he can't pay all his bills. Bad debt problems definitely happen to good people. Maybe he feels overwhelmed every time he checks his mail or when he starts getting calls from creditors. But what he absolutely cannot do is ignore the problem. When it comes to federal student loans, there are ways to delay or reduce payments. (See the box on p. 88.) But those options exist only if he doesn't go into default. With credit card companies, the best time to negotiate a better interest rate or work out an affordable payment schedule is when he still has good credit. If your kid is truly drowning in debt, he should seek help from a nonprofit credit counselor, who can be found at the Financial Counseling Association of America (FCAA.org) and the National Foundation for Credit Counseling (NFCC.org). The bottom line: Avoiding bills is bad news.

- **Shoot for a home down payment of 20%—or at least 10%.** Today the typical American rents for six years before buying her first home, while in the early 1970s, she rented for less than three. As a result, many young adults don't buy a place of their own until they're in their thirties. Still, it's smart to start the mortgage conversation early. (See p. 39 for more about saving for a down payment.)

    Deciding when to buy can be tricky. It's more complicated than simply comparing your kid's monthly rent with the mortgage payment. If your child isn't likely to stay in the home for at least five years—say, she gets married and needs a bigger place or gets transferred for a job—buying isn't usually a good deal. That's because the expenses that come with buying and selling can add up to thousands of dollars. If your kid moves too soon, she won't have built up enough equity (the amount the home is worth minus what she owes) to make that investment smarter than renting over the same period. The *New York Times* blog *The Upshot* has a calculator to help make the decision easier, at nytimes.com/buyrent. And once your kid is ready, steer her to *Get a Financial Life: Personal Finance in Your Twenties and Thirties*, written by (ahem) yours truly, for in-depth coverage of this topic.

Don't Miss Your First Student Loan Payment

Sometime during the final semester of your college-graduate-to-be's senior year, you should nudge him to take a few minutes to fill out this checklist. It will help him avoid missing that first student loan payment. To get this info, he needs to contact his lender(s). If he doesn't know who they are, he should check out nslds.ed.gov for a list of his federal loans. For info on any private loans, he can contact his college's financial aid office or get a copy of his credit report on AnnualCreditReport.com if he doesn't have the paperwork at hand.

Loan Name or Number	Loan Servicer	Total Balance Owed	Monthly Payment	Due Date of First Payment	Servicer Contact Info (Website/Phone/ Email)
1					
2					
3					
4					
5					
6					
7					
8					
9					
10					

If you're thinking of loaning your kid money for a down payment, think again: Most banks and mortgage companies will require you to certify in writing that any cash from you is a gift, since a loan would mean that your kid would have to pay that money back in addition to the mortgage. One possibility worth having your kid investigate: mortgages via the Federal Housing Administration (FHA), which require as little as 3.5% down for first-time buyers. Another place to look is your state housing finance agency, which can be found through the National Council of State Housing Finance Agencies, at ncsha.org/housing-help.

A low down payment, however, means higher monthly payments. After all, if you are putting down less money, you are borrowing more—and that means more interest. Another drawback is that if home values drop, your kid could end up owing the bank more than the house is worth. This is known as being "underwater" or "upside down"—and if she needs to sell for some reason, she'll actually lose money. This was one of the factors that led to the mortgage crisis that began a decade or so ago.

- **Parents: Don't bail out your kid.** Sound harsh? Perhaps. And, of course, there's no hard and fast rule. What you ultimately do depends on your attitudes about debt, your relationship with your kid, and your own financial situation. But letting your kid live at home for a while is one thing; enabling bad financial behavior is another. It's not that you shouldn't ever give your kid money. But paying his bills when he can't has a big psychological cost, in that it only perpetuates a cycle of debt. If you decide that you want to help your child get out of debt, do it in a way that helps him—and doesn't hurt you. For instance, if you're willing to pay off his credit cards, ask him how he proposes to avoid getting right back into debt, and make sure his plan is realistic. Handing him cash without having a practical strategy can make the problem worse. Instead, ask him to send you the bill he's unable to pay and make the payment directly. Or if you want to help with groceries, give him a gift card from a supermarket.

  You should never withdraw money from your retirement funds to help out your kid because, in addition to the sizable penalties and taxes you'll likely owe, you are jeopardizing your own retirement, which is coming up much sooner than your kid's retirement. If you're lending rather than giving your kid money, see the box below for some pointers. And remember what I said earlier about loaning to loved ones: You might not get that money back. No matter what, don't cosign any loans or take on your kid's debts; it can hurt your own credit score big-time.

Lending Money to Your Kids

Sometimes adult kids get in a bind, and parents are tempted to help them out with a loan. Although you aren't obliged—after all, they are adults—if you are able and willing to, make sure you do it right.

Be sure the deal is good for both parties. It's okay to charge your adult kid interest, especially if you're cutting her a break (say, lending her money at 5% to pay off a credit card with 21% interest). Show her how much she will save. If she owes $10,000 to a credit card company at 21% and paid only the monthly minimums, she'd pay nearly $17,000 in interest alone. A loan from you at 5% would cost her just under $4,000 in interest.

Put the deal in writing. Sounds a little weird and overly formal, but it helps everyone remember what was said. Write up an agreement that includes the interest rate charged and the payment due dates. Believe me, this helps avoid confusion and potential heated discussions later. You can find documents and contracts at Nolo.com.

Beware of any negative tax implications. The IRS sets a minimum interest rate—the applicable federal rate (AFR)—that family members and friends are required to charge on certain types of loans. So if you want to lend your kid money without charging interest, you might owe tax on the interest you would have received had you charged the AFR. If you lend your kid less than $10,000 to buy an item such as a car or to pay off debts, you don't have to worry about these rules. But if you lend more than $10,000, you might be expected to charge interest. For the current AFR, see the "Index of Applicable Federal Rates (AFR) Rulings" at IRS.gov.

5

Better, Smarter Spending

I still remember coveting the Izod shirt a girl in my first-grade class wore. Although I knew my parents were not fans of name-brand clothes, I desperately longed for a polo shirt with an alligator logo on it. And then one day, a fashion miracle happened: My mom's wealthy aunt Mildred sent us a bag of her teen daughter's hand-me-downs, which included a green Izod dress. It was four sizes too big for me, but it had that prized reptile on it. I carefully cut the logo off the dress and sewed it onto my favorite green sweater. The next day, I proudly wore my creation to class.

Immediately, Alligator-Wearing Girl lasered in on my sweater. "That is *fake*," she announced in front of the whole class. "You sewed that on yourself!" I'd been outed by my frayed stitching. Mortified, I stashed the sweater at the bottom of my cubby at school and never wore it again. (Not long ago, Alligator-Wearing Girl friended me on Facebook. I accepted her request, but I still haven't forgotten what went down in Mrs. Friedman's class.) What's most striking to me is that I was six years old when all this happened. It was the 1970s, the decade of peace, not Prada, and I was a fairly nerdy, unsophisticated child. But that alligator was everything.

It's hard to remember the intensity of those feelings when our kids tell us how essential a certain purchase is to their happiness, be it name-brand sneakers or the latest tech toy. We're horrified when our young children make cringe-worthy distinctions between "just regular boots" and Uggs, or "just a regular T-shirt" and an Under Armour T, or "just regular headphones" and Beats. We start to wonder what we did wrong to end up with such materialistic spawn.

But it might not be entirely our fault.

Sure, kids take a lot of their cues from us. But parental signals are often over-ridden by the marketing industrial complex, which spends billions of dollars each year to reach our kids well before they can talk or walk. As an example, let's look at breakfast. A Cornell University study found that cereals marketed to kids are placed half as high on supermarket shelves as those for adults, and—here's the creepy part—the gaze of the elves and pirates and rabbits on kids' cereal boxes is strategically angled downward an average of 10 degrees to catch a small person's eyes, whereas the characters on adult cereals look straight ahead. (I always thought Cap'n Crunch seemed kind of sketchy.)

The idea that kids are bombarded by marketing isn't novel. Experts have been aware for a long time that small children don't distinguish between ads and TV shows. But what's new is the sheer number of ways that marketers can get to our kids—from social media to websites to iPhones, and even in the classroom. And we know from brain studies of adults just how powerful the urge to buy is. In subjects' MRI scans, portions of the brain "light up" when they are presented with a shopping spree scenario.

The good news is that even in the face of this barrage, we can help our kids make better, smarter choices.

Often, it starts with having to revise our own assumptions about what it means to be a wise consumer. For instance, though we might believe that having lots of choices is a good thing, psychologists now know that having numerous options not only makes it harder to reach a decision but also can render us less happy with what we choose. (Just think about how stressed out you feel staring down a salad bar.) On the flip side, even a manageable number of options can be tricky, since studies also show that everything, including mood, memories, friends, and the weather, influences how we choose to spend our money.

As parents, we need to teach our children to be smart consumers. Their buying decisions don't have to be perfect every time, just good enough most of the time. And helping our kids helps us, too, since they influence *our* purchases. By one estimate, tweens alone channel $150 billion of parental dollars annually to the brands they want. That's a lot of buying power, and it could explain all those trips to McDonald's for dinner—not to mention the family MacBook you bought instead of a Dell desktop.

The good news is that most kids quickly develop a snarky, skeptical inclination to stick it to the Man—or at least they don't want to be fooled by him. Capitalizing on kids' natural wary-of-being-manipulated instincts can help make them independent money thinkers and spenders.

PRESCHOOL

Kids this age might be small and adorable, but they are already big consumers with strong opinions and fierce desires. Here are a few pointers to give your child as he navigates the minefields of materialism.

- **Play the "wants" versus "needs" game.** The distinction between things we have to have and things that are optional sounds superbasic, but it's not necessarily obvious to a little kid, who might feel she *needs* that cupcake you just cruised by in the bakery section. (I know I sometimes do.) Understanding this concept also happens to be the foundation of making wise spending choices. So use those "Gimme!" moments in the grocery store to teach your kid the difference between items she really wants and those she actually needs. We *need* milk and apples; we *want* chocolate milk and Oreos. Walk down the aisles, and ask each other, "Want? Or need?" *Needs* go in the cart. *Wants* stay on the shelf—except, perhaps, for one or two. Once your kid gets the gist, this game can become more nuanced. Clothing is certainly a need, but a Spider-Man raincoat qualifies as a want.

One mom told me that she started calling her five-year-old daughter's buying fevers "want attacks." But when her daughter asked her whether the family's new big-screen TV was a want or a need, Mom was taken aback. She admitted to her daughter that she, as a grown-up, had want attacks—a pair of gold hoop earrings or a Kate Spade wallet—from time to time too. That marked a turning point: They both got better at stepping back when want attacks hit, and they even giggle about them once in a while.

- **Don't trust advertising.** Here's how insidious—and effective—advertising to children is. In a Stanford University experiment, 63 kids between the ages of three and five were each given two identical portions of five foods. The big difference was that one portion was wrapped in McDonald's packaging and the other wasn't. When asked which they preferred, the kids overwhelmingly selected the items with a McDonald's wrapper—whether those foods were carrots or chicken nuggets.

   One way to fight the McInfluence of advertising is to tell it to your kid straight: "Don't believe everything you see on TV or online, especially if it's an ad." Next time the two of you are watching TV and an ad for soda comes on, for example, you can say something like, "That company makes money from selling soda to kids, so they pretend that soda makes people really happy. It's interesting—and kind of fun—to spot how ads are trying to trick you." Explain that the people on the screen are actors who are saying words from a script that a bunch of workers in an office approved; the ad uses bright colors and music to make you associate soda with joy. Another, more elaborate lesson: Try the McDonald's wrapping game or some other branding test on your kid.

- **Parents: Don't avoid situations that require you to say no.** Some parents I know refuse to take their kids to the store for fear they'll scream and cry unless they get what they want. I get it. But still I say, grit your teeth and let 'em scream. Truth is, in these situations, it's often the parent who ends up being more traumatized than the child, as other people stare. Even worse is the sense of guilt or regret that parents sometimes feel after they say no.

   Take my friend Paula. When her daughter Sally was three, they went shopping for a dress for a cousin's wedding. "We went into a store, and she saw a pink princess-type dress in fancy linen with a petticoat that would twirl well—her test for a good dress," recalls Paula. "It even had a pearl brooch that she kept running her fingers over. And it cost about a hundred and twenty dollars! I said no, she threw a tantrum, and I had to carry her out—so embarrassed." A couple weeks later, Paula ended up buying Sally the dress for her birthday, having felt so guilty about the teary scene. "She looked at me like I was crazy—she did not remember the dress, couldn't care less about it. What she really wanted by then was a set of small plastic horses that cost about fifteen dollars. I learned a lesson: Stick to your guns. The moment passes."

If your kid is prone to melting down in the supermarket aisle screaming for Lucky Charms, your best bet is to come up with a solid game plan before you walk through the doors. (For strategies to help your kid resist temptation in a store, see the box on p. 112.)

- **Parents: To limit nonstop nagging, limit screen time.** TV used to be the main way that advertisers tried to sell to kids—and it's still a big culprit. But increasingly, it's tablets and smartphones that push ads in front of their shiny little faces, whether they're watching their favorite TV show or playing a game online. These ads can be particularly inviting, since they're often disguised as games or include some fun interactive feature. Marketers know that the secret to selling their products is to get kids to bug their parents—what one marketing study infamously dubbed the "Nag Factor." Not surprisingly, researchers who surveyed mothers about their children's behaviors while shopping found that kids who could identify television characters like SpongeBob SquarePants and Dora the Explorer were much more likely to hound their mothers to buy stuff that had those characters on the packaging.

No wonder the American Academy of Pediatrics recommends zero screen time for children younger than two. (This includes giving your kid a cell phone to distract her when she's crying.) Of course, don't allow a TV in your kid's bedroom. And don't sit in front of one yourself all day watching *Friends* reruns. A recent study found that the amount of time parents spent watching TV had a stronger connection to how much TV their kids watched than did family rules about time limits or even whether the children had TVs in their rooms.

ELEMENTARY SCHOOL

This is the age when marketing and peer pressure join forces to take over your kid. Your job is to help him stay above the fray with these important lessons.

- **No means no.** If you let your kid nag you into buying that toy/piece of candy/Xbox that you insisted previously you weren't going to get him, you're guilty of "intermittent reinforcement," and in effect you've turned yourself into a human slot machine. Your kid thinks that if he keeps "playing" (that is, nagging), it will eventually pay off—at least some of the time—and so he will continue to do it until he gets what he wants. That's why it's important to say no only when you mean it—and not change your mind. Although your child might cry a lot at first, in the long run you are unburdening him from having to throw a fit in an effort to get what he wants. If he knows it won't help, he'll be less apt to go all histrionic when he sees a candy bar. He'll also learn to see decisions about spending as deliberate, rather than as a response to a whim or momentary desire.

- **Always check the price, no matter how small the item.** When Sam asked his 11-year-old son, Jason, to go around the corner to buy a few groceries, he gave his son the cash he figured the boy would need. Soon he received a panicked call from the checkout line: "I don't have enough money—what do I do?" As Jason rattled off the items and their prices to his father, they realized that the culprit was the fancy European cheese, which was nearly $10, much more than the generic brand he'd been sent to get. The lesson he learned the hard way: Check the price before you buy. Although most adults know the importance of looking at the cost of an item before they put it in the shopping cart, kids are not born with that habit. This is also a good time to teach your kid to do what my dad calls a "reality check" of what you expect the final tally to be at the register. That way, if you figure in your head that the few items in your shopping cart will cost roughly $20, but they cost $29, you'll know to review your receipt before you leave the store.

- **Save your receipts and ask about return policies.** Again, this principle might seem really basic to you, but it can be an epiphany for a kid, who is used to things breaking and not having any recourse. So here's a good habit for your kid to learn early: Make sure to take and then save your receipt for a period of time after you buy anything of value (at least as long as it's under warranty), and ask the sales clerk about the store's return policy. (If you buy a product online, find out if you have to pay the postage to return it or even pay a pesky "restocking" fee.) Ask whether the store will give your money back, only issue store credit, or only allow you to exchange the item for another. Do you have to have the receipt? How long do you have to make the return? And here's something that large department stores will often do but don't advertise: If you show up without the receipt, or with a price tag removed, the person at the customer service desk will take back the merchandise anyway assuming it wasn't used. It's always worth trying.

- **Parents: When possible, let your kid make some tough spending decisions.**
  As kids go through elementary school, awareness of what classmates think, wear, and buy takes on huge importance. A father named Hank, for example, told me that he grew up wearing cheap sneakers from a discount store that embarrassed him in front of other kids. So when his own son turned 11 and started wanting really nice sneakers, Hank felt torn because he knew the pain of not fitting in. At the same time, he didn't want his son to get the message that it was important to have the most expensive things in order to belong. He decided to give his boy a gift card to a sporting goods store and allow him to decide whether to spend the entire amount on the pair of sneakers he wanted or get a midpriced pair, leaving enough to also buy a basketball. In the end, his son opted for the less expensive shoes. "He was willing to resist the peer pressure to have the flashiest shoes when he realized that would leave him with more money to buy something else," Hank said.

- **Parents: Explain why you buy the things you do.** Instead of hiding the cost of big-ticket items such as TVs and cars for fear your kid will think you're loaded, draw her into the purchase process. Let her observe your decision making, and even chime in. Explanations like "We're choosing the minivan instead of the SUV because it holds more people and gets better gas mileage, and is therefore better for the planet" are powerful messages. In general, capitalize on those moments to explain to your kid how your choices reflect your family's priorities and values. The next time you're shopping together, show him several similar versions of the item you're going to buy and point out the price differences. Then tell him why you chose the item you did. Explain, for instance, why you're willing to buy generic-brand yogurt but would never skimp on your family's favorite bath soap.

- **Parents: Include your kid in the family budgeting process.** Joyce, a woman I know, remembers vividly how, as a young girl, she learned about setting priorities. When she was 10, she really wanted a bike. Her father drew a pie chart on a piece of paper that showed how much of their money was spent on needs (such as food, rent, basic clothes), how much on insurance to protect them, how much on gas for the car, and so on. It was plain that they had none left over for both a family vacation *and* a bike. Her father then asked Joyce to help him and her mother decide whether they would go on a camping trip or use that money to buy bikes for the family. When you can, be open about the trade-offs you make in your family spending decisions. And ask your kid for input.

- **Parents: Let your kid experience consumer dissatisfaction.** Daphne was excited when she bought her little sister a makeup kit that she had seen advertised and then spotted in the toy aisle of the grocery store. It was one of the first times she had used her own money to buy a gift for someone else. But when her sister unwrapped the kit at her birthday party, Daphne was devastated to discover that the makeup tube, eye shadow compact, and blush were all just plastic facsimiles. To calm her down, her parents were tempted to give Daphne the money to buy a different gift for her sister. But instead they wisely took her back to the store, receipt in hand. When she explained to the manager that the commercials, and the picture on the box, made it appear that she was buying real makeup, he refunded her money. Her parents also suggested that she write a letter to the manufacturer complaining about the product labeling, which she did, and she received a coupon discount in the mail for some of the company's other toys. (It might have been calculated PR on the part of the toy company, but Daphne was thrilled.) Most important, what felt like an emotional disaster at the time became part of family lore. Bottom line: As parents, we instinctively protect our kids from disappointment, hurt feelings, and cruddy merchandise. But that won't teach them to be savvy shoppers.

- **Parents: Know what your child is buying online—and where he's buying it.** Aside from helping your kid protect his personal info, you want to protect yourself from having him blow a bundle before you realize it. Well-known companies, including Apple and Google, have gotten in trouble with parents for offering apps—often for free—that then require kids to fork over real money for virtual currency, such as treats or coins, to be used in the game. The apps allowed parents to authorize one purchase with a credit card, then, unbeknownst to them, left a window of time open when other purchases could be made without further authorization. As a result, children have run up hundreds and even thousands of dollars in in-app purchases. In a recent case, a dad got a $5,900 bill from Apple after his son used his password to purchase Dino Bucks for the mobile game Jurassic World.

  Many smartphone providers allow parents to use their own devices to approve app purchases their kids want to make or to restrict the purchasing power their kids have on a phone or tablet. Parents can also remove the payment info from their own account, so that it has to be put in manually before a purchase is completed. If these methods fail and your kid winds up charging crazy amounts to feed a virtual pet, insist on a refund. Most important is to know where your kid is doing her online browsing. One friend of mine promised her daughter that she'd buy her a Nike tank top when it went on sale at the local Dick's Sporting Goods. The girl googled the word *dicks* with the goal of searching for the shirt online. You can guess the rest.

MIDDLE SCHOOL

Tweens spend more than $43 billion of their own money every year. Here's what to say to help them use that power for good.

- **Pay for your own impulse purchases.** This is a way to help your kid measure how much she actually wants something. If you're in a store and your child wants to get a pack of gum or a T-shirt on impulse, don't automatically say no. Instead, offer to front your kid the cash, but tell her, "I'll need you to pay me back out of your own money when we get home." Very often, she'll decide that the candy or shirt she was dying for just a minute ago isn't necessary now that she's the one paying for it. Of course, this works only if your kid does have some money of her own—but if she's been saving, she should. (And if she's not saving, read Chapter 2 for some tips about how to help her do that.) Huge reminder: If you pay up front, don't forget to collect on the debt as soon as you get home.

- **Research before buying big—online and off.** It's not necessary to spend hours studying the pros and cons of a $10 portable phone charger—as long as you know that it works for your brand of phone. But for a bigger purchase—say, a new Bluetooth speaker or a telescope—it's definitely worth the effort. Teach your kid to tell the difference between marketing efforts (such as product placement in TV shows, movies, and articles; TV commercials; and print ads in magazines and newspapers) and independent assessments (opinions about a product or service by someone who's not trying to sell it to you). Tell her to seek out known, unbiased sources of information like *Consumer Reports* (you'll need a subscription for full access) and reviews by journalists and other experts who aren't being paid by the company. The brand's website doesn't count.

  Point out, too, that many regular people post product reviews online. Go with your kid to a website such as Amazon and scroll through some of the reviews of toys your kid has. Do the reviewers make good points? Do their ratings and comments reflect your kid's own experience with the toy? She'll see quickly that not all reviews are reliable. That's why it's important to verify the ratings of other consumers with those from professional sources.

- **Don't let marketers brainwash you.** If your kid follows a TV star or professional athlete on Instagram, Snapchat, Twitter, or any other social media platform, make sure he knows that some of these people make millions by casually mentioning to their fans how much they like a product. Although Federal Trade Commission regulations require celebrities to 'fess up when they are being paid to shill, it's still often unclear to kids—or anyone else, for that matter—when their recommendations are actually paid endorsements. What's more, popular companies have succeeded in turning kids themselves into unsuspecting minimarketers. I have a friend whose 13-year-old son has hundreds of Instagram followers who like and comment on the sneaker designs he creates on a popular shoe brand's website. Make sure you know whether your kid is using social media to unwittingly spread marketing campaigns; if he is, point out that he's being exploited by the company as an unpaid salesperson. Many kids today understand this—and even embrace their role as an unofficial brand ambassador—but it's still a good conversation to have.

- **Factor in sales tax.** When your child saves up money to buy that coveted karaoke machine, she might face a big surprise—and not a good one—when she goes to the store and realizes that she doesn't have enough money to cover the tax. As we adults are reminded every time we look at a receipt, cities and states often charge sales taxes, which can boost the cost of a toy or, in many states, a piece of candy by anywhere from around 2% to 10%. You can explain to your kid that sales taxes mostly help pay for things such as roads, libraries, and schools. Sometimes they're used to try to change behaviors; most states, for instance, impose a special tax on cigarettes to discourage smoking. Certain items—including groceries—are exempt from sales tax because they are viewed as necessities, and some states have designated tax-free shopping days to encourage people to buy essentials like back-to-school supplies.

  One fun way to drive home this lesson is to play a version of *The Price Is Right*. On vacation, at Target, or just at the grocery store, give your kid $20 (or whatever amount you choose) to spend on whatever she wants, within reason. The condition: She has to calculate the sales tax, and you have to hold firm and not give a penny more if she guesses wrong. Not only does this exercise hammer home the idea that you always have to factor in tax, but it also proves that you can have as much fun on a budget as you can on a spree.

- **Don't be a brand-name zombie.** Whether it was Jordache in the 1980s or it's Joe's Jeans today, middle schoolers are obsessed with brand names. It's hard to talk them out of it, but one creative mom I know told me about a way she finally managed to get through to her son, Tom. She noticed that American

Eagle Outfitters was having a great summer sale on shorts, and she bought Tom, then 12, a couple pairs in the bright colors he liked. But when he saw the store logo on her shopping bag, he told her outright that he hated American Eagle, because none of his friends wore it. Plus, he said, the brand's clothes didn't fit well and didn't look cool. After looking for shorts elsewhere and finding them ridiculously priced, she went back to American Eagle, bought the same shorts in slightly different colors, removed all tags that showed the brand name, and put them in a different store bag. Her son loved them. "When I told him the truth, after his initial shock wore off, he laughed and got the point. He wore them happily all summer," she said. If your child has a specific yearning for a name-brand item that would normally be outside your budget, you can make that a special present or something he pays for with his own money.

- **Pay more only when it's worth it.** A few years ago, some researchers served adult participants several wine samples, telling them that they ranged from cheap to expensive. In reality, the "$10" and "$90" wines were the same stuff. But participants consistently reported preferring the vino that was labeled with the hefty price tag. Although wine tastings are definitely out for the tween set, you can run a similar test on your kids—with shampoo, ice cream, or nearly anything. Give them two samples of a product (using the very same stuff), but assign two different prices, and ask them which one they like better. The lesson you will drive home is that we let the price of something influence how much we like it. When Katy's son was 11, he asked for a $200 leather jacket. Realizing that he was about to hit a growth spurt, she told him no, since he'd outgrow it in less than a year. But then she looked online, and found a number of fake leather jackets for a fraction of the price. She showed him his options, and he was thrilled with the one that was $39.99.

That said, there are times when you will decide it is worth the expense to pay more. Maybe it's a loaf of whole-grain bread that's healthier and tastier than the store brand. Maybe it's a set of high-quality kitchen knives, one that'll last you the next 20 years (and may save money in the long run, even if it costs more initially). These are value calls. Maybe your kid isn't interested in consumer ratings of household gadgets, but it's smart to loop him into the conversation now and then, or bring him along when you talk to the store salesperson so that he can hear a discussion about the trade-offs between quality and cost and see how you weigh them—as well as how you are able to see through a sales pitch, since you've done your own research.

- **Be a smart restaurant diner.** Eating out is a favorite American pastime, despite the fact that doing so is usually much more expensive than cooking and eating in. Start by teaching your kid not to fall for menu tricks. Customers are much more likely to order a dish with a fancy description (for example, "New York Style Cheesecake with Sinfully Decadent Chocolate Sauce") than the same dish with a simpler label (such as "Cheesecake"), and they're willing to pay 10% more for it. An outrageously expensive dish on a menu might be there just to make you feel that the dish below it is a bargain, even if it's more than you'd intended to spend. And people who find themselves ordering on tablets—a growing trend at fast-casual restaurants—tend to order 20% more appetizers and 30% more desserts than people who order in person. (Probably because we aren't feeling the same food shame over these indulgences when ordering via computer as we might when giving the order to a real-life waiter.) Finally, make sure your kid understands that tipping is part of the cost of eating out. Many servers make just $2.13 an hour before tips. (For more on the minimum wage, see p. 51.) So make sure you tip at least 20%, and let your kid help you figure out the right amount once he's old enough.

HIGH SCHOOL

Research from the University of Michigan finds that teens tend to spend most of their earnings from part-time jobs on clothes, music, movies, eating out, their cars, and other personal expenses, and (shock of shocks) very little on savings for future education. Here are some tips to help rejigger their priorities.

- **Spending mistakes are okay if you learn from them.** If, after discussing it with you, your son insists that he wants to blow six months' worth of savings on a pair of designer sunglasses, don't make him feel bad about it. But allow him to live with the consequences. Too broke later in the month to join his friends at a concert? No need to rub it in, but remind him of his earlier choice. Having kids think about choices and trade-offs is important. Of course, if you are paying for these items, it's your prerogative to refuse to buy stuff that you consider inappropriate or just a mistake. If your kid wants you to foot the bill for the latest cell phone upgrade or a night out at a dance club that you don't want him to go to, say no, loud and proud—and stick to it.

- **Follow Shirley's "Do I love it?" rule.** One question I ask, and have gotten my kids to ask, before pulling the trigger on a purchase is "Do I love it?" My mom, Shirley, taught me this when I was young. We all have clothes and gadgets stuffed in our closets that we bought impulsively when we didn't ask ourselves this important question. Of course, many kids (and adults) fall head over heels on shopping trips a bit too often. Encourage your teen to invoke a 24-hour rule: Take a day to mull over any major purchase. If she's worried the item will disappear, you can let her know that many stores will put clothes on hold until the following day. Plus, she can use the waiting period to shop around to see if she can find the item at a discount or on eBay. Mostly, this pause gives her time to go home and check her closet to see if that shirt goes with what she has—or if she already has another shirt that's similar.

- **Haggling can save big bucks.** A surprising number of businesses are willing to bargain if you just ask, particularly if your request is reasonable and you ask politely. One friend told me she recently got a half-day rate at a hotel just by requesting it. Who knew? It's good to explain to kids that sellers at flea markets and garage sales often expect you to haggle, and they mark up items to account for it. Talk strategy. It's easy for your kid to lose her leverage when she smells a bargain and blurts out, "I love this! How much?" Tell her to act coy instead; maybe ask a question or two about a few different items without showing that she has her heart set on one of them. There's a special pleasure in scoring a coveted item for less. Of course, there are limits to the method. You want to remind your kid that courtesy counts, and vendors, particularly at small flea markets and fairs, need to make a living, too.

- **Happiness is cheap.** Research shows that people tend to be happier when they make small purchases frequently rather than splurge on a big treat for themselves once or twice a year, as University of British Columbia psychology professor Elizabeth Dunn and Harvard business professor Michael Norton explain in their book, *Happy Money: The Science of Happier Spending*. No matter how amazing that expensive car or big-screen TV, the rush we get from it wears off fast. (The scientific phrase used to describe this process is "hedonic adaptation.") So before your kid cleans out his savings to buy that one big thing, encourage him to think about all the smaller things he could get for the same amount. For instance, if your kid is saving up to buy a $1,000 top-of-the-line drum set, you might suggest that he consider buying a used beginner's kit for a third of that and spend the rest on lessons. Same goes for deciding how to allocate the family budget. Instead of one weeklong trip to Florida this spring, three or four weekend camping trips amortizes that fun over the year. Another way to fight the effects of hedonic adaptation is to underindulge. If we buy new clothes or eat out at fancy restaurants all the time, we get used to the experience, and it doesn't make us as happy as it would if we did it only occasionally.

- **Always buy a used car.** When your kid has fantasies about driving down the highway with the wind in her hair, chances are she isn't picturing herself in the driver's seat of a secondhand Ford Taurus. But here's why she should: First, it's obviously more affordable for a high schooler. (And if you're thinking of buying a car for her, read my advice on p. 78 about why you shouldn't. Also, see my tips for getting a smart car loan.) The average new car costs around $34,000. What's more, the very second it's driven off the lot, it loses value, and after one year, it's worth $9,000 less. After three years, it's lost nearly half its value. While I'm on the subject of cars: Tell your kid that leasing a car is generally a bad deal. At the end of all those payments, your kid will have nothing to show for it.

  At the same time, cars today are more reliable than ever—many can be driven for 200,000 miles with no trouble if they are properly maintained. If your kid buys her car from a dealer, she should ask for the vehicle's inspection history. If she's purchasing the car from a private owner, she can run the car's VIN (vehicle identification number) at the used-car listing service Carfax (Carfax.com) to get info about its history, for a small fee. No matter how she buys, she should pay an independent mechanic to inspect it. Of course, safety should never be compromised, so you and your kid should check out the National Highway Traffic Safety Administration (NHTSA) website Safercar.gov for crashworthiness and rollover safety ratings of any car she's thinking of purchasing.

6 Shopping Tricks to Teach Your Kids So That They Choose Smart and Spend Less

When you shop, you're often your own worst enemy—and the same goes for your kids. Here are some strategies to pass on to help them outsmart their brains, their desires, and their bad habits, as well as the marketers eager to lure them to buy.

1 **Use cash.** I can't stress this enough. For a famous MIT study, researchers asked volunteers to bid on NBA tickets. Those who used cash spent less—sometimes half as much—as those who used credit. Why would that be? One explanation is that spending cash is more "painful" than putting down plastic. In MRI scans of the brains of people faced with a purchasing decision, their pain centers activate when they see high prices; using a credit card seems to numb that response. The theory goes that parting with bills actually feels like you're giving something up; less so when you swipe a card.

2 **Be suspicious of sales, discounts, coupons, and online vouchers.** I'm not against coupons per se. My mom saved literally thousands of dollars by clipping coupons and using them for items we actually needed. That said, think of any "bargain" you see like bait—and don't fall for it unless you were already planning to buy whatever the item is that's on sale. Sounds simple, but our minds play tricks on us. We leave the store with four shirts because of a "Buy 2 Get 2 Free!" deal and end up spending more than we would have on just one shirt, which was all we needed in the first place. And here's the thing: We think we saved money, when the reverse is true.

3 **Don't trust your senses.** Stores use fragrances, lighting, and music to create an atmosphere that makes you want to buy. Hearing classical music has been shown to make shoppers buy more expensive stuff, for example. And there are entire companies devoted to "ambient scenting," or creating custom aromas, for retailers and other businesses. The Hard Rock Hotel at Universal Orlando Resort, for example, hired a company to position the aroma of sugar cookies at the top of a staircase and waffle cones at the bottom in order to draw customers to its lower-level ice-cream shop. It can be fun to walk into a store with your kid and point out how the ambience was created to entice you to buy.

4 **Don't get "anchored" to high prices.** This is a fascinating one. According to research, we tend to pay more than we typically would have for something when we see it in the context of a high-priced item. So if you're shopping at a store that has $50 sweatshirts, paying $40 for one might seem reasonable. But if you're at a discount store where all the sweatshirts are $20, paying $30 suddenly seems like a rip-off. Anchoring takes advantage of the fact that everything is relative. This is a retail trick that you can point out to your kid whenever you shop. (For a deeper dive, check out Gary Belsky and Thomas Gilovich's excellent book *Why Smart People Make Big Money Mistakes and How to Correct Them.*)

5 **Don't shop just to feel better.** The pull of retail therapy when you're sad and introspective is real. In one study, participants who were asked to watch a film clip about the death of a boy's mentor and then write an essay about themselves were willing to spend up to 300% more on a sports water bottle than people who watched an emotionally neutral clip from a National Geographic documentary about the Great Barrier Reef.

Buying stuff to make yourself feel better temporarily has a hangover effect when the bills come in.

6 **Don't shop with shopaholics.** Research confirms that our friends influence our weight and whether we smoke, so why wouldn't they also influence our spending? A survey conducted by the American Institute of CPAs (AICPA)—who better?—found that nearly two-thirds of people in their twenties and early thirties feel pressure to keep up with their friends when it comes to spending in areas such as dining out and tech gadgets. The solution isn't for your kid to dump her debt-laden friends, but she should probably skip going to the mall with them.

COLLEGE

It's pretty much a given that college students are *supposed* to be broke. Really. Tuition, room and board, and books are the essentials. Everything else is an extra. Giving your kid the strategies below will prime her for this reality.

- **Prepare for money culture shock.** A young woman I know named Meadow recalls that when she was in college and living in a house with a group of friends, one of them refused to split the grocery bill equally. She said she didn't eat the wasabi peas and salmon fillets that her roommates ate, and she didn't want to pay for them. At the time, Meadow was irritated. Now, as an adult, she realizes that the girl was on a budget and likely having to count every penny. It's important to talk with your kid about the reality that there might be many students at his college whose families are much wealthier than yours, as well as others who might have dramatically less. Your kid might barely be able to pay his fraternity dues while his frat brothers fly to the Bahamas for spring break. On the flip side, maybe your kid is the one who wants to go out for dinner on Saturday night while his roommate can't even afford pizza outside of the meal plan.

  If your kid's friends are doing stuff she can't afford, tell her it's okay to be up front about that. Sometimes that might mean staying home when they're going out, but it might also mean coming up with less expensive alternatives, such as a dorm room movie night on her laptop. On the other hand, if you're financially comfortable, you don't want your kid to be the one who always picks up the tab. Not only is it expensive but it can be just plain awkward—for everyone. Your kid might wind up feeling resentful (or entirely too blithe about passing the costs on to you), and his friends might come to see him less as a pal and more as an ATM.

- **Think ahead to save money.** The cost of a fan—or even a bottle of shampoo—at a store on or near campus will often be higher than at a big-box store near your home. Prior to your child's first day of college, a shopping trip can be a great time to underscore a life lesson about planning ahead rather than buying on the fly, which almost always costs more—whether you're traveling halfway across the country or just moving across town. If your kid is going to live in a dorm, have him check the school's housing website for a list of what he needs and to see if certain appliances, such as coffeemakers and hot plates, are banned. (He's probably already communicating with his future roommates about who brings the minifridge.) It goes without saying that your kid will need a laptop, but skip the fancy sound system. (For a college budgeting worksheet, see p. 202.)

- **Be smart when selecting a smartphone plan.** Since most teenagers are on some kind of a family plan, college is the time to research the best deals for everyone. Shop around at sites such as Wirefly.com to compare the prices for various combinations of data, minutes, and texting options among dozens of cell phone plans. (Some phone companies offer discounts through colleges, so your kid should also check the websites of her university's information technology department as well as her service provider for details.)

    Whether you ultimately end up switching plans or sticking with the one you have, now is the time to have the cell phone bill talk with your kid. It's likely cheaper for her to stay on your plan while she goes to college than to switch to an individual plan. So if you can afford it, maybe you want to maintain the status quo. (Or even if your kid does start taking responsibility for her own charges, it might make sense for her to just pay you and stay on your plan.) But here's a suggestion: Data is a huge money suck on many phone plans, and you can let your kid know how much she's using. If it's more than everyone else in the family, she can either figure out a way to reduce it or chip in extra.

YOUNG ADULTHOOD

Spending choices your kid makes now have an effect on her lifestyle today—and down the road. She isn't going to want to hear from you about every purchase she makes, but here are a few guiding principles to slip into conversation.

- **Don't buy stuff just because it seems like the grown-up thing to do.** When faced with her first job interview, my friend's daughter used her credit card to buy a $100 black leather briefcase, a $300 suit, and $200 black pumps, since she felt she had to dress for success. The good news is that she got the job; the bummer is that the items ended up gathering dust in her closet since the office had a laid-back vibe—and all she really needed were her college clothes and her backpack. Another friend's son, feeling flush with a $40,000 salary after he graduated, rented a two-bedroom apartment. A few months later, he was begging his landlord to let him out of the lease so he could rent a studio instead. He could barely afford to make the rent payments—because of all those other expenses, such as gas for his car, utility bills, and groceries. The moral of these tales: Start small. That doesn't mean that people in their twenties need to deprive themselves of everything, but it's a good idea for your kid to adopt the mantra that making do with what you have is part of being young. And as we all know, your kid will probably look back with fondness on his years of cooking with a banged-up frying pan and using a milk crate for a nightstand.

- **Travel cheap or not at all.** Years ago, my dad and I spoke to a college audience together. When he told the crowd that he and my mom had never been to Europe until their 25th wedding anniversary—because they couldn't afford to go sooner—we heard a collective gasp. I'm not saying you have to wait until your silver anniversary to see the Eiffel Tower. In fact, research has found that people get more satisfaction when they spend their money on experiences rather than on material things. Traveling when you're young—and having adventures that will stay with you—can be truly valuable. But putting a trip to Cancún (or anywhere else) that you can't afford on a credit card is a bad idea: A plane ticket, a hotel, and a few evenings out can sit on a credit card bill for months or even years, gathering interest, if you overextend yourself.

If your kid does want to travel, she can get creative. One enterprising young woman I know, Amy, posted a profile on an au pair website and was matched with a bilingual family in Portugal that was in need of a temporary babysitter during the kids' two-week school break. In exchange for watching the children, Amy received room and board, a modest stipend, and time off during the mornings, evenings, and weekends to sightsee. All she had to spring for was her ticket, which she found on a discount travel website. She returned from her trip having broken even and having improved her Portuguese.

- **Whether you have a taste for pasture-raised steak or fast-food burgers, be a frugal foodie.** When a friend of mine met her niece and her niece's boyfriend for dinner at a restaurant they suggested, she noted that they casually ordered the foie gras appetizer and a second bottle of chardonnay. They knew the waiter by name and asked where the oysters were from that day. My friend was surprised because she knew from her sister (the niece's mother) that the couple were always complaining about having trouble paying their bills. Clearly, there was a disconnect between their stomachs and their wallets.

Young people starting out might legitimately have trouble making ends meet. However, if your kid earns a decent salary but is regularly scrambling when the rent is due, food (or bar tabs) could be a culprit. In such a case, tell your child to check his grocery and restaurant receipts. Even if you yourself are not an artisanal cheese eater or a craft cocktail drinker, don't preach to your small-batch-bourbon-savoring child about the price. Instead, help him weigh the trade-offs. Suggest that he shop for basics at the local chain grocery, then pick and choose a few "treat" items at a specialty market, like that fancy olive oil he so enjoys.

The New Money Rules for Weddings

When parents think of their kids, it's often the milestones they remember most. Their first words. That first piano recital. Their high school graduation. But perhaps the most poignant—and potentially pricey—one-shot event? Their wedding.

Although there was a lot wrong with the 1950s marriage paradigm, one aspect must have been kind of nice. When it came to weddings, it was fairly clear who paid for what. Etiquette maven Amy Vanderbilt laid out the rules: The bride's family paid for the ceremony and the reception, and, of course, the dress; the groom covered the marriage license, the minister's fee, and the honeymoon. Today it's a free-for-all. What isn't free is the wedding itself: The average cost of nuptials in the United States, according to *The Wedding Report*, an industry publication that tracks expenses, is $27,000. Many cost a lot more. It's become such a sizable investment that many couples are purchasing wedding insurance. To see why you probably shouldn't, take a look at p. 136.

So where does this leave you? Well, first and foremost, don't feel obliged to pay for a child's dream wedding, particularly if your own finances are precarious. No tapping retirement savings or going into hock on your credit cards. That said, if you can and want to put up some cash for your kid's wedding, do so, but realize that it doesn't give you the right to impose your own preferences on the couple's wedding plans.

The good news is, with people marrying several years older than they did decades ago, they are often more established financially. A *Consumer Reports* survey found that, on average, couples today pay for nearly half the cost of their reception. Many foot the entire wedding bill. Still, it's tough for many couples to come up with that kind of money. Here are some tips to pass along.

- **Buy a ring you can easily afford.** Forget the myth that the cost of an engagement ring should equal two months' salary. That rule was created in the 1980s by the marketing department of the giant diamond company De Beers. (This shamelessly upped the original suggested price of one month's salary, which the same company's marketers had proposed decades earlier.) Researchers from Emory University found that when a man spent between $2,000 and $4,000 on an engagement ring, he and his spouse were 1.3 times likelier to divorce than were a couple who had paid between $500 and $2,000 for the ring. One explanation suggested by the researchers: The less debt the couple has at the outset, the less stress on the marriage.

- **Weigh the opportunity cost.** It's easy for your kid to get swept up in planning a celebration to rival the Royal Wedding, but remind him of how the money he might spend on just this one day could help him with other goals. For instance, that average wedding price tag of $27,000 is almost equal to a 20% down payment on a $150,000 home. It's also nearly enough to pay off the average amount in student loans that kids owe when they graduate from college. Ask your kid to weigh those numbers against his determination to invite every person he played Little League with 15 years ago to his wedding.

- **Don't pay a wedding premium if you can help it.** Caterers, florists, photographers, and other vendors often jack up their prices for a wedding, counting on the couple to be inexperienced first-time shoppers and to fear seeming "cheap" on their big day. A British survey found that vendors as much as quadrupled the price for a family party if it was described as a wedding. Encourage your kid to price a few places for a "family gathering," and then call back and get the price for the same number of guests if it's a "wedding." Your kid can then try to negotiate the price—or abandon the vendor altogether if the difference remains too high. Given these economics, many couples are opting for a do-it-yourself wedding in a low-cost venue such as a neighborhood bar, a public park, or someone's backyard.

- **The less money you spend on the wedding, the longer your marriage is likely to last.** Contrary to what marketing by the wedding industry suggests, couples across all income levels who spend big on their weddings are likelier to split than frugal couples are. (Remember, that $27,000 figure is an average, which means that many people spend much less.) According to the Emory University study mentioned above, couples who spent more than $20,000 on their nuptials were 3.5 times more prone to break up than ones who budgeted modestly ($5,000 to $10,000). The researchers speculated that, like an expensive engagement ring, a big wedding can result in debt that strains a new marriage. Plus, having an over-the-top affair takes the focus off what's most important: the relationship itself.

- **If you're asked to be in a friend's wedding, find out what you are expected to pay for before saying yes.** I know: Awkward, right? But I've heard so many stories of young women (and men) who end up in debt trying to be the perfect friend: shelling out for a blowout bachelorette party, a bridesmaid's dress (picked out by the bride), plane tickets and hotel tab, and a fabulous gift. Not many young adults can afford to do this even once, let alone multiple times in a summer. So when the bride-to-be starts describing a destination wedding in St. Barts or names a fancy dress designer for the bridesmaids' gowns, it really and truly is okay for your kid to say that she totally supports her friend but isn't in a position to spend that kind of money. Paying $300 for a dress she might wear only once isn't a sign of loyal friendship.

6

Get Insured

You probably think insurance is too boring, too confusing, or just too darn depressing to discuss with your kids. Guess what? You are *correct* about it being boring, confusing, and depressing! But you're wrong about it not being a fit subject for familial conversation. Let's talk about what you're right about before we talk about what you're wrong about, because I am all about bucking up your self-esteem.

It's *boring* because *blah, blah, blah* deductibles and *blah, blah, blah* co-payments.

It's *confusing* because it's sold as a way to protect *everything*: purchases (a cell phone, a trip to Aruba), property (a car, the contents of a dorm room), and your very personhood (your health, your life, even your identity).

And, most of all, it's *depressing,* because who wants to think about car crashes and cancer? Fire and theft? Dents and death? (If you feel like getting bummed out, why not read *The Bell Jar* and then watch *Titanic* a few times instead!)

Still another reason insurance isn't a fun topic? Odds are, you are going to lose money on it. That's because insurance is actually designed to be what's called an expected value loser. Here's what I mean: Although you might think the point of health insurance is to cover your few doctor's appointments a year, that simply isn't so; you'd actually, in all likelihood, be better off not buying a policy and just paying for those few visits in cash. The reason we need health insurance—and pay monthly premiums to get it—is to cover those rare but devastating medical bills triggered by a serious illness or a major accident. Those situations can wipe you out financially, so having coverage is essential. The irony, of course, is that we buy insurance hoping our policy never has to pay out big, since that would mean we've suffered a medical disaster.

But to get back to your kids: Despite the whole boring/confusing/depressing thing, avoiding the topic isn't the answer. If you don't teach your kids about insurance, they won't know whether they're being savvy or suckers each time they decide to purchase some—or say no thanks.

In this chapter, you'll learn everything you need to about insurance—and the best ways to pass that knowledge along to your kids. I promise to leave out the extra stuff that doesn't matter, like the boring, confusing, *and* depressing. Better yet, I'll cut to the chase to give you the basic concepts your kid needs to know.

PRESCHOOL

Even at this age, your kid can understand the basic concept of insurance. Here's how to drive the point home.

- **There are things you can do to protect yourself and your stuff.** When you spray your kid's shoes with Scotchgard to protect them from rain, or help her tie her mittens to a string she loops through the arms of her coat, point out that there are ways to protect your stuff. And when you teach her to brush her teeth or wear sunscreen in the summer, that's a chance to talk about the idea that there are things we can do to protect our bodies. This idea of "insuring" yourself against future harm by taking actions today is one that even a young kid can understand.

- **Parents: Be prepared for the unexpected with a family "insurance fund."** Keeping a cookie jar in the kitchen filled with $1 bills and coins—and using that stash to replace your kids' occasional lost umbrella or pair of gloves—is a concrete way to demonstrate why it's helpful to have some insurance as a backup if something happens that you didn't expect. Try hard not to cheat by dipping into it yourself, but if you do, replace the money as soon as possible. Otherwise you'll be undermining your message to your kid about being prepared for the unexpected.

- **Parents: Explain how insurance was invented.** The first modern insurance policies were created by ship owners hundreds of years ago. When one of their ships sank, they lost everything aboard. So some of them got together and said, "When a ship goes down, we will chip in to cover the cost." They determined the amount they had to ante up based on the number of ships they owned; the more ships, the more money they had to put into the insurance pot. (This is still the way insurance works. We chip in—in advance now—to create a single common pot of money from which claims are paid.) The ship owners finally decided to hire a bookkeeper. That bookkeeper eventually become known as the "insurance company." Today people can buy insurance for everything from health care to celebrity body parts.

ELEMENTARY SCHOOL

Kids this age can start to understand the role that insurance—particularly health insurance—plays in our daily lives. Here's how to help them connect the dots.

- **There are costs if you don't take care of your stuff.** If a kid damages something intentionally, you might feel that a punishment or at least a reprimand is in order. But what if he mistakenly throws out his retainer along with the trash on his school lunch tray? (Like I did in fifth grade.) Or puts a hole in the wall while wrestling with a friend? (Like my brothers did.) This can get tricky, particularly with a remorseful child. The first time your child loses something, it's fine to give him a pass while explaining that each loss costs money. Everyone makes mistakes. But if you find that the losses are piling up—a pair of glasses every few months, a jacket every spring—your child probably needs an incentive to be more responsible and to learn that there are real costs incurred when we lose or break stuff. Ask him to pay, but be realistic. The price of a replacement jacket might be a couple months' worth of allowance, so maybe split the bill or just have him pay a small flat fee, either all at once or in installments. Even in families where parents can easily afford to fix or replace the item without financial hardship, consider the message you want to send your kid. When a friend's fourth-grader lost a school library book and received an overdue notice from the librarian, my friend required her daughter to split the cost of replacing it. The result: no more lost books.

- **Parents: Explain health insurance during your child's next doctor's visit.** At your child's annual checkup, instead of having him roam around while you pay for the visit, talk him through what you are doing. Explain that the doctor is a worker just like all the others we've talked about, and his or her job is to help kids stay healthy by doing checkups or giving them medicine if they are sick. We need to pay the doctor for that job. And here's the cool part: We don't have to pay for it all ourselves; the insurance company pays for a chunk of it. So when we go for a checkup, the visit might cost $150, but health insurance typically covers most of that, leaving you to pay only $20. Then you can explain in basic terms where you get your insurance, whether through your job, your spouse's job, the government, or a company from which you have purchased it on your own.

MIDDLE SCHOOL

Allow me to present two important insurance concepts that a middle schooler might find kind of interesting.

- **Insurance protects us from really big losses.** We all take risks in life—some of us more than others. We wear the jeans with a hole in the pocket, and if our lunch money falls out, we may go hungry that day or have to share a sandwich with a friend. We hang out with a cousin who has a cold, and sure enough a few days later, we have it too. Usually we don't prep for what happens if something goes wrong. We take these small risks and deal with the consequences. But there are some consequences that are so big that we would be financially drained if the worst-case scenario happened: Say, you trip and fall on the sidewalk and need new front teeth, the family gets into a fender bender, or a huge storm damages the roof. For these risks, we buy insurance. The basic categories of insurance we need are health insurance, car insurance, and home insurance. When your kid gets older, he'll probably need life insurance too, but no need to freak out your middle schooler about this topic.

- **Liability insurance protects you if you accidentally hurt someone else.** While we think of insurance as something that protects us if we get sick or hurt, or if our stuff gets lost or stolen, you can also buy insurance to cover the cost of any damage you cause to others. Auto liability insurance might cover the damage you accidentally cause to someone's car or even to the people in that car; your home insurance liability protection will cover your neighbor's medical bills if he trips on the thick-pile area rug in your living room.

  "But what exactly is liability?" your kid might ask. When my friend Lidia's aunt Rose slipped on a greasy floor in the butcher shop and broke her hip, the store's owner paid the entire hospital bill. If he hadn't, Aunt Rose might have hired a lawyer and sued the shop. Had he purchased liability insurance in the first place, the butcher could have avoided paying out of his own pocket. You can explain that there's been a lot of discussion about frivolous lawsuits that people bring against companies, hoping to get a big payout even if the damage they incurred wasn't serious. On the other hand, if a butcher fails to sprinkle some sawdust or put out signs alerting customers to a slippery floor and a customer winds up severely injured as a result, doesn't it seem fair for him to cover the costs of the damage done? Liability is a tricky topic but worth discussing.

You Can Insure Just About Anything: Why Lloyd's of London Is in Business

It's been widely reported that supermodel Heidi Klum's legs were once insured for an estimated $2 million. (One, which had a scar on it, was worth less than the other.) Soccer legend David Beckham insured his legs, too, as well as all ten toes. Singer Bruce Springsteen insured his voice. And it's rumored that actor Daniel Craig's entire body was insured for millions while he was filming a James Bond movie in which he performed his own stunts.

As you introduce your kids to what insurance is and what it does, you can tell them about Lloyd's, an insurance network in London that connects people who want to insure something unusual with companies (known as underwriters) that are willing to offer such unique insurance. Lloyd's isn't the only place to purchase this kind of insurance, but it's the best known.

If you're a movie producer, you can buy "key-man insurance" on the actor starring in your action film, so that if he dies or is injured, you don't lose all the money you've invested in the project. Same goes for a company that depends on its CEO. If she has a heart attack and the company's profits suffer, there's insurance for that. Ditto a football team with a star quarterback. A business can even insure its reputation, so that if an environmental accident or a scandal damages how people view it, and profits go down, it will be compensated.

HIGH SCHOOL

Although insurance isn't a thrilling topic for a teen, driving sure is. Whether your kid takes a driver's ed class or you teach him yourself (brave you!), this is the time to talk not only about auto insurance but about all types of insurance.

- **You'll need to chip in for auto insurance.** Plain and simple: Your kid will need car insurance whether he drives your car or has his own. Explain what the policy does—and doesn't—cover, and explain deductibles (the amount you have to pay before the insurance kicks in) and premiums (the amount you pay for insurance). There are three basic parts to car insurance: liability, medical payments, and collision/comprehensive. Liability will pay your legal expenses if you get sued after an accident, as well as the medical and repair bills for whomever you hurt. Medical payments insurance covers the hospital bills for you and your passengers. Collision insurance pays for damage to your car from an accident. Comprehensive insurance covers damage caused in just about any other way, including if a tree falls on it. Some states also require uninsured motorists coverage, which protects you if an uninsured driver crashes into your car and you're injured or your car is damaged.

Tell your kid that adding him to your policy will likely at least double your premiums—not to make him feel *guilty* or anything. (Oh, you have a daughter? Well, lucky you: Teenage girls will raise your premium only about 70%.) Make sure to have this talk before your kid gets his own car. Factors including his grades in school can affect the cost of his car insurance. (You might get a discount if your kid makes Bs or better.) Also, insurance generally costs less if you have a boring car. (It's cheaper to insure the driver of a Toyota Corolla than someone with a BMW convertible.) Of course, the most important thing your kid can do to keep rates low is to avoid tickets and accidents. To drive the point home (hard to resist this pun), you can let him know that he will have to pay for any increase in your insurance rates that results from a traffic ticket or fender bender that is his fault. Whether or not your kid has his own car, require him to pay at least some portion of the premium. This will make him more aware of how insurance works—and give him a real incentive to try to bring down that cost.

COLLEGE

Sending a kid off to college can make even the calmest parents feel nervous. But with just a few moves, you and your kid can both relax. A smidgen, anyway.

- **Health insurance is a must.** Now is the perfect moment to drill this idea into your kid's brain so that it becomes a lifelong mantra: Having health insurance is a must. Many colleges require students to prove they have it before they can even start classes. Your kid's school might offer a health insurance plan, or it might leave it to your family to provide one. (As of this writing, you can keep your child on your health insurance until she turns 26—or is even older, in some states.) No matter how your kid ends up covered, it's important for her to know that health insurance, now and in the future, is nonnegotiable. While you're at it, if you haven't already had the talk with your kid about the health risks of smoking (a habit many college students take up), get on that. To underline your point, mention that smoking is also wildly expensive. Cigarettes can cost anywhere from $5 to nearly $13 a pack, meaning that a half pack a day—the national average for young smokers—will set her back from about $1,000 to almost $2,500 a year. And it can boost her health insurance premiums by up to 50%.

- **You need homeowners or renters insurance.** When your kid leaves for college, it's important to make sure her stuff is covered, and it's also a great time to talk about the concept of homeowners and renters insurance. These can help replace personal property that is damaged or stolen, provide liability coverage if a visitor to your child's place gets hurt, and even help cover the cost of staying in a hotel if a fire or other incident leaves her place uninhabitable for a while. If your kid is living in a college dorm or at home with you, her belongings are probably covered under your renters or homeowners policy—but check with your company to be sure, and ask about any limits (especially if your kid is living in campus housing instead of with you, because there might be a dollar-amount cap on coverage).

  If your kid is living in an apartment off campus, she'll need a renters policy. College students have lots of possessions that would cost thousands to replace: laptops and other electronics, furniture, clothing, maybe a bike, and all those textbooks. Renters policies are inexpensive, and there's a special policy available to college students through National Student Services, Inc. (NSSI.com) that offers year-round coverage for their stuff no matter where they are. Policies range from $65 to $240. But bear in mind that unlike regular renters insurance, this policy covers only personal property. So talk to your kid about what she owns that might need to be covered, as well as whether that insurance is coming from your policy or from a policy of her own. Even if she's covered by a policy of yours, she should know that.

- **Get the highest deductible you can afford.** When buying insurance, your kid might be tempted by a low deductible, the amount he has to pay out of his own pocket, if he files a claim, before insurance kicks in. Ultimately, though, having a low deductible will end up costing him more in two ways. First, the lower your deductible, the higher your monthly premiums. Second, consider this scenario: Your kid rear-ends another vehicle. His car sustains $1,200 worth of damage. His car insurance has a $500 deductible, so he files a claim and receives a check for $700. Which feels pretty sweet, until his insurance company deems him a higher risk and jacks up his annual premium by $800. By paying for smaller repairs himself—those for which the cost is less than his deductible—he'll keep his premiums down and save money in the long run. Note that this strategy works only if your kid has an emergency fund to cover the repairs.

- **Consider "self-insurance."** These days you can insure just about everything— a cell phone, an airplane trip, or even your credit card debt. But while you definitely need health, home, and car insurance, you can skip most of these other categories. Why? Well, in general, you don't need to buy insurance on an item if the cost of repairing or replacing it would be small enough that you could cover it with your savings. Beyond that, it might be covered already in some other way: for instance, by your home or renters insurance or a manufacturer's warranty included with the cost of the item. And with all the exclusions and disclaimers, and maybe a hefty deductible, an insurance policy or a warranty might not cover as much as you think. Laptop insurance, for example, generally won't cover you if your laptop is infected with a virus. So your first instinct when asked if you want to insure something should be to say no. (See the box on p. 133 for more about how to weigh these decisions.) Ideally, you'll set aside the amount you would have spent on that extra coverage in a savings account that you designate for self-insurance (and that might even pay you a little interest), so that if you really do need a replacement or a repair, you'll have the cash.

One more really good reason to absorb smaller bills: If you file a claim against a homeowners or renters policy for something that costs a few hundred dollars—say, a stolen bike or a broken ceiling fan—you might get a little money if the deductible is low enough to cover some of the cost. But when it comes time to renew that policy, your premiums are likely to shoot up, or the insurance company could refuse to renew at all. It might feel unfair, but that's how it works. In the company's eyes, there's a high risk that you'll file a bigger claim down the road. Save the claims for the truly big stuff.

- **Parents: Figure out if your child should stay on your health insurance plan or go with the campus health insurance.** As I said earlier, your child can remain on your health care plan until she reaches age 26. But depending on your plan's details, it might be smart to switch to the college's coverage. One of the biggest downsides of keeping your kid on your current plan is that he could be restricted to doctors in its network, which might include only doctors near to where you live—definitely a problem if your child attends college out of state, since seeing physicians outside of the network is much more expensive. My friend's 20-year-old son Tony had just moved to San Antonio for a summer job when he started having excruciating back pain. He was referred to a local doctor for an MRI. To his surprise, his parents' insurance didn't cover out-of-state doctors, and Tony had to wait to undergo the scan until he was back in New York. If your child is living at home, or going to a local school, it might be a better deal to keep him on your plan. The only way to figure this out is to compare both plans' costs and coverage.

YOUNG ADULTHOOD

You'll always want to protect your kid, but now that he's grown, it's time to teach him how to do it for himself. Here's what to say.

- **You need to get health insurance.** As a parent, you are not responsible for your adult child's medical bills (even if he is living in a miasma of his own sweaty-sock smell in your basement) unless he still qualifies as a dependent on your taxes. To see if he does, check out "Who Can I Claim as a Dependent?" on IRS.gov. But many parents feel responsible for their kid's health care, so it's in your interest to make sure he is covered. Keep in mind that the majority of personal bankruptcies filed each year are due to unpaid medical bills.

For many young adults, the best option is insurance provided by an employer. This option might be a nonstarter for your kid if (1) his job doesn't offer insurance, (2) the insurance provided is way too expensive, (3) he's a freelancer or part-timer, or (4) he's unemployed. Don't fret—there are other options.

If your kid is under 26, and your insurance allows you to cover dependents, start by looking at the cost of adding him to your policy. In a few states, remember, insurers are required to allow parents to cover their grown kids for even longer; in New Jersey, for example, the age cutoff is 31. To find out the rules in your state, check with the National Conference of State Legislatures (NCSL) at ncsl.org/research/health/dependent-health-coverage -state-implementation.aspx. Chances are, insuring your child through your plan will be less expensive—and it probably offers broader coverage—than what your kid would pay to obtain coverage on his own. As of this writing, Healthcare.gov may offer an affordable plan as well as tax breaks or subsidies if an applicant's income falls below a certain threshold. No matter which way he gets coverage, you might decide to help him pay for a portion of it if you're in the position to do so. (For much more on how to choose a health insurance plan, see Chapter 8 of my book *Get a Financial Life: Personal Finance in Your Twenties and Thirties.*)

- **Don't skip renters insurance.** When I returned home the day after I moved into my first solo apartment—a tiny studio in what seemed like a safe building—I discovered that the few pieces of gold jewelry that my grandmother had given me were missing, as were a computer and some cash I'd left on the dresser. I didn't have renters insurance. Whether your kid's apartment building has a fire and all of his valuable stuff goes up in smoke or a neighbor cuts himself on your son's glass coffee table and wants to sue for the medical bills—these are the times when your kid needs renters insurance, also known as tenants insurance. Contrary to what many people assume, the landlord is generally not responsible for theft or most of the damage that could happen in a rental. So if your kid's possessions are destroyed or stolen, items such as clothes, computer equipment, and furniture could end up costing tens of thousands of dollars to replace. Renters insurance is relatively cheap—nationally, the average premium ranges from $15 to $30 a month, depending on what is covered and where your kid lives. Have your kid start at Knowyourstuff.org from the Insurance Information Institute to log what it would cost to replace lost items, then shop at NetQuote.com to compare rates.

- **You don't need life insurance—yet.** Despite the sneaky commercials that make it seem that the person buying life insurance gets a windfall, it actually pays your loved ones, not you, when you die. If your kid doesn't have anyone who depends on him financially, who's going to get that money? His pet hamster, Lord Killington? Let's be honest: Nine times out of ten, those who push life insurance on young people who don't have kids are life insurance agents themselves. At least that's been my experience. So until your kid has kids of his own, tell him to skip life insurance, and just give Lord Killington some lettuce. And don't let an insurance agent lure your kid into buying so-called cash-value life insurance by telling him it's a great forced savings plan and offers tax-favored growth. Yeah, nice try. But if your kid doesn't need life insurance, he doesn't need life insurance. And even if he does, because he has a child of his own, he's better off getting simple, inexpensive term insurance and investing the savings in his 401(k) or IRA. (For more on those, see Chapter 7.)

- **Buy insurance that protects against general risks rather than against specific events.** It's tempting to buy quickie insurance for one-off situations: flight insurance (when you're taking a trip), laptop insurance (when you buy a new computer), credit card insurance (in case you lose your job). But that isn't a good use of your money. When it comes to insurance, think big and cover the underlying risks, such as your life (life insurance), your health (health insurance), and your possessions (homeowners or renters insurance). Then pay the small stuff out of pocket. (See the self-insurance advice on p. 129 and the following box.)

Insurance Your Kid Probably *Doesn't* Need

As your kid gets older, she'll have to make decisions about all kinds of insurance. Here's what she needs to know.

Extended warranty or service contract

What It Covers Repair or maintenance of things such as appliances or vehicles.

The Lowdown These tend to be hugely profitable for the companies offering such policies, but they are generally a lousy deal for you.

Do You Need It? Almost never. Most major appliances and electronics include a one-year manufacturer's warranty in the purchase price. Buying coverage for a few years after that rarely makes sense because many of these products last for years beyond the extended warranty period. At that point, you're typically better off paying out of pocket for any repairs or replacements.

Trip cancellation insurance

What It Covers Usually, the cost of flights, hotels, and car rentals.

The Lowdown A policy will cost anywhere from about 4% to 10% of your trip's total prepaid, nonrefundable expenses. Check out the website InsureMyTrip.com to get quotes and more info.

Do You Need It? Only for big trips. Buy it when you're spending lots on travel—particularly overseas trips or long stays. Most policies cover cancellation only for illness or natural disasters and won't cover your costs if you cancel just because you decide not to go. If you do have reason to believe you may cancel, you can buy a special policy, but you'll have to pay extra.

Flight insurance

What It Covers If you buy a policy before boarding an airplane that crashes, your beneficiaries collect if you die.

The Lowdown The average American's odds of dying in an airline accident are just 1 in 11 million. You're more than 2,000 times more likely to die in a car crash.

Do You Need It? No. But if you're really worried, spend a couple bucks to download the Am I Going Down? app, which will reassure you, since it calculates the very, very small chance of a particular flight crashing. It'll at least keep you entertained at the airport—if you have a certain sense of humor.

Pet insurance

What It Covers A portion of your pet's bills for routine medical care, surgeries, and so on.

The Lowdown Starting prices for dogs average $35 a month, and coverage for your cat starts at around $25, plus the deductible. But older animals and those with chronic conditions cost a lot more to insure.

Do You Need It? No. Most plans don't cover yearly "well visits," which means you're better off simply paying the vet bills yourself.

Smartphone insurance

What It Covers Either a new (or like-new) replacement device and/or the cost of repairs.

The Lowdown Sure, it sounds reasonable to get this when you hear that a cracked screen can cost upwards of $100 to repair. But the truth is that many policies give you only a used phone as a replacement, or a different model altogether. This is a big moneymaker for the companies that offer it.

Do You Need It? Skip it. Only one in five people surveyed by *Consumer Reports* has needed to replace a lost, broken, or stolen phone. If you know your kid has a case of dropitis, buy him a heavy-duty smartphone protector such as the OtterBox or Life-Proof case.

Rental car insurance

What It Covers There are three parts to it: (1) liability, which covers damage to other vehicles as well as medical bills if anyone else is injured in an accident you cause; (2) personal accident insurance, which covers your medical bills if you get injured; and (3) a collision damage waiver (sometimes called a loss damage waiver), which pays for damage to the car itself. Some companies also offer "loss of use" insurance to cover any costs incurred if the rental car company can't use your car for a few days after you're in an accident.

The Lowdown Many people panic at the rental car counter and cave to the pressure to buy this coverage. Often it ends up almost doubling the cost to rent a car.

Do You Need It? Yes, but you may already have the coverage and not know it. If you own a car, your auto insurance policy probably covers rentals too (both collision and liability), so check your policy. If you don't own a car but you pay for the rental with a credit card, you will likely be covered for collision (but not liability), so check your credit card agreement too. If that's the case, you'll want to decline the rental company's collision damage waiver, but you definitely need to buy liability coverage at the counter. Note that card companies often exclude certain locations or types of rental vehicles (like SUVs or pricey cars). As for personal accident insurance, your medical insurance will cover your bills if you are hurt while driving a rental, so skip it.

Laptop insurance

What It Covers The cost of repairs to a laptop if you spill coffee on the keyboard or drop it—things not covered by the usual one-year manufacturer's warranty.

The Lowdown For many people, it's nearly impossible to live without a laptop, which is why laptop insurance can seem appealing.

Do You Need It? It depends. If you set aside enough money for a repair or even a new computer, skip it. If you consider yourself clumsy, you may benefit from a one-year policy.

College tuition insurance

What It Covers The cost of tuition (and other expenses) if a college student gets sick or injured at school and needs to leave before the end of the term.

The Lowdown GradGuard, A.W.G. Dewar, and others charge 1% to 5% of tuition, room, and board. Many don't give refunds for mental health reasons unless your kid is hospitalized. Nor do they give money back for drug or academic problems.

Do You Need It? Probably not. It's expensive and doesn't cover many of the most common reasons kids leave midsemester.

Identity theft insurance

What It Covers Help with monitoring your credit records for fraud, and guidance through the time-consuming process of repairing and protecting your credit if your identity is stolen.

The Lowdown These services prey on people's fears and can charge hundreds of dollars a year. Sometimes they throw in insurance (up to $1 million) to pay costs associated with identity theft, but what they don't tell you is that federal protections mean that victims often pay no out-of-pocket costs anyway.

Do You Need It? No. The best (and cheapest) insurance against identity theft is the do-it-yourself kind. Monitor your bank and credit accounts regularly, check your credit reports at least once a year at AnnualCreditReport.com, and if you are a victim of fraud, go to IdentityTheft.gov for next steps.

Credit insurance

What It Covers Pays off your car loan, mortgage, or credit card balance if you die or become disabled.

The Lowdown It's really expensive and always caps the number of months it will pay your bills. You're much better off using your money to pay down your debt instead.

Do You Need It? Nope. When this does pay out, it's usually not much. Plus, if your kid has a credit card, in the unlikely event that he does die young, the only one who takes the hit is the credit card company.

Wedding insurance

What It Covers Nonrefundable deposits if a wedding (or other special event) is canceled or interrupted because of a natural disaster, death, illness, vendor bankruptcy, or other problems.

The Lowdown Policies generally cost $155 to $550, plus about $200 for up to $1 million in liability coverage.

Do You Need It? Not likely. You might have liability protection through your contract with the vendors, and you might already have coverage for some of these risks through your homeowners insurance. Plus, most wedding policies exclude the biggest risk: cold feet.

7

The Plain Truth About Investing

At a brunch not long ago, a woman pulled me aside and said she'd come up with a great idea to get her 14-year-old son interested in the stock market: She gave him $500, opened a brokerage account in his name, and told him to buy some stocks.

Smart?

Errrrr, not so much.

If the stocks' value goes down, her kid is likely to conclude that investing is a sucker's game and decide to avoid the market altogether. That's a problem. And if the stock goes up, he'll think he's got the touch and continue to place bigger and bolder bets. Which could wind up being an even bigger problem. Win or lose, he won't learn the right lessons.

Now, I'm not saying this mom was off base on all counts. Kids *should* learn about investing. They just need to be taught what really matters. That's what you'll learn in this chapter, whether you're a financial whiz who can't explain what you know in simple terms or a parent who doesn't know the difference between a value stock and chicken stock.

You might find yourself wondering whether you could just avoid the whole shebang and let your kid stick her money under the mattress—or in a bank account—so it's safe. Problem is, the money won't *really* be safe. And I'm not talking about a thief stealing it. I'm talking about inflation, the tendency of prices to rise over time. If your money isn't earning a rate at least equal to that of inflation—which has averaged about 3% a year over the last three decades—you're losing buying power. (I'll explain later.)

One investment that, over time, has beaten inflation is stocks. And though no one knows for sure, it's the best guess of experts that, over the long run, this trend will continue. (See the box on p. 139.)

Fine. Great. Sure. But it'll be a long time before your kid has enough money to invest, so most parents can skip over this part, right?

I'm afraid not, Dear Reader.

I get why it's tempting to think that you can put off investing discussions until your kid has a stable job or a stockpile of cash. But don't. Postponing these lessons will mean that your kid loses the big advantage that all kids have: time for investments to grow. Making sure that your child learns the fundamentals early and starts putting away small amounts while he's young will be a valuable gift. Even if your kid is flat broke right now, if he becomes comfortable with the market, he won't miss out when he does have money.

Don't panic if you don't understand the market at all yourself and have never even bought stock in your life. Most people believe mistakenly that if only they had the "right" broker, contacts, or pipeline of information, they'd absolutely know which stocks would make them money. This chapter will give you the few simple investing rules that matter most. If you pass them along to your kid, you'll ensure that he's smarter than most people who invest today. That's a promise.

Where Should You Put Your Money?

This chart shows you approximately how much money you'd have if, in 1985, you had taken $1,000 and done one of four things: (1) invested it in the stock market, (2) invested it in bonds, (3) put it in a savings account, or (4) stuck it under the mattress.

One thing to note: Although, as you'll see, stocks definitely beat the rest of the investment options over the long haul, there were individual years in which you could have lost *a lot* of your money. In 2008, for instance, stocks plummeted by 37%. (If you'd had to withdraw your money in 2009 to pay your kid's college bill, you would have suffered a big loss. That's why I recommend never investing money you'll need in the short term in the stock market.)

Overall, however, you still would have come out way ahead if you'd kept your money in the market. Generally speaking, the higher the return, the higher the risk.

Where You Put $1,000 in 1985	Average Return*	What You'd Have 30 Years Later
Stocks (S&P 500)	11.0%	$22,892
Bonds (Barclays Capital U.S. Aggregate Bond Index)	7.2%	$8,051
Savings account (1-month U.S. Treasury bills)	3.6%	$2,889
Under the mattress	0%	$1,000**

* Compound annual total return, 1985 to 2015. Return not adjusted for inflation.

** If you adjust for inflation, the money under your mattress would have *lost* value. It would really only be worth about $472.

PRESCHOOL

When your kid is very young, you're not going to launch into a lengthy treatise on price-to-earnings ratios. But here are some lessons to teach your little one the concept of investing. At heart, it's really a way of looking at the world.

- **An investment is something that pays off in the future.** Get a copy of *The Little Red Hen* and read it to your child. You remember the story, right?

There are various versions of this old fable floating around, but the gist is the same: The hen invested the time and effort to turn wheat into bread—sowing the grain, harvesting it, and making and kneading the dough. The lazy animals who were her friends blew her off and didn't help until it came time to eat. Then they were all in! But that Little Red Hen was no pushover; she held her ground and refused to share her bread with the slackers, and everyone learned a lesson. The Little Red Hen was thinking long term, and reaped the rewards of her investment of time and hard work. Introduce the concept of being an "investor" when your kid completes a puzzle or an art project: "Wow, you really invested time and effort—and look at what you've come up with!"

- **Parents: Help your kid plant a garden or put some seeds in a flowerpot.** Because young children have a difficult time understanding the concept of the future, wrapping their little minds around investing can be tough. One way to introduce the idea is to relate it to something that a kid can see, like the process of a seed growing into a flower or vegetable. Talk about the time it takes the plant to grow, and the fertilizer and water that you need to "invest" in it so that you get the payoff of a beautiful sunflower or a ripe tomato at the end. You can extend that to your community. When you go with your kid to the independent grocer a couple blocks away rather than to the giant chain supermarket up the block, you can explain that the smaller store is owned by someone in the community, and that by shopping there, you are choosing to invest in your neighbors and, ultimately, your own town.

ELEMENTARY SCHOOL

Kids this age are able to absorb more than you think when it comes to simple investing concepts, and many will be more interested than you'd guess. Here's how to explain the basics.

- **A stock is a small piece of a company that you can own.** The next time you watch a Disney movie or sip a Coke with your kid, you can use the occasion to teach him about stocks. It's good to try to have this conversation when your kid is in third or fourth grade, when he'll be old enough to grasp these basics. Start by explaining that a lot of the stuff he likes is made by companies. The Coca-Cola Company makes that drink he loves (but may not be allowed to have very often). And his favorite remote-controlled car is made by Hasbro. These companies make these products and then sell them. They need money to make the products, and to get it many companies sell what is called stock. When people buy stock in a company, they are investing in that company. Basically, they own a little piece of it. Your kid isn't going to do much with this knowledge now, but it's good for him to start thinking that his buying decisions play a part in the bigger financial picture.

- **Don't put all your eggs in one basket.** Tell your kid to imagine opening a restaurant that sells only hamburgers. As long as people really like hamburgers, she'll make lots of money. But what if people hear that some cows got sick, and those people begin thinking that beef is tainted and burgers aren't safe to eat anymore? Or what if people decide they want to eat French fries, too, and start going to a restaurant that sells more than just hamburgers? The point: It's good to serve a few different things so that there will always be something on the menu that people want. This meaty example illustrates one of the most important investment concepts, known as diversification. And here's how it applies to stocks: While it's really tempting to buy the stock of a single company you like—say, Krispy Kreme—if you do, you're making a big bet on that one company and the future popularity of donuts. If, however, you own stock from many different companies, you're reducing the risk that you'll lose all your money. That's because if some companies' stocks do poorly, there's a chance that other companies' stocks will do well, and so overall you'll do okay.

- **Parents: Play the lottery with your child—just three times.** Ask many kids the best way to make a lot of money fast, and they'll answer, "The lottery." Your kid might have noticed the "All you need is a dollar and a dream"–type ads or seen news stories about jubilant lottery winners and decided, "Ah, there's the ticket." If your kid has lottery fever, let him learn the hard way.

Have him use his own money, if he's willing, to play the next time there's a big jackpot. When your kid doesn't win (and he won't), explain that often the chance of winning the really big, highly publicized lotteries is less than one in 250 million. That is very, very, very small. So small that it is a big ol' waste of money to play at all. A few years ago, the *New York Times* ran a story about a doorman who was spending $500 to $700 a week on lottery tickets hoping to strike it rich but couldn't catch a break. Naturally, I couldn't resist calculating how much he'd have if he'd sunk that money into a stock fund investment. Let's say he spends an average of $600 a week. That's $31,200 a year. Now suppose his investment earns 7% per year. In just 10 years, he'd have well over $400,000. Within 18 years, he'd have $1 million. No gimmicks, impossible odds, or scratch-off tickets required. For talking points for your kid about his real chances of winning the lottery jackpot, see the box below.

Things More Likely to Happen to You Than Winning the Lottery

If your kid thinks the lottery is the best way to get rich, show her this chart about how the odds of winning the big lotteries stack up against other unlikely events within her lifetime.

The Freak Occurrence	Likelihood
Being struck by lightning	1 in 12,000
Being in the Olympics if you're a high school basketball player	1 in 45,000
Becoming a movie star	1 in 1.2 million
Dying from a shark attack	1 in 3.7 million
Becoming president of the United States	1 in 10 million
Buying the winning Mega Millions ticket	1 in 259 million
Buying the winning Powerball ticket	1 in 292 million

MIDDLE SCHOOL

If there's one subject that'll catch middle schoolers' attention, it's making money. Although their first thought might be to start some far-fetched business, you might be able to pique their interest by telling them how their money can make money.

- **Compound interest can make you rich one day.** The phenomenon of compound interest has been called the eighth wonder of the world. Here's why. When you invest your money, you earn interest on the initial amount you put in, known as the principal. That's great. But here's the beyond-great thing: The interest you earn *also* earns interest. And that keeps happening over time. When interest earns interest on itself, it's known as compounding, and your money grows quickly. Rumor has it that even Albert Einstein spoke of this with awe. What's amazing is that the longer your money compounds, the faster it grows. Which is why it's so important to clue your kid into this early. Using a compound interest calculator like the one on Investor.gov, from the U.S. Securities and Exchange Commission (SEC), you can show your kid this: Let's suppose he set aside $7.50 a month (essentially a quarter a day) starting at age 10 and earned an average of 7% a year. By the time he hit 65, he'd have $51,800. If he didn't start saving until age 35, he'd have only $8,250.

    The moral is that starting early pays off. One big thing to note: Compound interest cuts both ways, so if you owe money, the interest you owe gains interest, too. That's why buying something on credit and taking a long time to pay it off just isn't smart. (See Chapter 4 for more about debt.)

- **Know the "Rule of 72."** By about fourth grade, your kid is probably learning division. This is a great time to show her a neat trick for figuring out how many years it will take to double her money if it is earning interest. Here's how it works: You divide 72 by the interest your money is earning, and the result is the number of years it will take to double your principal (which, as you'll recall, is the amount you started with, before interest). So, for instance, if you invest in an account that earns 8% interest, you'll double your money in nine years. (72 divided by 8 is 9.) There's a complicated mathematical explanation for this (and if you really love math, go on and google "Rule of 72" and knock yourself out explaining it to your child). But all your kid needs to know is that it works.

- **Guard against inflation.** The issue of inflation is about as interesting to most kids—and parents—as listening to your uncle complain about his sciatica. But as I explained at the beginning of this chapter, inflation is an issue that, if ignored, will smother your kid's long-term buying power. So you can explain it to your kid this way: Over time, the price of all the stuff we buy tends to increase. For example, today a Hershey bar might cost $1, but in 1970 that same bar might have cost 10 cents. Obviously, $1 buys you much less today (1 chocolate bar) than it did 45 years ago (10 bars). So how can your kid protect his money from losing value? By putting it where it will grow at least 3% a year, which, as I said earlier, has been roughly the average rate of inflation over the last three decades. (Our Hershey's example also demonstrates another key point about inflation: Not everything rises at the same rate. Some products rise in price faster or slower than the inflation rate. In this case, the price of the iconic candy bar has risen at an average rate of 5% since 1970, slightly outpacing inflation during that period.) But today bank savings accounts often pay much less than 1%. That's why investing is so important. Having your kid understand this concept now is critical. It will also help him understand the need to put some of his 401(k) into stocks. (More about this on p. 153.) For now, it'll give him a snappy comeback when his grandparents gear up for one of their rants about the 1950s, when shoes cost $10: "Grandpa, that might be true, but you're not factoring in inflation and the fact that people earned a lot less too!" Bam! (If your kid is intrigued by the concept of just how much or how little a certain sum was worth in a different era, he can play around with the Bureau of Labor Statistics inflation calculator at bls.gov/data/inflation_calculator.htm.)

The Price of Stuff Goes Up

There's no more persuasive way to illustrate the realities of inflation than by using real examples. Share this chart with your kid to show him why it's necessary to invest to have a fighting chance at keeping up with inflation.

Item	Price in 1970	Price in 2016
Barbie doll	$3	$10
Football (official size)	$5	$30
Lego set (about 350 pieces)	$7	$30
Movie ticket	$1.50	$8.50
Bicycle (Schwinn cruiser)	$85	$215
Annual in-state tuition, room, board at a 4-year public university	$1,400	$19,500
New car (average price)	$3,500	$34,000
Home (average price)	$25,700	$273,600

- **Stock market games and investing camps can be fun, but they don't teach real investing smarts.** Stock market games are all the rage in schools around the country. In clubs or even in class, kids create a portfolio that tracks real stocks, though the money they invest is usually imaginary. And in recent years, investing camps have become somewhat trendy too. Send your kid away for two weeks, and he returns a veritable Wall Street whiz! These classes, clubs, and camps tend to promote the same idea: that with some research you can pick stock winners. Sounds doable, right? Two problems: There are thousands of analysts whose job it is to follow a company's stock price and analyze whether it will go up or down—and *they* often get it wrong. In order for your kid to pick a winner consistently, she'd need to know *more* than all these analysts combined. And that just isn't possible, even if your kid's favorite channel is CNBC. The other big problem with these games and camps is the short time horizon. Most give kids only a few weeks or months to pick stocks that will beat their competitors' returns. That means going for risky stocks that have the potential for a big, quick payoff. This approach contradicts the diversified, long-term investing strategy that will be more likely to succeed in the real world. Of course, finance games can be fun for your kid and might even pique her interest in investing in general. But instead of buying her a briefcase and a subscription to the *Wall Street Journal* and plotting her career at Morgan Stanley, give her the real scoop. For that, read on.

- **An index fund is the smart, easy way to invest.** Okay, by now you know my strong belief that investing in individual stocks is a sucker's bet. But now what? I admit it might seem nutty to tackle this subject with middle schoolers, who often appear barely capable of remembering the combination of their gym lockers. But I've found that most kids this age actually can understand the basic concept of investing in index funds—and love learning it. So let's review. As discussed, diversifying—or investing in lots of stocks rather than just one—reduces your risk. That's because even if some stocks go down, others will probably go up.

  The best way to diversify is to invest in a few hundred or even a few thousand stocks at once. And the simplest way to do that is with a so-called index, which is simply a grouping of stocks. One popular index, called the Dow Jones Industrial Average, tracks 30 stocks of large companies. Another, the Standard & Poor's 500, or S&P 500, contains 500 large stocks. There's even one called the CRSP (Center for Research in Security Prices) U.S. Total Market Index, which has nearly 4,000 stocks.

  The simplest way to invest in an index is to buy what's called a stock index mutual fund. This is an investment that pools the money of lots of investors; that money is then invested in the various stocks that make up a particular index. So an S&P stock index mutual fund would gather money from investors and use it to purchase the different stocks that make up that index. Of course, most middle schoolers aren't ready to invest real money yet. But it is great to get them thinking about what actually works. (And if your kid is precocious, see the high school section for more detailed info.)

- **Parents: Talk to your daughter about investing.** No matter how progressive a parent you are, make sure you aren't subconsciously skipping the investment talk with your daughter. A recent North Carolina State University and University of Texas study of kids between the ages of 8 and 17 found that parents are much more likely to talk to boys about investing than to girls. And that may have consequences: In a poll of people between the ages of 22 and 35, just 56% of women had started saving for retirement, versus 61% of men.

Of course, the fact that women still *earn* less is one reason that fewer women are saving, but another may be their lack of knowledge about investing.

HIGH SCHOOL

Many teens have some money from part-time jobs or other sources. Use this time to get your kid to think of herself not just as a saver but also as an investor putting away money for the long term.

- **Open a Roth IRA with money you earn from your job.** When I was giving a lecture at a college not long ago, a student raised his hand to tell me about one of his most memorable moments from high school. It happened when his history teacher announced that the class would not be studying the Civil War that day, as previously planned. Instead, the teacher devoted the entire period to talking about individual retirement accounts and how opening one was the single smartest thing someone could do to grow his money over time. The student told me he had followed his teacher's advice and already had thousands of dollars in his IRA. I wish I'd asked who that teacher was, because I'd call him right now and tell him he's a genius.

   Individual retirement accounts, known as IRAs, are supersmart places to put your money. As I mentioned in Chapter 3, it's a mistake to think of them as "retirement" accounts, since they are really good investment accounts for people of all ages. The hitch? The money you put in an IRA needs to be earned from a job. (It can't be allowance or birthday money.) The kind of IRA your high schooler should open is called a Roth IRA. Your child can withdraw the money that he has put into a Roth at any time—without paying any taxes or penalties. He would have to pay taxes and penalties on any interest he earns and then withdraws before he turns 59½.

   So why am I so gung ho about Roth IRAs? The money in these accounts grows tax free, which will make it multiply like crazy, especially if your kid starts early. Let's say he puts $1,000 of his summer earnings into a Roth IRA for each of the four years from age 15 to age 18. If he stops and never puts in another penny, but lets the money grow, by age 65 he'll have about $107,000, if the money earns 7% a year. But if your kid waits until age 25 and then puts away $1,000 for each of the four years until age 28 and stops, that account will be worth only a little over $50,000 by age 65. Starting early and having the extra years when the money compounds tax free makes a huge difference.

If you can afford it, match your kid's contributions to his IRA. Let's say that your kid worked as a lifeguard and made $3,000 over the summer, and he decides to put $500 of that in a Roth IRA. You can offer a $500 match, allowing him to deposit a total of $1,000 in his IRA. This will not only double the amount that will compound over many years but prime your kid for the day he can take advantage of the 401(k) match that many companies offer, once he gets a full-time job. Remember, though, the most your kid can sock away is the amount he earned during the year.

- **Invest your Roth IRA in index funds or index exchange-traded funds (ETFs). Forget everything else.** Okay, so now you know that your kid should put part of his paycheck into a Roth IRA. Then what? Once your kid puts money into a Roth IRA, he'll need to pick investments that will allow it to grow. The good news: My advice can be boiled down to two choices.

  Option A is an index fund. (For a review of what these are, see p. 146.) It's important to explain that when you invest your money pretty much anywhere, a portion of it gets siphoned off by the investment company in the form of expenses and fees. This is known as the investment's expense ratio. The good thing about index funds is that they tend to have low expense ratios. That's because with an index fund, you're not paying for a manager to pick and choose stocks; your money is used to buy stocks in a preset index such as the S&P 500 or the CRSP U.S. Total Stock Market Index. So now here's an amazing truth: Research shows that, on average, those funds in which an expert picks the stocks don't do better than index funds. That's why index funds are a great choice.

  I like the Schwab Total Stock Market Index Fund from the Charles Schwab brokerage firm (0.09% expense ratio), which requires a $1,000 initial investment. Second place goes to the Vanguard Total Stock Market Index Fund (0.16% expense ratio), which requires $3,000 to get started. For more information, visit them at Schwab.com and Vanguard.com.

Your kid doesn't have $1,000 to invest? No worries.

Option B is similar in many ways to an index fund: It's an investment called an exchange-traded fund. An ETF can also be invested in a preset index such as the S&P 500 or the CRSP U.S. Total Market Index. And, like stock index funds, index ETFs also have low expense ratios. One big difference is that the price you pay for an ETF goes up and down throughout the day, whereas an index fund's price changes just once a day. Though some companies charge a commission to buy and sell ETFs, you can find ones that don't.

For about $100, you can invest in an ETF like the Vanguard Total Stock Market ETF, which tracks the CRSP U.S. Total Market Index. As of this writing, you can purchase as little as one share, commission free, from Vanguard and not worry about the $3,000 Vanguard minimum. You can also purchase the Schwab U.S. Broad Market ETF, which has a slightly lower expense ratio.

One warning: Although you can buy and sell index ETFs daily like an individual stock, you shouldn't. ETFs should be treated like stock index funds—you're not playing the losing game of trying to outguess the stock market. You just want to participate in the performance of the market as a whole over a long period of time.

Don't Get Snookered

Who can forget Bernie Madoff, the notorious scam artist who swindled his clients out of nearly $20 billion?

Well, apparently, lots of young people have: A 2014 survey found that nearly half of 18- to 29-year-old investors didn't know who he was.

That worries me, since his story is important for everyone to remember.

For decades, Madoff, a guy who everyone assumed was an investing genius, was actually running a classic Ponzi scheme—named after the notorious Charles Ponzi, a huckster who in the 1920s "guaranteed" 100% returns in 90 days. Like Ponzi, Madoff promised investors a guaranteed return, but he was clever: He promised returns of 10% to 12% every year, which, as Princeton University professor

Burton Malkiel points out shrewdly, doesn't *sound* all that crazy. But over the long haul, stocks have returned an average of just 7% a year after inflation—and that average includes some years with extremely high returns and others with *losses* of 40%. It's impossible to guarantee that an investment will earn double-digit returns every single year, as Madoff was claiming. He was able to keep up the charade by employing Ponzi's method of using money from new investors to pay off old ones, who believed that the money flowing into their accounts was coming from stock-market profits. As long as he had lots of investors willing to give him money, Madoff could keep this financial house of cards standing.

What made Madoff's scheme particularly crafty was that he fostered a vibe of exclusivity: Basically, you had to know someone to get in, and many people were turned down. Of course, when his fraud came to light in 2008, all the dejected souls whom he'd rejected were very happy not to have become members of that ultraselect club.

The obvious but often overlooked moral of this story: If it sounds too good to be true, chances are it is. That doesn't mean you should avoid investing—that's a mistake, too. You just need to educate yourself.

- **You can invest for good (and not evil) if you want.** Recent studies have found that young people are superfocused on buying from companies that support social causes they think are worthy. So it makes sense that when it comes to investing, your kid also might want to sink her money into what are called socially responsible funds. If, say, she gets fired up about the environment or hates smoking, you have a natural hook to discuss how socially responsible funds work. Some don't invest in certain industries, such as tobacco or firearms, while others seek out corporations that treat their employees well or, if they're international, have good human rights records. Still others home in on companies that deal with energy conservation or environmentalism. You get the picture. These funds will let your kid invest in a way that allows her to stick to her principles, but you need to help her make sure she doesn't get suckered by slick PR. As always, steer clear of any fund that charges a commission or has a high expense ratio. To help her find lower-cost options, go to SocialFunds.com. I recommend the Vanguard FTSE Social Index Fund (0.25% expense ratio), or, if your kid is looking for an ETF, check out iShares MSCI KLD 400 Social ETF (0.50% expense ratio).

COLLEGE

College is usually the biggest onetime expense you'll incur when it comes to your children. It also can be a great investment. On average, kids who finish college make a lot more money over their lifetimes. But college students have little money to put away in investment accounts. That said, you should still make your kid aware of the following investment-related concepts.

- **You can have a say in how your school invests its endowment.** Back in the 1980s, divesting from South Africa was the big issue, in protest of that country's apartheid policies. Today college students are demanding that their schools' endowments rid themselves of investments in fossil fuels, and some prominent universities have responded. If your kid expresses interest, show him that his beliefs in environmentally friendly business practices and companies with good human rights records can have a meaningful impact. Suggest that he check out the Responsible Endowments Coalition (Endowmentethics .org), a student-founded organization that helps other students figure out how to launch their own divestment campaigns.

- **Put your savings into money funds.** Not only do most college kids not have spare money but they also don't want to lose any money. And while over the long haul, stock investments have on average outperformed bank accounts (see the box on p. 139), they also have ups and downs from year to year. A college kid probably can't afford that level of risk for her savings. A money market fund, also known as a money fund, is a specific type of mutual fund that offers an alternative to bank savings accounts. Money funds are safe, stable, and liquid, meaning that you can withdraw your money whenever you need it without a penalty. Also, in the past, money funds paid higher returns than the interest rates you would get on bank savings accounts. (Though they are not FDIC-insured like bank accounts, only two have ever lost money, and even then it was just a few cents on the dollar.) In recent years, money funds have paid rates just as low as bank savings accounts, in some cases even lower. But as anyone who has ever ridden a roller coaster (or invested) knows, what goes down often comes back up. And though there are no guarantees, stay aware of money funds, since by the time your little one is in college, they might have made a comeback. Your kid can compare money funds at iMoneyNet .com and CraneData.com.

Picturing Yourself with Wrinkles Can Make You Richer

Not long ago, researchers conducted a study at Stanford demonstrating that young people are lousy savers, in part because they can't imagine themselves old. In a virtual technology lab, one group of college students was shown avatars of themselves at their current age. The other group was shown avatars of themselves aged to look 70 years old. Students in each group were encouraged to identify with their avatar by controlling its movements and interacting with another avatar in the same room. Members of both groups were then asked several questions, including how they would divvy up a windfall of $1,000: buy a gift for a loved one, invest in a retirement account, splurge on a fun event, or put it into a checking account. Amazingly, those who had seen themselves as septuagenarian avatars said they'd save more than twice the amount in their retirement accounts than the subjects who'd seen themselves at their current age. Score one for the prematurely gray.

YOUNG ADULTHOOD

Investing might seem like a far-off dream for many recent college graduates with their entry-level salaries, student loans, and other big new bills. Here's what to say to encourage your kid to invest, even if that means starting with a very small amount.

- **Know where you stand on the risk scale.** It's not surprising that polls show that young people in their twenties are more than a little gun-shy when it comes to investing in stocks. The economy has been shaky, Wall Street has been vilified (often justifiably), and many in this group came of age hearing their elders lament bitterly that the market is rigged against the small investor. My favorite summary of this generation's fear and loathing of investing actually came from Ryan Cooper, a young business reporter at *The Week*: "Just looking at a 401(k) booklet feels like the hotly acidic fingers of Satan are clutching at my trachea. It's almost as if I'd rather die in poverty than figure out which investment option would shaft me the least."

  By now, I hope I've made it clear how important it is for your kid to have some money in the stock market. How much depends on her age, her goals, and her overall feelings about taking risks. There's that old rule of thumb that you subtract your age from 100, and that's how much of your investment money should be in stocks; the rest should be in bonds and money funds. (See p. 157 for more on bonds.) Like any general rule, this one has to be tailored to your specific situation, but it can be a useful guide for new investors. The idea is that you gradually reduce your risk over time as you get closer to retirement. That's also why you don't want to invest in stocks for short-term goals, meaning less than five years away—like a down payment for a house. Investing is for those who are in it for the long haul.

- **If your company has a 401(k) plan with matching, sign up ASAP and max it out.** Two words: free money. No matter how little your kid is earning, if his company has a 401(k) plan that matches at least part of what he puts in, and he doesn't contribute, he's leaving money on the table. There are two types to choose from at many companies: traditional 401(k)s and Roth 401(k)s. Roth 401(k)s are generally the better choice. Although they require you to pay taxes on your contributions now, you don't have to pay taxes on the earnings when you retire. With the traditional 401(k), you get to avoid paying taxes on the amounts you put in today, but you have to pay up when you make withdrawals. Generally speaking, you can assume that, in an entry-level job, your child's income and tax bracket today are likely lower than they will be when he reaches retirement age—hence my preference for going Roth.

Of course, your kid needs to be smart about how he invests that money. The expectation is that it will stay untouched for many decades. (Official retirement age, when it comes to 401(k)s and IRAs, is 59½, oddly.) Since your kid is in his twenties, it will be a long time before he retires, so it makes sense for him to put the bulk of his 401(k) into stock investments such as low-cost index funds and ETFs. (For a general explanation of what these are, and my recommendations, see p. 148.) Some employers offer free investing advice through companies like FinancialEngines .com, which can help you pick and choose among your 401(k)'s options. This can be really helpful to get started. No matter what, though, recommend that your kid skip his own company's stock if it's offered. Putting money into one stock, especially if it's your own company's, is just too risky. If the company does poorly, not only will his retirement savings be in jeopardy but his job will be too.

Your kid might also want to consider a target-date fund (TDF), which is likely to be among his 401(k) investment options. TDFs automatically and gradually shift their composition from mostly stock investments to safer bonds and even to money market funds as the investor nears retirement. One warning: The expense ratios for TDFs are sometimes higher than for index funds, with a recent average of 0.55%.

10 Investment Rules for Your Kid to Live By (or at Least Know)

1 **You don't need to be a perfect investor to be a good investor.** When you're a beginner, it's common to agonize over every investment choice and then stress out that you're not making the optimal decision. But you can stop worrying. According to a recent National Bureau of Economic Research study of people with retirement accounts, those with basic knowledge about investing were on track to have 25% more in their accounts than those who knew squat. These people weren't necessarily investing whizzes. They just understood the simple fact that stocks outperform bonds and cash, and they invested accordingly.

2 **Be lazy.** Put your money in a stock index fund (Warren Buffett's a big fan of these) or stock index ETF, and leave it there. If you follow this strategy, you'll beat the returns, on average, of professional money managers who spend their lives tracking stocks. In fact, one study found that in a large group of investors, the 20% who traded the most earned 38% less than the 20% who traded the least.

3 **Don't pay high fees.** You're probably sick of hearing me make this point, but here's the math: Say that you put $1,000 into a fund with an expense ratio of 1.5%, and at the same time you put another $1,000 into a fund charging just 0.2%. If they both earn 7%, after 30 years, the first fund would have accumulated $4,984, and the second would have $7,197. That's why expenses really matter.

4 **Reduce your taxes.** Put money into 401(k)s and IRAs, and watch it grow fast, since these are tax-favored accounts. Period.

5 **Hot tips will burn you.** When your uncle Melvin mentions at the next family reunion that he has the inside scoop on a new biomedical youthful regeneration company whose stock is guaranteed to zoom through the roof, you can smile sweetly, thank him kindly, then go home and do absolutely nothing. Because there's no such thing as a hot tip for the average investor. They always go to the Wall Street hotshots first. If it's truly an insider's tip that no one but uncle Melvin knows, he may be behind bars instead of at the next family get-together. He could be passing inside information, which is illegal.

6 **To save enough, automate.** Often people assume that the best way to accumulate a significant nest egg is to be a great investor. Of course, that would be nice. But even the most amazing luck won't make up for not saving enough. With your 401(k), once you sign up, the money will be deducted from your paycheck automatically. (Which is what you want: little pinch now, big payoff later!) With an IRA, make sure to have a set amount funneled from your checking account every payday.

7 **Diversity is important.** As I've said repeatedly, it's key to invest in a stock index fund or stock index ETF, for example, rather than bet the farm on one stock only. Diversification helps reduce your risk.

8 **When you need that money soon, skip stocks.** If you have cash set aside for a home down payment in three years or a wedding in several months, keep that money in supersafe places such as savings accounts, certificates of deposit, and money market funds. Don't jeopardize it by putting it into stocks. Although over the long term stocks have offered higher returns than other types of investments, they're also more volatile. If the market dips at the wrong moment, your money might not be there when you absolutely need it.

9 **Think globally.** International stocks used to be viewed as risky investments suitable only for the truly daring. No longer. Today, investing a bit in international stock index funds—say, 20% of your total investments— can add diversity. If the U.S. stock market goes down the tubes, the markets in other countries might not.

10 **Your vintage toys, antiques, and figurines are not investments.** Remember Cabbage Patch Kids, Beanie Babies, Precious Moments figurines, and *Laverne & Shirley* lunch boxes? All once hot collectors' items with prices through the roof. But now many of these clutter eBay and fetch a fraction of what people paid for them back in the day—if they sell at all. Buy these things, if you're lucky enough to be able to afford them, for nostalgia or for love. Because that could well be all they are worth in the future.

- **Open an IRA (if you haven't already).** Your kid's first priority should be trying to contribute as much to his company's 401(k) as the company matches, but after that, he should contribute to an IRA. I've already sung the praises of Roth IRAs in the high school section. But now I want to talk a bit about traditional IRAs. The way they work: You get a tax break on your contributions now, but you pay tax many years from now when you withdraw the money at retirement.

Here's why I prefer the Roth for young adults. First, as I mentioned earlier, odds are good that your kid's salary and tax bracket are lower now than they will be in the future when he makes the withdrawals, so he's better off paying the taxes at his current lower tax bracket. Second, Roths allow you to withdraw your contributions free from taxes and penalties, unlike traditional IRAs. And third, it's more difficult to qualify for a traditional IRA and get the full tax break; if you have access to a 401(k) at work, your income must be $62,000 or less. To open a Roth and make a full contribution, you need to earn less than $118,000. Both kinds of IRAs have a $5,500 annual contribution limit as of 2017. To help with this analysis, use the Roth versus traditional IRA calculator on Bankrate.com.

No matter which IRA you choose, you'll need to decide where to open it and how to invest it. My first choice, once again, is a mix of low-cost stock index funds (or stock index ETFs) and, eventually, some low-cost bond index funds from a company like Vanguard, where you can open an IRA for the price of one share of one of its stock index ETFs—about $100. You can also consult a robo-advisor such as Wealthfront.com, Betterment.com, or SigFig.com for free guidance. You don't need to sign up or pay to see the recommendations of these robo-advisors. Instead, your kid simply fills out a short questionnaire about her income, age, and tolerance for risk. These companies then recommend various low-fee investments that meet his profile.

- **Invest a little—but not too much—in bonds.** When you buy a bond, you're basically lending a sum of money to the company, government, or other institution that issued it for a fixed period of time. In return, the issuer pays you interest. Generally, as we've discussed, bonds offer lower returns but less risk than stocks do. Bonds come in funds just like stocks, and the way to choose a bond fund is to look at expenses and choose the fund with the lowest one. There are long-, medium-, and short-term bond funds. No matter which type you choose, make sure its fees don't exceed the average, around 0.5% at the time of this writing.

Another, different type of supersafe bond is called an I Bond. It's designed to help your money keep up with inflation and can be purchased with as little as $25 directly from the U.S. Treasury. Your kid will have to keep the money in the I Bond for at least a year, and there are tiny penalties for redeeming the bond before five years—but that's why I Bonds are a great way for your kid to save for a long-term goal such as a house down payment. Although the interest rates haven't been much higher than those of savings accounts in recent years, not long ago, they offered relatively attractive rates. So if your young adult has a chunk of money he wants to keep safe, I Bonds are worth considering. Check out TreasuryDirect.gov for details and instructions for opening an account.

- **Invest your raise and/or bonus.** The more money we have, the more we tend to spend. But when you think about it, there's no reason you need to spend more just because your paycheck goes up. In fact, two behavioral economists, Richard Thaler and Shlomo Benartzi, figured out that employees could dramatically increase the amount they funnel into savings if they adopted a plan that the economists dubbed SMarT (Save More Tomorrow). Employees commit to automatically putting a certain percentage of future raises into retirement, so that when the raises come, they never have to take the deliberate action of increasing the amount they contribute to their 401(k), or have a chance to "miss" that money before it's set aside for investing. You can encourage your kid to start his own SMarT program, even if he's the only member, by committing to invest his raise, or even a portion of it, in his 401(k) or an IRA.

8

Give Back

Right after Hurricane Sandy hit the East Coast in 2012, just about everyone I knew rallied to help the families affected by the storm. Many people suffered huge losses, and the devastation was beyond anything that most of us, especially our children, had seen.

Deirdre, the mom of a girl in my then eight-year-old son's tae kwon do class, told me that when she informed her daughter that their family was donating food to a shelter for people whose homes were destroyed by flooding, her daughter said she had something important she wanted to say. Deirdre readied herself to hear some profound concern about the tragedy. Then her daughter said, "Please don't give away my peanut butter!" Deirdre was speechless. So many of her friends' kids, who were not much older than her daughter, were spending weekends on cleanup duty at sites all over New York, and here her usually sweet girl was hoarding her favorite snack. Disgusted and confused, she asked me, "How could she be so selfish?"

We've all been there as parents. We are sometimes shocked—even mortified—by our kids' lack of empathy. Sure, there are the mini Mother Teresas who hand over their shovels and pails in the sandbox to any kid who wants them. But children are naturally acquisitive. Asking them to give away material goods, even something as minor as an old T-shirt or, yes, peanut butter, can trigger the survival instinct.

You might want to shout, "Are you really telling me that you won't give a Jenga set that you *never even opened* to a homeless child?" Don't. It'll only alienate your kid. Instead, make it clear that giving to others in need is an important part of your family's values. You do it, and he has to do it, too. Plain and simple.

And don't worry if your child just isn't "feeling it." An ancient Talmudic tenet holds that going through the motions is just fine—the old "fake it till you make it" idea. The deed itself is what's important, no matter if you're doing it out of sheer obligation, to get school credit, or out of the goodness of your heart. And cheer up. Economists have found that kids become more altruistic as they get older.

Take the case of the Peace Corps. Just a few years ago, at the peak of the recession, applications to the organization soared. While some viewed this increase as a testament to the younger generation's sense of what was truly important in life, others suggested that the real motivation was just that the job market was so bad for new college grads. (When the economy picked up, Peace Corps applications dropped dramatically.) No matter the motivation, it doesn't take away from the good work that those volunteers did.

Still, finding a charitable activity or project that your child does take a shine to is great for her in all kinds of ways. Research shows that charitable giving—particularly when it's voluntary rather than mandatory—actually makes people happier.

Raising a generous child requires some real soul searching on the part of parents. A Harvard Graduate School of Education survey of 10,000 middle and high schoolers points to a "rhetoric/reality gap" that seems to get in the way. The study found that although most parents *say* they want to raise caring kids, in reality they focus on personal success and achievement above all else. It's no wonder that in the survey children were three times more likely to agree than disagree with the statement "My parents are prouder if I get good grades in my classes than if I'm a caring community member in class and school."

This chapter will show you how to raise a kid who pays it forward and eventually experiences the joy—and I do mean joy—of giving.

PRESCHOOL

Most young children are capable of showing kindness to friends and family. And by age four, they are developmentally ready to show kindness even toward people they don't know. So send the following messages early to nudge your kid toward generosity.

- **The sharing jar matters.** Many families like the three-jars approach to managing money that I discussed in Chapter 2, in which money is divided among jars for saving, spending, and sharing. But some parents feel that having their kid put one out of every three dollars into a giving jar is unrealistic, since, after all, most adults don't dedicate nearly that much to charity. It's important not to get too hung up on the details. Decide on *some* portion of your child's money to have her set aside for charity—it could be 30%, 20%, or 10%. And then make sure your kid consistently puts away that set amount each time she gets cash—whether it's dollars from Grandpa, coins she finds on the floor, or birthday money from you.

  Then comes the fun part: giving that money away. Kids this age often won't have clear ideas about the causes they want to donate to, so you'll need to guide them. Carol Weisman, the author of *Raising Charitable Children*, recommends that parents ask, "If you could change one thing in the world, what would that be?" and then follow up the answer by drilling down to what's bothering your kid. Is it a disaster reported in a distant country or an issue closer to home, like a person she saw living on the street or a cousin's genetic disease? A young kid might not be able to connect the dots between the earthquake reported on television and a donation to a disaster relief organization, so it's up to you to help with that. But even at this age, kids will latch on to causes that feel concrete and relevant. For organizations that are good at showing kids where their money goes, see the box on p. 163.

- **Some people have "plenty" and others "not enough."** As a little girl, my friend Denise asked her father for a new bike, and he said, "I'm sorry, but we can't afford that."

  "Why are we so poor?" Denise whined.

  "Poor?" he replied. "I'll show you poor!"

  It was dinnertime, but her father was so steamed that he made the entire family get in the car, and he drove to an unfamiliar area of town that she could see right away was much different from her own middle-class neighborhood. Her father finally stopped in front of a house with peeling paint and an old washing machine on the porch. Two small girls squatted in the yard behind a chain-link fence playing in the dirt. "That's poor," her dad whispered. They drove home, and as they pulled into their driveway, their modest house suddenly looked like a palace. There were times after that when Denise wished her family could buy certain things they couldn't afford, but she never complained about being "poor" again.

  While this type of in-your-face tactic might not be your style, this dad was smart to teach his kids that everything is relative—as well as to hammer home some humility in a very memorable fashion. One way to do that, actually, is to avoid using the word *poor* altogether, since such words can put distance between the child and the person who needs help. That's why Connie Burton, cofounder of the Speyer Legacy School in New York, talks to small children using terms like *plenty* and *not enough* to describe what people do or don't have. This notion of a spectrum—and that there are kids out there who have less—is key.

- **Giving is rewarding.** This isn't just some feel-good parenting spin. Psychologists at the University of British Columbia found that young kids can experience the joy of giving. The researchers introduced toddlers to a monkey puppet, then gave both the kids and the puppet empty bowls. The researchers poured goldfish crackers in the kids' bowls, which made them happy, as measured by a group of "emotion coders" who analyzed their facial expressions. But when it was pointed out to the children that the puppet didn't have any crackers, they gave some of their crackers to him and became even happier than they already were. Don't underestimate your kid's capacity to give, even at some cost to himself.

- **Parents: Start a charitable matching plan.** Studies confirm what fund-raisers have long known: People give more to charity when their money is matched—say, when a donor announces that she'll chip in another $10,000 if that amount is raised within a certain period. You can do a variation of this with your child. For example, you might offer to contribute a dollar to a charity she cares about for every dollar she contributes. But don't feel like you have to offer wild incentives to get your kid to be a giver, since research also shows that matching, say, two dollars for every dollar saved rather than a one-for-one arrangement doesn't seem to boost giving. It's the idea of leveraging a donation, rather than the actual *amount* of the match, that can motivate givers. Starting this practice when your kid is young and perhaps able to afford donations of only a quarter or 50 cents will help her see the power of her charitable dollars (and pennies).

6 Great Places for Kids to Give

When encouraging kids to give, it's important to help them find causes in which their smaller contributions can make larger, concrete impacts. If your kid needs ideas, here are some amazing charities that make the results more tangible.

1 **Heifer International** (Heifer.org). This nonprofit donates animals (goats, pigs, ducks, llamas, honeybees, and, of course, heifers) and farm supplies to families around the world to address hunger and poverty. Donation amounts are correlated with what they can purchase, so your kid gains a sense of what his dollars are helping to buy. What kid wouldn't get excited about giving $10 to help buy a goat in Zanzibar, $25 for a water buffalo, or $50 for a cow?

2 **No Kid Hungry** (Nokidhungry.org). This campaign by the nonprofit Share Our Strength addresses the huge problem of hunger in our schools. No Kid Hungry provides nutritious food to students who need it and teaches their families how to prepare healthy, affordable meals.

If your kid can't imagine going through the school day hungry, this is a great place for him to donate his giving dollars. For $10, your kid can provide up to 100 meals for another child who doesn't have enough food.

3 **KaBOOM!** (KaBOOM.org). Kids who play are healthier and more creative and have better social skills than kids who don't have playtime. KaBOOM! collaborates with local and national partners to create play spaces and playgrounds for communities that need them most, often in lower-income areas. When it's time for your kid's birthday party, you can set up a page for donations in lieu of gifts.

4 **The Nature Conservancy** (Nature.org). This environmental organization allows your kid to "Adopt an Acre" in an endangered area for a donation of $25; your kid can "pick" an acre in one of five regions, and he will receive an adoption kit with certificates, photos, and more.

5 **Pencils of Promise** (Pencilsofpromise.org). This nonprofit works in developing countries such as Guatemala and Laos to build schools, train teachers, and provide scholarships to students in need, with 100% of all online donations going straight to projects—rare for a charity. If your kid sets up a monthly donation of as little as $10 through PoP's "Passport" program, he'll receive photos and videos of the children he helps and communities where his money is being used.

6 **DonorsChoose** (DonorsChoose.org). This organization connects donors with public school teachers who post requests for necessary supplies to complete classroom projects. Kids can pick projects and donate as little as $1 to help purchase crayons or transportation for a class field trip, or even fund a project such as building a butterfly nursery for an elementary science class in Arizona.

ELEMENTARY SCHOOL

At this age, kids begin to better understand the needs of others. Here's what to say to help them see how they can use their time and money (even if it's not very much) to help.

- **Donating time is valuable too.** When my friend Phil's kids were 13, 11, and 6, his family visited a soup kitchen in their church to serve Thanksgiving dinner to the guests. The staff was glad to have more hands in the kitchen, but Phil realized that while there seemed to be lots of help around the holidays, the staffing was quite a bit thinner the rest of the year. So he and his family started going in to help one Saturday every month. The soup kitchen was able to feed more people on a regular basis and truly appreciated the help during the not-so-popular times. If you can, find a project that your whole family can participate in that will make a meaningful impact. Volunteering is a great way to show that money isn't everything.

- **Give a gift to someone else on your birthday.** What kid doesn't love to get gifts on his birthday? What's more, for some kids, a trip to the store to purchase a gift for a child whose family can't afford presents can be just as satisfying. Melissa, a mother I know, matched her five-year-old son, Jude, with a kid from a lower-income family living in New York City through an organization called Birthday Buds (Birthdaybud.org). One child supplies the other with birthday presents—fun toys as well as some essentials—that he otherwise wouldn't receive because of his family's financial situation.

  On a recent birthday, Melissa and Jude learned not only that his birthday bud loved Thomas the Tank Engine but also that he needed rain boots and a toothbrush. The list was eye-opening for Jude but also for Melissa. "The next time I complain about something, please remind me how fortunate I am that I have no trouble finding money to buy my son a toothbrush," she said. Mother and son went to the bank and withdrew $40 from Jude's savings account so he could buy the gifts on the list. Making a habit of giving on birthdays and other occasions is a great way to cultivate generosity in your kid, as well as gratitude for all he has.

- **For every new thing you get, give away an old one.** This was the rule in my friend Sadie's house growing up, and now that she's a mother, she's asked her kids to follow it too. "If we got a new pair of shoes, we'd have to donate a pair we no longer wore very much," she recalls. "It was a great way to think about what we really needed—and how others needed it more. It also helps me reduce clutter!" The nice thing about this rule is that it gives your kid some discretion—you aren't telling her *which* thing to give away. She just has to give away something. Keep a bag in a closet or another designated place that everyone in the family contributes to regularly. If it doesn't fit or you won't wear it, it goes to someone who will get some use out of it. Donate it to the Salvation Army or Goodwill and get your receipt. If your child is resistant, don't force it. Some kids just aren't ready yet. Tell your child that when she is old enough, you're sure that she will get as much out of this as you do.

- **Parents: Don't ignore people who ask for money.** Anyone who lives in a large city has had the experience of being asked for money while walking down the street with his kid. Some people always throw a buck into the hat. Others feel that doling out dollars to people begging or panhandling isn't a good idea. Regardless of your personal policy, you shouldn't pretend that you don't see or hear the person in need. Saying something like "Sorry, not today" is a better response when possible. Sometimes, your kid might ask you about someone she sees sitting on the street with a sign or sleeping on a grate, even if that person isn't asking for money directly. Don't brush off those questions. That isn't to say that you must get into a deep discussion as you rush off to school and work, but take the time later to explain your philosophy. If your policy is not to give, let your kid know how you direct your charitable dollars instead (for instance, to a local organization that helps those who suffer from addiction, or to an entirely different cause that you feel is equally important).

- **Stay local.** With natural and humanitarian disasters around the globe making headlines with alarming frequency, it's understandable that a child will be drawn in and want to help. But for young kids, it can be difficult to connect the dollars raised at bake sales to the needs of tsunami victims in a faraway locale. Choose local activities that children can see through from contribution to payoff. Whether it's handing out fliers for a local community election or collecting signatures to support a neighborhood park, hands-on local activities offer a tangible benefit. Keeping your giving local will also give you and your kid a window on issues affecting your community that you might not otherwise be aware of, such as hunger and homelessness.

Your kiddo into animal rights? If a local animal shelter is in need of food donations, raising the money for kibble and then actually purchasing and bringing it to the shelter can be rewarding and fun. Just be careful you don't walk out with two cats, a mutt, and a guinea pig of your own!

- **Parents: Talk about why you give—and why your kid should too.** Simply modeling giving behavior—by having your kid see that you donate time or money—isn't enough. To turn her into a giver, you also need to talk about what you are doing and why it's important. That's the surprising finding of a recent study by the United Nations Foundation and the Women's Philanthropy Institute at Indiana University. Researchers tracked the charitable behaviors of 900 kids over the course of a year, then checked in with them six years later. Those whose parents talked to them about giving were more likely to contribute to a cause than kids whose parents donated money but didn't discuss why it was important. Don't worry that you'll appear to be bragging about your good deeds. Instead, you can explain what cause you're contributing to, the way that money will help specifically, and how that donation fits into your budget. The holidays can be a good time to tell your child that you set aside a certain amount to give to others every year, just as you set aside certain amounts for gifts to family and friends.

Practice What You Preach

When each of our three children was born, my parents donated an antique *tzedakah*, or charity, box from the 1800s to a local Jewish museum in his or her honor. The idea wasn't just to commemorate our kids' births but also to hammer home the point that *tzedakah*, which literally translates as "righteousness," is a moral obligation in Judaism (as opposed to a kind act one chooses to do from time to time). The same is true for *dana*, the charitable giving tradition in Hinduism and Buddhism, and for almsgiving in Christianity. Some religions get very specific about what you're expected to give: Mormons, for example, are required to tithe, or donate, a full 10% of their annual income to the church, and the Koran calls on Muslims to give away 2.5% of their accumulated wealth in excess of their basic needs, a practice known as *zakat*.

Whether you give because it's a religious obligation or you're simply an altruistic agnostic or atheist, make sure you pass along your charitable inclinations to your kids. One international study led by University of Chicago professor Jean Decety found that children between ages five and twelve from families who self-identify as religious were actually *less* generous. (The researchers measured altruism using a test called, ominously, the Dictator Game. Each child was given an opportunity to share a gift of stickers with peers. Some gave more generously than others.)

How could this be? Professor Decety and his colleagues theorize that it may be a product of an unconscious phenomenon called "moral licensing"—living an upstanding life in the past gives us permission to make less than virtuous choices in the future. In religious terms, someone who regularly performs the rituals of her faith might feel the moral authority to skimp on the good works. So make sure, no matter your religion or lack thereof, to teach your kids to value giving.

MIDDLE SCHOOL

Kids this age might feel that they don't have money or time to give. But truly being charitable means giving from what you have, even if it isn't much. Donating a small amount of allowance or birthday money, or volunteering between extracurricular activities, not only is possible but also will make your kid grateful for all she has. Here's how to convey those expectations.

- **Treat charitable work and violin lessons with the same respect.** When your kid wants to skip tennis practice or religious school, you probably say no because it's important for him to honor those commitments. A habit of following through is a trait that will stand him in good stead with teachers, not to mention future employers. The same goes for projects that help other people. That said, be realistic about your kid's schedule—and yours. Don't let the desire to be noble and heroic lead him to make promises he can't keep. Instead, discuss the options and decide what's doable. If your kid can't swing volunteering every week, how about every other week? If he can't fit in the standard three-hour shift in the community garden, how about shelving books from the returns cart in the school library for an hour instead? If you urge your kid to commit to more than he can actually deliver, not only do you teach him a lousy lesson about follow-through, but you've left a charitable organization in the lurch.

- **Think about what other people really need.** This may sound obvious, but it's important to find out what an organization needs before you and your kid go to the effort and expense of donating. Take food drives, a kid-friendly and very common form of charity. There's something fun about going to the store, having your child pick out his favorite soup, and bringing over a few cans of it to a food drive. But here's the thing: Most food banks in the United States have access to a vast network of food donated by the food industry, which includes perfectly good items that for some reason can't be sold—for example, mislabeled cans. Giving cash allows food banks to purchase exactly what they need from this network for a handling fee of a few cents per pound.

  Looking to do their part, a friend of mine and her son donated laptops to a local homeless shelter and offered to give computer lessons. Months later, the laptops sat unused and few people had signed up for classes. When they asked what the shelter actually needed, the answer was something much more basic: blankets. If you really want to do the most good, call or drop by with your child and ask about a given agency's needs. Let your kid listen in on the conversation. He'll get the message that being a good giver means being a smart giver.

- **Parents: Help your kid understand other people's economic realities.** Susan took her twin boys to a homeless shelter, and on the way home, one of them asked, "If they have enough money to go to McDonald's, why don't they just make their own meals, which would be even cheaper?" At first she was annoyed that her kids seemed so flippant—not to mention clueless. Then she considered the fact that her kids didn't understand how little their own experience applied to the lives of the men they were helping. "I explained that cooking fresh food might not always be cheaper than buying fast food, and reminded my boys that these men didn't have stoves or refrigerators or pots and pans," Susan recalled. "Only after a long conversation did they get it."

One important way that kids learn about economic inequality is by discussing current events with their parents. In fact, a study of nearly 600 Midwestern middle and high school kids found that the ones whose parents talked about what was happening in the news had a more nuanced understanding of income disparities. They were less likely to buy into the idea that people are poor because they aren't intelligent or they don't work hard enough, which, research has shown, many Americans do believe. The more your kid understands about the world around him, the more he'll know that other people deal with circumstances far more challenging than his own.

- **Parents: When you give, encourage your kid to give as well.** If you regularly donate to an organization you care about, or you make it a point during the holiday season to give to people in need or to a particular cause, include your kid in those decisions. One woman I know who grew up without much money remembers that every Christmas, no matter how little her family had, her father wrote a check to CARE, an international humanitarian organization that provides food and health care to families in dire need. The messages she took away? Not only that it was important to give but also that lots of people in the world had less than she did, and she should be grateful. Your middle schooler might not have much money, but encourage her to set aside some to give to the causes she thinks are the most important. As I said earlier, there are no magic percentages when it comes to giving, but establishing the rule of thumb that your kid give 10% of any money she gets is not unreasonable. For example, 10% of $10 is just $1, but putting that amount in a jar each time money comes in can add up.

- **Parents: Don't overpraise your kid's charitable efforts.** A 13-year-old named Kim told me about the time she and her friend Ana volunteered at a church to sort donated clothes. After a couple hours, Ana's mom picked up the girls, then went on and on about how important the work they had done was and how extraordinary the girls were to volunteer. "Her mom was so over the top that it essentially killed the whole experience," said Kim. "It isn't about how it makes me feel; it's about doing the work." Smart kid. Your job as a parent is to help your child develop the habit of giving, not to infuse a holier-than-thou "Aren't we generous!" vibe into a small act of philanthropy. Keep your eye on what matters.

HIGH SCHOOL

According to research, teens who volunteer are generally more engaged in their communities and at school. The important thing is to let your high schooler decide where he wants to spend his time and dollars to make an impact.

- **Don't just follow the herd with your donating dollars.** Remember the "Ice Bucket Challenge" craze of a few years ago? The folks at the ALS Association who came up with it were brilliant to use social media the way they did to spread the challenge, especially among young givers. People who accepted the challenge filmed themselves having a bucket of ice water dumped on them. They posted the clip online and tagged friends to do the same. The idea was that participants would also donate dollars to the ALS Association, which uses the money to fund medical research and to raise awareness of the fatal neuromuscular disease also known as Lou Gehrig's. Though some people ended up dousing themselves with water just for fun, many donated generously, and the organization raised more than $220 million after the Ice Bucket Challenge went viral. While participating in these types of highly publicized charitable efforts can be wonderful, and this particular one was a record-setting success that helped fund an eventual breakthrough, there are all kinds of important efforts that never attract attention. It's good to discuss with your teenager the numerous organizations that are worthy of his attention even if they're not featured on BuzzFeed. Tell him to ask the three questions in the box on p. 173 before donating to any organization.

- **Don't pay to volunteer.** There are numerous organizations that package trips for teens to build houses or teach English in distant countries—then charge thousands of dollars so the kids can "give back." These programs no doubt offer children wonderful international experiences and perspectives they might not get elsewhere. But unlike true community service—where the vast majority of the proceeds go to the cause—these are often businesses that make money pitching themselves as basically socially conscious teen tours. And the "work" that the kids do may be manufactured. The comedian Louis C.K. described these boondoggles this way: "Yes, you went on a school trip to Guatemala, and they told you you helped, but you totally did not help. The guy was like, 'I got a mudslide on my house, and now I gotta babysit a *#@! college kid. Why do I have to do this?' Just take her picture with a shovel and send her home so she can put it on Facebook." Couldn't have said it better myself.

- **Giving shouldn't mean taking from others.** It can be easy for a kid to get caught up in his enthusiasm for a cause and assume that everyone has the same ability to give that he does. It's up to you to gently encourage him to consider people's differing circumstances and plan accordingly. For instance, the kids in a dance group at a school in an affluent neighborhood decided to hold a charity event and invited other local school dance groups to participate. At the door, tickets were $15. Although the money was going to a worthy cause (a community center in an underserved part of town), parents of kids from some of the less affluent schools were taken aback by the high fee. While $15 per person wasn't much for the well-off families, it was a budget-buster for others. Instead, a suggested donation—maybe $20—would likely have raised a good amount of money and allowed those who could afford it to give without preventing everyone interested from attending.

- **Get your hours in.** A number of schools and even school districts have started requiring community service hours in order to graduate. Maryland has a state requirement that starting in eighth grade all students must complete 75 hours of community service by the time they get their high school diploma. If your kid's school has a service requirement, make sure she's on track to meet it. But don't assume that it will make your kid a charitable superstar: Research shows that schools with mandatory community service requirements may make older kids *less* likely to volunteer in the long run, perhaps because such requirements sap the kid of a sincere motivation to help others. Make it clear to your child that giving both time and money is part of your belief system—requirement or not—and be sure to encourage her to support causes that are personally important to her.

- **Parents: You can't dictate your child's takeaway.** I've heard from many parents who are amused, puzzled, or outraged that their kids came home from a volunteer experience and started questioning their family's values and habits. One father told me that his daughter, after volunteering at a park clean-up, started a crusade against drinking straws, quoting a statistic she'd heard that Americans use 500 million drinking straws a day. This dad was glad his daughter had become environmentally aware, but he wasn't willing to listen to her yell at her brother that he was evil and didn't care if the entire country ended up choking on plastic when he ordered a Coke.

  When we think our kids have gone overboard, it's important not to feel personally attacked. They're just figuring out how to make sense of the world in their own way. If your kid *is* making personal attacks that seem unwarranted, you can say that you're glad she's developing her own values, but she has to allow other people to have their values too. Once she's on her own, she can weave her own clothes on a loom made of sustainable Guatemalan hardwood and lecture her buddies about their carbon footprint until their eyes cross and she has no more friends. But until then, she will have to reconcile herself to a family that uses a car and buys the occasional plastic straw.

3 Questions to Ask Before Giving

Just as you need to teach your kid to do research before making a major purchase, evaluating a credit card, or choosing an investment, you want to make sure she does the same when it comes to donating money. This process doesn't have to be so onerous that it drains the feelings of goodwill and beneficence that giving bestows. But your kid should learn to give smart.

1 **Is the charity an accredited nonprofit?** If you're considering donating to an organization, check to see that it's a registered 501(c)(3). That means the group is not making a profit off your donation. You can find out if an organization is a 501(c)(3) by using the IRS Exempt Organizations Select Check tool at irs.gov/app/eos. Confirming this status is the first step toward avoiding scam artists. It'll also prevent you from giving on the spot if you and your youngster are solicited, say, in front of the local supermarket. A polite "Thanks so much, but I always do research before I give to any organization" is a great message for your kid to hear.

2 **Is the charity spending the money you donate wisely?** Look at the progress that the charity is actually making as well as the work that it is doing. One helpful group is the Better Business Bureau Wise Giving Alliance (Give.org), which offers free reviews of 1,300 national charities and 10,000 local ones using 20 benchmarks, including effectiveness, board compensation, and fund-raising expenses.

3 **How does the organization measure success?** What info is available in its annual reports and audits, not to mention on its website? If you and your kid are really interested in learning more, two websites that offer free, detailed information on thousands of nonprofits are GuideStar.org and CharityNavigator.org.

COLLEGE

Realistically, most college kids won't have money to donate, what with tuition, housing, books, and other bills to pay. But that doesn't mean they shouldn't be giving their time. The side benefit: Volunteering during college provides a great way for kids to explore a career in the nonprofit world. Make sure you let your kid know how to do it right.

- **Use your college's resources and faculty as a launch pad for volunteering.** Campuses are overflowing with organizations and opportunities to volunteer. Yale University undergrads started the Prison Project to help inmates earn their GEDs. Students at the University of Maryland, College Park, noticed how much food went to waste in campus dining halls and started the Food Recovery Network, now a national organization, to get that food to the needy. Encourage your kid to see what's going on at his school.

- **Be wary of linking giving with spending.** Some companies promise to donate a percentage of profits or give some of their products (shoes, eyeglasses, bottled water) to people in need each time you buy. Some credit cards pledge to donate a percentage of the amount you charge to a cause. And sometimes the cashier at the checkout counter asks if you'd like to kick in a buck or two today to help a worthy organization. There's nothing inherently wrong in any of these scenarios. These efforts raise huge amounts of money—dollars that would have stayed in people's pockets rather than gone to people who are in need.

  But being mindful of your giving dollars can make you a much more effective giver. Would it, say, make more sense to buy cheaper shoes, glasses, or bottled water for yourself and then donate the money that you saved to a group you really want to support? Does that so-called affinity credit card come with a high interest rate and/or an annual fee that costs you money, and if so, could you save by using a different card and then plow that money into good works? Connecting charitable giving with buying can easily start you down the slippery slope of making purchases you might not have otherwise, and even make you feel good about overspending.

- **Parents: It's okay to remind your kid that volunteer work doesn't pay the bills.** Don't get me wrong. The altruism and social awareness on college campuses today is impressive. But here-and-now realism is important too, and parents have the right to speak up about the family's own economic circumstances. It sounds harsh, but you shouldn't feel guilty for putting the kibosh on your kid's desire to save endangered sea turtles in Costa Rica if your family budget requires her to get a paid summer job to help defray college costs.

If, during the school year, your kid starts expressing passion for a particular organization or cause, encourage him. But if he's hinting about forgoing his part-time job during the school year or ditching his plans for a paid summer internship, he might need a gentle reminder that he still needs to help pay for college. You don't want to squelch his enthusiasm for giving, but you also need to set realistic ground rules. A possible compromise is that your kid can volunteer after work hours in the summer.

YOUNG ADULTHOOD

When kids are in their early twenties, it's a great time to volunteer—and even donate a small amount regularly—because they likely don't have kids of their own or other responsibilities and expenses. Plus, they'll gain a whole lot of perspective.

- **Volunteer while you're looking for a job.** If your kid is like most grads, she wants a job right out of college. If she's lucky, she'll find one, but if she doesn't, she can use her downtime to help others and maybe even herself. People who volunteer have a 27% greater chance of getting a job than those who don't volunteer. Probably not all that surprising, because the kind of people who volunteer tend to be those who have the focus and determination to find jobs. Volunteering expands the network of people your kid knows, and sometimes those contacts end up being people who can offer her paid work. It'll also sound a whole lot better at an interview than saying, "Since graduation, I've watched 150 *Law & Order* episodes."

- **Give some of your salary to charity.** Starting out after college, a new grad has so many expenses that charitable giving may seem like an impossible goal. So suggest that he start with just 1%. The average college grad makes around $50,000 right out of school—and 1% of that is $500, or about $40 a month. For many young adults, that's doable. As your kid gets a handle on his expenses (and maybe, in a little while, a raise), he can bump up the percentage he contributes. And while he's at it, your kid should see if his company offers matching donations for charitable giving. Many do. (Another way your grown kid can use his money for good is to consider socially conscious investments. For details, see p. 150.)

- **Don't make snap decisions about giving.** Many of us tend to give on the spot: Someone stops you on the street, calls you on the phone, or posts a plea on Facebook, and you decide then and there whether to give. (Often you feel bad whatever you end up doing. Either you give too much and feel like a sucker, or you give little or nothing and feel guilty.) Although it may seem awkward, it's smart to do your homework before you say yea or nay. (See the box on p. 173.) Many times, that means delaying your decision to give, which isn't a bad thing. For instance, when you're solicited over the phone, it might be by a telemarketer, hired by the organization, who will keep a large chunk of your donation. It might also be a scam. Take the time to find out. And tell your kid that the next time someone with a clipboard hits her up for a buck on the street, or she gets a phone call asking for money, she can request a brochure or a web address instead and say that she's going to read up on the organization before donating. Few if any credible groups would argue with that.

- **Save those donation receipts.** Whether your kid is giving money, used clothing, or an old laptop, donations to organizations with 501(c)(3) status are tax deductible if he itemizes his taxes (meaning he fills out the 1040 form, not the 1040A or 1040EZ). Many young people don't itemize, but if your kid donates a lot to charity, he probably should. If he donates items, he's allowed to deduct their value, which is generally less than what he paid for them. Check out the valuation guides on the Salvation Army and Goodwill websites. How big a tax break your kid gets depends on his tax bracket. Donating an old couch valued at $100 will mean $25 in your kid's pocket come tax time (assuming he's in the 25% tax bracket). Warn him to follow the rules and always get a receipt from the organization to which he gives that shows the date of the donation, the name of the organization, and the amount donated. For donations of $250 and above, the IRS requires a receipt for a tax deduction to be valid. It must include a statement to the effect that no goods or services were given to the donor in exchange for the contribution.

9

Your Kid's Most Important Financial Decision: College

Alex was a dashingly handsome high school senior with a devastating grin, a rich social life, and a solid B average. When he was admitted to a pricey private university, he made a proposal to his parents: Allow him to skip college and take the $200,000-plus they would have spent on his education to create an app called Quick-E-kilt, a service that would deliver a rental kilt in one of 237 clan patterns and the renter's choice of wool, silk, or cotton fabric, within an hour, anywhere nationwide. (For an extra fee, an attractive Scottish woman would video chat with customers to explain proper wrapping technique and sporran placement.)

Alex's wealthy, supportive, extremely good-looking, and well-dressed parents agreed, and within 18 months, his start-up was funded by a top venture capital firm, was valued at $15 million, and had inspired a syndicated TV show hosted by Ryan Seacrest.

Okay. So I totally made that story up. But chances are you've come across similar suburban legends involving a quirky kid who skips college, then creates some improbable-sounding tech company and makes a bundle. The subtext is that college costs are out of control, and attending college is a big ol' waste of money.

So let's start with some truth.com: Never before has a college degree been more valuable. No matter what you hear, read, or feel deep in your soul, the fact is that the single most important thing you can do to make your kid a money genius is to help him go to college. On average, college graduates earn around *$1 million* more over their lifetimes than those who attain only a high school diploma. After you factor in college costs, lost earnings while in school, and inflation, a degree is *still* worth, on average, about $300,000. This isn't to say that every single kid has to get a four-year college degree to fulfill his potential. There are some well-paying careers—from licensed practical nurse to industrial machinery mechanic—for people who learn a skilled trade on the job, through a formal training program, or while earning an associate's degree. If your kid wants to pursue one, I say go for it. But for many young people, a college degree is the best path to a solid future, and that's what I'll be focusing on in this chapter.

While college is still necessary, the rules of the game have changed, and the process requires you to become a savvy education consumer—long before you write that first tuition check. The first step is reexamining some of the myths about paying for college. Perhaps you think your family makes too much to qualify for financial aid, but in fact 70% of students at private nonprofit colleges whose families earn between $150,000 and $250,000 receive grant aid. Or maybe you think a public school will definitely be the least expensive option, but after you factor in a private school's financial aid package, that might not be the case. Or maybe you're adamant that you don't want your kid to graduate with any student debt, or, on the flip side, you've resigned yourself to the idea that life-altering, Sisyphean college loans are inevitable. Both those attitudes might need to be adjusted.

This chapter is about educating you, the parent, with smart saving strategies, shrewd financial aid moves, and straightforward ways to talk to your kid.

A few years ago, I spoke with a young couple who had just graduated from college with a student debt load of about $100,000 each—much higher than the average, which is currently around $37,000. Each was a talented artist with a desire to be a children's book illustrator. Though they felt they had received a great arts education, they were seriously stressed out about how they would be able to afford to start a life together with that much debt. I couldn't help but wonder, Where had the grown-ups been? What if, for instance, someone had had a 20-minute conversation with each of them and explained what $100,000 in loans would mean back when visions of hat-wearing cats and inquisitive dinosaurs were dancing in their heads? Maybe they would have done some research and found an in-state public university or a different private college that offered more generous financial aid. Or perhaps they could have looked harder for grants and scholarships. I'm hoping that if you follow the advice in this chapter, your kid won't end up like them.

One final note: For the majority of this book, I've given you specific lessons to pass along to your children. This chapter is a bit different: I'm mainly talking to you, the parents. Listen up.

PRESCHOOL

Ensuring that your kid is on the path to higher education is less about piping Mozart's piano concertos on an endless loop into his crib and more about opening a college savings account.

- **Start saving for your kid's college when he's born, and when he's a toddler, tell him what you're doing.** This might sound ridiculous. After all, your little one can't even tell a dime from a quarter. But here's the thing: Children with savings accounts earmarked for college are much more likely to actually go to college than kids who don't have such accounts. This is the case for kids from all income levels, though it's most pronounced in families that earn $50,000 or less. Those families are at least three times as likely to send a kid to college if they start a modest college savings account when their child is young, according to research out of the University of Kansas. The idea is that simply having college savings accounts can be very influential in shaping the aspirations of kids (and parents). The evidence is so strong that San Francisco has established a program for its public schools that gives every kindergartner a college savings account with at least $50 in it. And this trend is catching on elsewhere in the country.

One good option is a 529 plan (see the box below), which allows you to save money without having to pay federal tax on the earnings as long as you use it for education expenses. You'll want to open this account in your name, not your kid's name, and I'll go into the rationale for that in a moment. Once you do, see if there's a way to automate a monthly contribution, either through your employer's payroll office or by having money drafted from your bank account, and watch your kid's college nest egg start to add up.

3 Ways to Save for College

When you're saving for college, you want to be smart about it. So here's a Savings 101 rundown.

1 **529 College Savings Plans.** A state-sponsored 529 plan is likely to be the best place to save for your kid's college education because it allows you to invest money without having to pay federal tax on the earnings, provided that you use it for college expenses. You can contribute to a 529 no matter how high your income.

Almost every state offers at least one 529 plan, and if you don't like your own state's choices, you can select one from another state. But there may be state and local tax benefits for staying in state, so check. (In Michigan, for instance, you can deduct up to $5,000 of 529 contributions per year—$10,000 if you're a married couple—when computing your state income tax.)

Some states offer a choice of an "advisor-sold" (sometimes called a "broker-sold") or a "direct-sold" plan. Definitely go with the direct-sold 529, since it will charge much lower fees. For instance, New York's broker-sold option could cost an investor 13 times more—which over the years could mean thousands in extra fees. And in general, as discussed in Chapter 7, investments that charge high fees do no better than those that don't. For a list of all the 529s as well as tips for choosing one see Savingforcollege.com.

Some states and one group of private colleges offer a type of 529 known as a prepaid tuition plan, which in theory enables you to lock in tuition at a particular college at or near today's prices, with the promise that you'll be able to afford it in the future even if costs soar. The guarantees are not always ironclad—and there have been cases of plans sometimes failing on promises. Another issue is that your kid might not want to go to the schools in the plan, or might not get in, and then you will have to decide whether to change the beneficiary to another kid, roll the money over to another education account, or withdraw it and face tax penalties if it's not used for education purposes.

Open a 529 plan when your child is born, and choose mainly stock investments like index funds. Although stock funds can be volatile, it's the best guess of experts that over the long run, despite the ups and downs, stocks will do well. As your kid nears high school, you'll want to gradually shift to safer investments such as money market funds. That way you won't run the risk that the stock market tanks just as it's time to pay tuition. Some 529s offer age-based portfolios that shift the mix of investments to safer choices over time, as college draws near. These funds can be good options, but make sure that the fees aren't higher than those of the index funds offered by your 529. One thing to note: Under federal rules, you can move money into different 529 investments only two times a year.

2   **Coverdell Education Savings Accounts.** Like 529s, Coverdells are investment savings accounts that allow your money to grow without your having to pay federal tax on the earnings, as long as that money is used for education purposes. These are fine, but you can put away only $2,000 per year in a Coverdell if you earn less than $110,000 as a single person or $220,000 as a married couple. The one big benefit of Coverdells: They also can be used to save for elementary or high school expenses, such as computers, after-school programs, tutoring, and even private school tuition.

3 **Custodial Accounts (UGMAs/UTMAs).** These accounts allow you to save money in your kid's name and reap the rewards of a child's lower tax bracket for some of that savings. Available at banks and mutual fund companies, UGMAs (Uniform Gifts to Minors Act) or UTMAs (Uniform Transfers to Minors Act) aren't just for college savings but also can be used to pay for just about any expense related to your child. (Some states call them UGMAs and others UTMAs, but they're equally unwieldy acronyms for the same concept. Po*tay*to, po*tah*to.)

Unlike 529s and Coverdells, these accounts don't let the money in them grow completely free from federal tax. In a given year, the first $1,050 of income typically is tax exempt, and the next $1,050 is taxed at your kid's tax rate (which is generally very low or nothing). Any income over that is taxed at your tax rate if the child is under age 19 (or is a full-time student under age 24).

The biggest downside: Your kid controls the money as soon as he turns 18 (21 in some states). That means you'll have to trust that the money you've carefully squirreled away for his room and board won't be used for a sweet, sweet Maserati. You also can't transfer the money to a new custodial account for another one of your kids who might need it for college. Another drawback is that these plans aren't good for families anticipating any financial aid, since colleges count money in an UGMA/UTMA as an asset your child owns and expect 20% of it to go toward college costs. That'll mean less aid for your family overall.

ELEMENTARY SCHOOL

Pressuring your kid to shoot for your alma mater at this age is crazy. But it's not too soon to prepare her for higher education in general.

- **Capitalize on your kid's interests to get her excited about college.** When Angela's daughter was in second grade, she noticed that her kid seemed oddly obsessed with blood. She was eager to bandage up any nick or cut on her family members and was enthralled by surgical close-ups on her favorite medical show. Although Angela found her kid's interest unusual, not to mention a bit creepy, she decided to talk to her about medicine as a career, how much good doctors can do in the world, and the college and medical school degrees required to be an MD. Her daughter, now in college, is premed, and Angela is relieved that she seems to be headed for a career in ER medicine, not serial killing.

There are all sorts of opportunities to create college-bound dreams in kids when they're young. If your kid loves animals, let her know that veterinarians need a college degree (as well as veterinary school) in order to take care of pets. If you move into a new house, talk about how the architect who designed it had to go to college (and probably grad school). You get the picture. You don't have to go into a lot of detail about the type of courses required for a degree. It's enough for your kid to know, at this age, that going to college is the surest route to doing lots of the cool jobs in the world.

MIDDLE SCHOOL

This is the age to start talking college. Just make sure you dial down any anxiety that you may have about the competitiveness of getting in—and the costs. Plenty of time to worry about that later.

- **Take your kid to visit a local college or your alma mater.** We all want our kids to find something to do that they love and can be successful at, and as long as it's in the realm of the probable—say, helping the world versus headlining at Madison Square Garden—a college degree is a definite plus. Visiting a college campus can get a kid excited about going one day and offers a great, even fun, way to talk about why college is important. (Have him invite a friend.) Explain that many jobs that used to require just a high school diploma now require a college degree. Case in point: A recent survey found that most people who currently work as executive assistants don't have a college degree (only 19% do), but 65% of postings to fill executive-assistant jobs now require that applicants have one.

If you loved college, talk about the upsides (an eye-opening professor, a lifelong friend, an incredible team experience playing a sport); if you would have done something differently (chosen a liberal arts path rather than an undergraduate business program, or found a smaller school rather than a giant state university), share that with your kid, too. If you didn't go to college and regret it, you can explain to your kid why. I've spoken to a number of people who are wildly successful in their line of work but never got a college degree and are wistful about what they missed, from knowing more about Aristotle or marketing to experiencing campus life. As I mentioned at the start of this chapter, on average, a person who completes college can expect to earn hundreds of thousands—even a million—dollars more than someone who doesn't. That's a nice point to drop along the way.

Bribes Can't Buy Good Grades

When my pals Arnie and Carolyn asked their son Cam's eighth-grade homeroom teacher how to get their smart but slacking kid to work harder at math, they were shocked at his advice: Promise Cam a PlayStation if he got an A. Though the teacher acknowledged it sounded ethically suspect, he said he had seen it work, particularly for middle schoolers.

Nearly half of all American parents with kids in school bribe their kids to do better in their classes. Moral questions aside, there's another big problem with bribing kids for grades: Research shows it doesn't work. Harvard economist Roland Fryer studied nearly 40,000 public school students in several cities and found that cash payments didn't improve math and reading test scores at all. Though he found a minuscule uptick in students' overall GPAs, it was roughly 0.1%, not a game changer. And I'd venture that the ethical downside and takeaway for students far outweighed that tiny bump in terms of the impact on their futures.

What hasn't been measured is the effect that bribes have on children's overall self-worth and their long-term performance. After all, a bribe can send a strong signal to your child that you don't think he has what it takes to motivate himself.

Another reason to forgo cash payouts for grades is that they can devalue the schoolwork your kid is doing. A famous psychology experiment by Leon Festinger and James Carlsmith performed decades ago revealed this counterintuitive finding: The more money people were paid to do mundane jobs, the less they valued the work itself. The psychologists concluded that lower-paid workers had convinced themselves that the work itself was inherently valuable, the rationale being: "Why would I have done it otherwise?" Those who were paid a lot assumed they were being highly compensated because the project was uninteresting and unimportant. The bottom line: Paying big bucks—or giving big prizes—to get the job done can backfire.

Of course, there are times when incentives can be effective. Professor Fryer found that offering a kid an incentive for the effort he puts in instead of the result you want works better. So, for instance, dangling the reward of the latest Madden football video game in exchange for your child's diligently completing his math homework for the next month is better than offering it in return for an A in algebra. This makes sense when you think about it: Rewarding a specific, concrete effort is a way to reinforce hard work, which is a major driver of achievement that is in your kid's control.

HIGH SCHOOL

The college admissions process can feel scary for both you and your kid. But taking it step-by-step and staying calm will help you both survive the process.

- **Have the college money talk starting in ninth grade.** It might feel like it's too soon, but starting this conversation early gives you and your kid a wake-up call. Going to college—and figuring out how to pay for it—is less than four years away, and beginning now gives you a chance to plan. The box on p. 189 explains how to get some estimates of how much your family will be expected to contribute to college costs. Note that this is very different from simply looking up a school's sticker price. These days, about four in five families receive financial aid (including low-cost federal loans). Getting a rough sense of the numbers—even though your kid is just a freshman in high school and the figures will likely change—will get the conversation going.

It'll also force you to think about how much you're willing and able to spend on college costs, whether you're okay with borrowing, and whether your kid will *have* to borrow. (Telling him that most of his peers have to borrow at least some money helps him know he is not alone.) The college money talk will raise some important questions: Should your family cut back on spending? Are there ways you and your kid could save more? And are there ways you can boost your income? There isn't one right answer. Some parents feel that if their kid gets into an Ivy League school, they'll do what it takes—meaning going into hock for years—to send her there. Others will do anything to keep themselves and their kids out of debt. Even if the very prospect of pondering all of this makes you sweat, staying factual rather than frantic is critical during these discussions. One bonus: This talk will also serve as a reminder to your child that grades in the freshman year of high school "count" for college admissions.

- **Realize that the Ivy League isn't necessarily the gravy train.** With admissions to elite colleges becoming insanely competitive, you might wonder if your kid will be at a disadvantage in life if he doesn't attend one of these superselective institutions. Two terrific studies from economists Alan Krueger and Stacy Dale found that, on average, kids who were accepted to an Ivy League college or other elite schools but ended up going to less prestigious institutions had salaries similar to those of the kids who went to the fancy schools. The same is true of kids who were rejected by these top schools but had the same SAT scores as kids who were accepted. There are exceptions. The economists found that kids who were Latino, black, or from low-income families, as well as those whose parents did not graduate from college, did get a salary bump from going Ivy. The economists speculate that that's because top-tier schools provide networking opportunities these kids wouldn't have had otherwise.

Your Step-by-Step Guide to Applying for Financial Aid

It's possible to write an entire book on the ins and outs of financial aid. In fact, many people have. Two guides to check out are Kalman Chany's *Paying for College Without Going Broke*, from The Princeton Review, and *Filing the FAFSA: The Edvisors Guide to Completing the Free Application for Federal Student Aid* by Mark Kantrowitz and David Levy. Get a copy of each. Beyond this reading assignment, here's a rundown of your best moves for the next few years.

- **9th grade: Get a sense of what colleges might expect you to pay.** It's impossible to know what college will cost you four years from now. But you can get a really rough idea by going to a prospective college's net price calculator, which you can find via collegecost.ed.gov/netpricecenter.aspx. These calculators look at your income and the number of kids you have in college, as well as family savings and assets, and spit out an estimate of what you'll be expected to pay freshman year. Although this number can be thousands of dollars off, and specifics will likely change by the time your kid applies, you'll get a ballpark idea of the cost of sending your kid to a particular school.

- **10th grade: Hone your financial aid strategy.** Time to roll up your sleeves and dig into the numbers to get a better sense of what your family will be expected to contribute. The financial aid forms you'll fill out during your kid's senior year will look at money you earned and assets you owned from January 1 of his sophomore year through December 31 of his junior year. Most colleges use a federal formula that takes into account factors such as your income, your savings, the number of children you have, the number of kids your family has in college, and so on to figure out your so-called Expected Family Contribution (EFC). Go to FAFSA.gov, select the FAFSA4caster tool, and answer the questions to generate your EFC as well as an estimate of federal financial aid you're likely to get.

    You may be shocked by this number, which may seem beyond what your family could come up with. And typically, a family will have to come up with thousands of dollars more. Here's why: In theory, colleges subtract your EFC from the total cost of attendance, and the resulting number is your "need." While some wealthy schools will meet a family's full need with grants that you don't have to pay back, some meet need with loans, and some simply say that they won't be able to meet your total need. What's more, some colleges use their own tailor-made formula to determine how much they expect your family to pay.

This is the time to be looking at a wide range of colleges and weighing potential costs and benefits of each. For lists of schools that are the most generous with financial aid, check out bestcolleges.com/features/best-financial-aid and *U.S. News & World Report*'s education resources (usnews .com/education).

- **11th grade: Do a realistic scholarship search.** Many parents have a secret fantasy that there is a perfect scholarship out there for their child, and all they have to do is unearth it. Sadly, that's rarely the case. The vast majority of money for school comes from federal and state governments as well as the colleges themselves, and your kid will qualify for it only if you fill out the financial aid forms during your kid's senior year—and every year of college. Even athletic scholarships, which many families hang their hopes on if they have a kid who's good at throwing things, hitting things, or running faster than other kids, are rare; fewer than 2% of students in a bachelor's degree program land any kind of sports scholarship at all.

  That said, junior year is a great time to see if there are any awards that target your kids' talents or characteristics and can bolster the financial aid money she might get from what's known as merit aid. Colleges and some state governments use this to recognize a student's academic, creative, or athletic skills. And grades that are above average for the schools your kid is interested in certainly can help. According to Chany, every one-tenth of a point a student raises her high school GPA can net her thousands in financial aid at the right school.

  Definitely don't pay for scholarship searches (they tend to be rip-offs), but do peruse StudentScholarshipSearch.com, Fastweb.com, and the College Board's scholarship search (bigfuture.org/scholarship-search) as well as the U.S.

Department of Labor's CareerOneStop (careeronestop.org/scholarshipsearch). If you're part of a military family, check out studentaid.gov/military.

Note: If your kid does earn a scholarship from a club, community organization, or contest, he usually won't be permitted to simply add that on top of the financial assistance he gets from the college. Instead, colleges replace the money they've offered your kid with the new money he is awarded. That said, many colleges will allow your kid's outside scholarship money to reduce the loans he is getting, which is obviously a plus.

- **12th grade: Fill out financial aid forms and compare aid packages from colleges.** I won't lie: Filling out the financial aid forms can be a tedious chore for families. But for the vast majority, it's worth it. The Free Application for Federal Student Aid (FAFSA) unlocks the bulk of the financial aid for which your kid might be eligible, from the federal government, your state, the colleges your kid is applying to, and many private scholarship services. It also will give you access to low-interest federal student loans. Fill out the form as soon as possible once it's released on October 1 of your kid's senior year.

  Some schools require additional financial aid forms. The most common, called the CSS/Financial Aid PROFILE, collects more-detailed financial information and is used primarily by a few hundred of the country's most selective colleges. Fill out all forms as soon as possible, since some schools and some states give out financial aid on a first-come, first-served basis.

  Once your kid has been admitted to schools and receives financial aid award letters from each, the work really begins. (I know, it's insane. But it needs to be done.) Financial aid offers are not standardized, but thousands of schools do use the Department of Education's Financial Aid Shopping Sheet, a format that attempts to make comparisons easier by putting all the offers in the same terminology. If the school your kid is interested in doesn't use the shopping sheet, use the federal government's Consumer Financial Protection Bureau's financial aid comparison tool (cfpb.gov/paying-for-college).

  For each college financial aid offer, calculate the net price. (See the ninth grade section above.) This is the difference between the total cost of attendance (including tuition, fees, room, board, books, supplies, transportation, and miscellaneous expenses) and the gift aid your kid is receiving (including grants, scholarships, and other money that does not need to be earned or repaid). This is the real college cost: the amount you'll have to pay from savings, income, and loans.

If you feel that the aid packages for your child's top choices don't provide you with enough help, try to negotiate with the schools' financial aid offices. (See how on p. 195.) By following all the steps outlined in this box, you will optimize the amount of aid you'll receive—and the choices your child will have.

- **Be leery of for-profit colleges.** Most colleges are not-for-profits, but a number of schools are run specifically to make money. You've likely seen ads for the biggest ones. Not only do these for-profit schools have high tuition—their graduation rates are abysmal. A government study found that it can cost between 6 and 13 times more to get an associate's degree at a for-profit school than at a public college. Students who attend for-profit colleges are less likely to graduate or to get a good-paying job and, as a result, are more likely to default on their student loans. If you're wondering if the school your child is considering is a for-profit, search the College Board's BigFuture.org or the federal government's CollegeNavigator.gov. And if it is, tell him it could be a bad deal.

- **Make sure your kid has a rock-solid plan if she's applying to less-expensive colleges with the intention to transfer.** To make getting a degree somewhat more affordable, many students consider the strategy of attending a dramatically less expensive school—say, a local commuter college—for a year or two with the goal of transferring to a more prestigious flagship public university or private college. This approach can definitely be a money saver, but your child needs to be supermotivated and focused to achieve this goal. Make sure at least a few four-year colleges that she's interested in will accept her credits from the two-year institution. (One study found that 14% of students who transfer from a community college lose most or all of their credits.) Also, she needs to know that the acceptance rate at some schools is actually lower for transfer students than it is for kids who are applying from high school. The GPA that she will need in order to have a shot at transferring in a year or two is available on many schools' websites. For instance, successful transfer applicants to Brown University have an average GPA of 3.8, transfers to the University of California, San Diego, have an average GPA of 3.5, and transfers to Ohio State typically clock in with at least a 3.2. So tell your kid to keep those grades up!

Insider Tips to Getting Money for College

With the complicated rules—and talk of tricky strategies—it's no wonder that most parents dread the financial aid process. And unlike the tax code, which has accountants to guide you, the financial aid system has few sherpas to help you find your way.

- **Don't save money in your kid's name.** If there's any chance that you'll qualify for financial aid, it's a bad idea to put college savings in your kid's name. The federal formula expects you to contribute up to about 6% of your assets and up to 47% (but often much less) of your income to college costs. Those numbers are more onerous for students: The formula asks for 20% of assets in a child's name and up to 50% of a child's income. So if you've saved $1,000 in your kid's name, the college may take up to $200—but only about $60 if it's saved in your name.

  If grandparents are eager to help, it's best to have them contribute to the 529 you've opened in your name (if your plan accepts "third-party" contributions, that is, and most do). If your kid's grandparents open a 529 in their *own* names, when they give that money to your kid at college time, schools will count it as income to your child, which overall means less financial aid.

- **Fill out the financial aid forms even if you think you're too well off to qualify for aid.** According to financial aid expert Kalman Chany, even if you earn more than $125,000, have a healthy 401(k), and own a home, there's a good chance you're eligible for financial aid. Factors including the cost of the college as well as the number of college-age children you have and whether money is saved in your child's name can make a big difference.

- **The sticker price of a school doesn't matter as much as you think.** What does matter is how much a school is going to expect you to pay after all financial aid is factored in. Two-thirds of students get financial aid in the form of grants or scholarships. So looking at the price of a school doesn't really help you get a sense of how much it will cost your family. For instance, an out-of-state public university such as University of Michigan or University of California, Berkeley, can end up being more expensive than a private college that has a lot more financial aid to dole out.

- **Pick a few financial safety schools.** A true financial safety school is one that your family could afford even without financial aid; a public university that's close to home will probably be one of your least expensive options. But beyond that, it's also good for your kid to apply to at least a few schools where her chances of getting aid money look particularly good. One question to ask the financial aid office: What percentage of a school's gift aid is merit aid, doled out based purely on a student's ability, such as playing a particular sport or an instrument, or some other expertise?

- **Read the fine print in financial aid award letters.** Just because a financial aid letter opens with the greeting "Congratulations!" it doesn't mean you should expect a windfall. I have a friend whose son got excited when he received a letter announcing his financial aid award from a small liberal arts school. On closer inspection, the $5,500 "award" was simply a federal student loan that his family would have to pay back.

- **Think ahead to maximize aid.** The amount of federal aid your kid receives is determined by the family finances you report for the so-called base year—January of your child's sophomore year through the following December. So you should take measures to decrease your net worth and income before that January 1. A couple good ways to do that? Use savings to pay down debt. And if a financial windfall such as a bonus is headed your way, try to receive it before the base year begins. One more thing to consider: If you've put any assets in your child's name, remember that 20% of that money will be counted in the Expected Family Contribution. You should move it into accounts under your name, where it will be assessed at a lower rate, which means more money for your kid's college. Of course, your family's finances will be reassessed each year you apply for aid, but the freshman year is key. You don't get a second chance to make a first-year impression.

- **Don't use money from your 401(k) or IRA to pay for your kid's college.** Not only will this jeopardize your own retirement, but it's also a dumb financial aid move. If you have an IRA, for example, you can take money out of it for education expenses without paying the usual 10% early-withdrawal penalty. But next year, the school will treat the money that you've taken out of your retirement account as new income and reduce your family's financial aid accordingly. The good news is, the FAFSA doesn't ask how much money you have sitting in retirement accounts. And though some individual schools do ask for that information, it rarely factors in to your aid package, as long as it remains in the account.

- **Financial aid is negotiable.** Although you need to do it gingerly, it is crazy not to at least see if you can get more financial aid from a school that your child is really interested in if the aid package falls short of what you expected or what you can truly afford. Make sure the financial aid office knows if there has been some change in your financial situation—such as a lost job, an illness, a divorce, or high dependent-care costs for a special-needs child or elderly parent—so it can rejigger your financial aid package. Always be honest and polite. And as Chany points out, financial aid officers aren't exactly raking in the big bucks—the median salary is around $40,000 a year—so don't cry poverty if you earn twice that much.

COLLEGE

If your kid is in college, congrats! Take a few breaths, give yourself a high five, and put up your feet. But just for a minute. Now your job is making sure that you and he can afford college long enough for him to get a degree.

- **Tell your kid to graduate from college in four years.** Just under half of students at four-year colleges earn their degrees in the traditional, uh, four years. But an extra year to finish means extra tuition, not to mention extra time during which your kid isn't earning a salary at a full-time job. Recent studies have put the average cost of an extra year of college at $68,000 to $85,000. Yikes! So unless your young adult has a really, really good reason not to, she needs to graduate on time. Prepare her for all the challenges that she and her fellow students will face that could put a crimp in their plans to graduate in four years. They include being crowded out of required classes (particularly at large public schools), falling behind when switching majors (which will require additional credits), losing credits when transferring schools, working too many hours at a job, or simply taking too few credits each semester. Insist that your kid discuss her course choices with a good advisor so that she is clear on the requirements for her major.

- **Come up with a college budget.** As a family, you'll have to decide what you'll cover and what your kid will cover with his own money—either from savings or from a part-time or summer job. (For more on working in college, see Chapter 3.) I've heard a range of parental monthly allowances—anywhere from $100 to $1,000—to cover everything from pens to movie tickets to haircuts. (And, of course, there are plenty of families that make their kids pay for these expenses themselves.)

  If you're going to give some sort of allowance, I strongly recommend coming up with a monthly lump sum and telling your kid up front that that is *all* he will be getting. If he blows it all on a big night out with friends, he'll have to figure out how to come up with the money for campus movie night. This lump-sum-and-nothing-more approach hands your child the responsibility for budgeting in a way he probably has never had to before. The amount needs to take into account both your own finances and your kid's expenses. Even if you have enough cash to cover all of your kid's expenses comfortably, limiting your patronage—and requiring your child to live within a budget—provides a valuable lesson. See the worksheet on p. 202.

6 Rules for Borrowing for College

1 **Accept that your kid will probably have to take out loans.** More than two-thirds of students graduate from college with debt, and on average they owe about $37,000. Since that's an average, it's skewed by a much smaller number of students who take on huge loans. The median number—closer to what most recent grads owe—is about $20,000. Either way, the reality is that your kid will likely have to borrow, either from the federal government or from private lenders. The key is to do it right.

2 **Do the math with your kid when deciding how much she will borrow.** I've heard various rules of thumb about how much a college student should borrow. For instance, financial aid expert Mark Kantrowitz recommends that a student not borrow more than she is likely to make in her first year out of college. Of course, you can't know exactly what that will be, but if your kid is majoring in art or engineering, you can find average starting salaries for jobs in those fields on PayScale.com, the Bureau of Labor Statistics site (BLS.gov), Salary.com, Glassdoor.com, and the salary search feature on Indeed.com (indeed.com/salary). Another excellent resource is the U.S. Department of Education's College Scorecard (collegescorecard.ed.gov), which provides information about how much a particular college's graduates earn. (Nationally, college grads earn an average of around $50,000 in their first year on the job.) Whatever you and your kid decide, the point is to consider your own situation. In the end, if you and your child feel that attending a particular school is worth borrowing more than that guideline, you need to talk about how she'll pay it back and what that might mean after graduation—for example, living back at home for a year to save money.

3 **Tell your kid to stick with federal loans if he possibly can.** If your family qualifies for financial aid, chances are the college your kid attends will expect him to take out federal Direct Loans. Also referred to as Stafford Loans, they are a good deal, since they tend to have low rates (recently about 4%) that are locked in, or fixed, for the life of the loan. Also, your kid won't have to pay them back while in school, and when he does repay them, he can choose from a range of repayment options.

4 **Let your kid know it is almost always better to avoid private student loans.** Because there's a limit to how much you can borrow in federal loans, your child might be tempted to apply for private loans offered by banks and other lenders. Private loans generally have much higher interest rates—some greater than 18%—except for borrowers with sterling credit, and they also have stricter repayment rules. Plus, the interest rate on private loans can be variable rather than fixed, meaning that it could rise much higher in the future. You as a parent will likely need to cosign your kid's private loan, which is far from ideal. If she has trouble paying it back, both of your credit scores will take a hit. Some private loans even require the borrower to begin repayment while still in school, so it is critical to understand the terms as well as the fees.

5 **In general, stick with federal loans yourself.** To help out with college costs, many parents look into borrowing. Federal Parent PLUS Loans have a fixed, relatively low interest rate that tends to be the best deal. Recently, it was around 7%. But there are a couple caveats to Parent PLUS Loans: Bad marks on your credit history might disqualify you. And since the Parent PLUS program allows you to borrow as much as you need to fill the gap between how much financial aid a student is receiving and the total cost of attendance, be careful that you don't overborrow and jeopardize your own financial health. Remember: Your kid has the option of choosing a less expensive school.

One exception: If you have really good credit, you might qualify for a private student loan that's a better deal than the Parent PLUS Loan. Check if the interest rate is fixed; remember, if it is variable, it could rise in the future. In addition to loan origination fees, check a loan's repayment terms.

6 **Talk to your kid about why he needs to finish school once he starts.** The student loan borrowers who are in the worst shape are the ones who drop out. They're four times more likely to default on their loans—which, to state the obvious, does very bad things to their credit. Your kid needs to know that taking out loans means a commitment to finish school, because without that degree, he probably won't be able to earn enough to make his monthly loan payments.

- **Shop around for textbooks.** Students spend an estimated $1,200-plus on textbooks and supplies every year, and one survey found that 65% of students have skipped buying at least one textbook because of the cost. Even if you can afford to foot the bill entirely, why pay $400 for a new textbook when you can rent it used for $200? (Yes, parents, that's how much a textbook can cost.) By getting your kid involved in shopping for her books, you'll be instilling in her the habit of shopping around for the best deal. Many campus bookstores rent used and new textbooks on a first-come, first-served basis. You can also rent or buy used from sites such as Amazon.com, Barnesandnoble.com, Half.com, IndieBound.org, and Chegg.com. Some college textbooks now come in e-book versions that can cost quite a bit less. If your kid does decide to buy, she can almost always sell her textbooks back to the bookstore, though she could probably get much more by selling them at one of the websites listed above.

- **Parents: Take advantage of college-related tax breaks.** Don't miss out on your chance to save money on your child's college costs when you file your taxes. The American Opportunity Tax Credit allows you, if you earn less than $160,000 as a married couple or $80,000 as a single taxpayer, to subtract up to $2,500 from the tax that you owe if you have a kid in college. This is particularly attractive, since a tax credit is a dollar-for-dollar benefit, which is much better than a tax deduction that simply reduces your taxable income. And this credit is $2,500 per student in school for each of the first four years of higher ed. Eligible expenses include tuition, fees, textbooks, and equipment. Also, as a parent, each year you can deduct up to $2,500 in interest on federal and private student loans you took out in your own name to pay for your kid's education.

YOUNG ADULTHOOD

The years right after your kid leaves school can be about starting a career or realizing she wants to change tracks and perhaps go to graduate school. This is also the time when she will likely be counting every dollar she spends while struggling to pay back her student loans.

- **If your child has student loans, he needs a solid repayment plan.** Don't feel you need to pay your kid's student loans. Instead, help him evaluate his repayment options. In brief, federal Direct Loans, the most common, go into repayment six months after graduation. That's why he needs to figure this out soon after he graduates. Fortunately, there are some great online tools that will make paying back federal loans more doable than it might sound. Make a copy of my four steps for repayment outlined on p. 88 and send it to him.

  If your kid was among the roughly 30% of undergraduates in a bachelor's degree program who had to borrow money from private lenders, he'll need to take additional steps to make sure he understands his repayment obligations for these loans as well. He should start by contacting his lender to find out (1) whether there is a grace period, (2) when the first payment is due, (3) what his payments will be, and (4) what repayment choices are available. Whatever your kid's situation, make sure he knows that he can't be late on a loan payment—ever—or he'll get slapped with late fees and mess up his credit score. The consequences really can be draconian. If your kid has a public-service-type job such as social work or teaching, he should check out the info on Public Service Loan Forgiveness on p. 90.

- **Do the grad school math.** If your kid wants to go to graduate school, it can be a good move: People with master's degrees might find it slightly easier to find a job, and they earn, on average, $11,700 more a year than someone with just a college diploma. But most people also emerge from graduate school with a chunk of debt—around $60,000 is typical, including undergrad and grad school loans. Remarkably, one in ten borrowers ends up with over $150,000 in debt. You don't need a PhD in number theory to understand how burdensome that can be.

  Of course, you also need to factor in the kind of degree your kid is getting. Someone with a doctorate in computer science earns a lot more money, on average, than someone with a bachelor's degree in that same subject. Though in certain fields, even a graduate degree doesn't guarantee you'll get the job you want. One study found that only about half of people who get a PhD from the country's top six graduate programs in English find jobs as tenure-track professors! Even a profession such as law, which once seemed a surefire path to a stable career, has seen some upheaval in recent years, including massive layoffs at some of the toniest firms. For a sense of what graduate degrees in different fields are worth, see Georgetown University's Center on Education and the Workforce at cew.georgetown.edu/valueofcollegemajors.

My recommendation: Don't pitch in for your kid's grad school if it will jeopardize your own financial security. If you can't contribute, tell her so. This will be a nudge for her to figure out if it's worth it to go into more debt to finance the degree. The federal Direct Loans and Grad PLUS Loans for grad students don't offer interest rates as low as some of the undergrad loan programs.

- **Tell your kid to get paid for going back to school.** If your grown kid decides to seek an additional degree or take some classes while remaining on the job, pass along these ways to possibly get some financial help.

  - **Ask his boss.** Many employers offer financial help to employees to further their education. An employer might be able to help pay for tuition, fees, books, supplies, and equipment, up to $5,250, without that money being considered taxable income. (To get a bit IRS-y here, there are limitations to this generosity; for instance, this tax-favored rule won't cover meals, transportation, tools, or supplies other than textbooks that you keep after your class ends or, in most cases, courses focused on sports, games, or hobbies.) If a company pays more than $5,250, the extra money is likely to be taxable income to you. There are exceptions, so go to IRS .gov and access Publication 970, "Tax Benefits for Education," for details.

  - **Deduct it on his taxes.** If your kid's employer won't pay for school, he might be able to deduct the cost of classes on his taxes, saving him hundreds if not thousands of dollars. But the rules are tricky. He can qualify for the deduction, for instance, if the course is required by—or will improve his ability to do—his *current* job, but not to get a *new* job. One example: If a math teacher works at a school that requires him to take a course each year and the school doesn't pay for it, he can deduct this expense even if he will eventually earn a master's degree from all these courses. He wouldn't get the tax break if he were a math teacher taking lion taming classes to eventually leave academia to join the circus. Again, see IRS Publication 970 for details.

Who Pays for What When Your Kid Goes to College?

Once your child has chosen a school, the financial aid is determined, and you're planning what to pack, it'll dawn on both of you that you need to come up with a reasonable budget. This can be tricky. Use this worksheet to write in what you expect to pay for each item and what your kid can expect to pay. It's perfectly reasonable to expect your kid to chip in for most if not all discretionary spending, such as snacks and entertainment.

Expense	Estimated Costs per Year	Parent(s)	Student
Tuition, fees, room, and board	Money your family is paying this year for college. (This will vary depending on your kid's financial aid package.)		
Books and supplies	$1,200 to $1,600		
Laptop and printer (probably onetime costs)	$1,000 to $2,000		
Travel to and from school for holidays and breaks (total of three round-trips)	Bus: $200; Train $450; Air: $1,200		
Food and snacks (outside of meal plan)	$50/week, or $1,800/year		
Toiletries	$250 to $350		
Entertainment	$800 to $1,250		
Basic clothes	$500 to $750		
Bedding, towels, hangers, and so on (onetime cost)	$200		
Gym	Up to $350		
Sorority/fraternity dues	$1,100 to $5,500 for sororities; $1,500 to $4,500 for fraternities		
Club/activity fees	Up to $700		
Birthday gifts/dinners	$350 to $600		
Haircuts	$125 to $325 for men; $200 to $350 for women		
Laundry	$125 to $200		
	Total		

– **Take a tax credit.** The Lifetime Learning Credit reduces your taxes by up to $2,000 per year. The full credit is available to single taxpayers making less than $56,000 and married couples who make less than $112,000 in 2017. You can claim this credit even if your program of study doesn't lead to a degree, and there's no limit on the number of years it can be claimed, which is why it's often claimed by grad students. It's one of the many lessons that, unfortunately, you won't learn in school.

- **Parents: Make sure your kid gets a tax break on his student loan interest.** As long as your young graduate earns less than $80,000, he should be able to deduct up to $2,500 from his taxable income in interest on both his federal and private student loans. (The interest paid, not the principal.) This is true even if *you* made some of those payments. Don't let him pass this up. One of the reasons the tax break is so great is that your kid doesn't have to itemize his taxes in order to take it. Tell him to look for a Form 1098-E that he will receive from his loan servicer. If your kid is in the 25% tax bracket and deducts $2,500 from his taxable income, that's $625 less he has to pay in taxes.

10

Financial Advice for You, the Parent

All together now with my money mantra: You don't need to be a money genius to raise a money genius!

But, Dear Reader, the reality is, if you're going to have the talk, you should do your level best to walk the walk. And in the same way that you probably tried to clean up your act after having kids—whether that meant easing up on junk food, getting to bed at a reasonable hour, cutting out smoking, or closing down the ol' meth lab in the basement—it makes sense to give thought to changing some of your bad money habits too. Not only will this make your own life better, but it will also set a great example for your kids. Think of it as the circle of financial life. (*Naaaaaants ingonyaaaaaama bakiiiiithi baba!*)

Of course, if you're like most people, the idea of putting your finances in order seems about as fun as tackling a year's worth of dirty dishes in one night.

It's an overwhelming, distasteful job, and you're not sure what unsightly horrors you're going to find. This chapter will prove that getting a grip financially doesn't have to be that bad. Even if you latch on to just one or two of these ideas, you'll have changed your money profile from that of someone who's given up to that of someone who's trying. And those small tweaks can really make a difference over time.

To make this process as painless as possible, let's approach this as if we're chatting over coffee—just you and me, two parents talking. If you're already financially savvy, we can zip through my recommendations over, say, a drink instead. Either way, I know you don't have all day, so I'll keep it short and sweet. Let's begin.

PROTECT YOURSELF, PROTECT YOUR FAMILY: GET HEALTH, LIFE, AND DISABILITY INSURANCE

If you're a parent, part of your job is to plan for what happens when things go wrong—specifically, if you or someone in your family gets sick or injured, or even dies. This isn't fun, and it can be stressful to ponder, but it's necessary. So gird yourself and get it done.

- **Health insurance.** This one is a no-brainer: You need to make sure that you and your children are covered. Practically speaking, even if your adult kid is on his own, you'll want to make sure he's covered, not only for his own health (clearly the biggest issue on the table) but also to protect your financial livelihood. If your child has a major accident or comes down with a serious illness and doesn't have health insurance, don't you think you'll go to whatever lengths necessary to get him the care he needs? Fortunately, as of this writing, federal rules say you can keep your kids on your insurance plan until they turn 26. (Some states allow them to stay on even longer.)

  If you're insured through your work, review your company's offerings to make sure that the plan you picked a few years ago is still right for you and your family, because your needs might have changed since you first signed up. If you're not covered through your or your spouse's job, you need to figure out how to get coverage. As of this writing, you can go to Healthcare.gov or comparison shop for a plan on a site such as eHealth.com, through an insurance agent, or directly from insurers.

- **Life insurance.** It would be a whole lot easier if we could all agree to rename this "income protection coverage," since that's what it is. If a family breadwinner dies, the people who rely on him or her financially get a chunk of money that is supposed to last until they are able to earn on their own. If your kids are already grown and can take care of themselves, and your spouse earns his or her own income, skip it. And despite what those heart-wrenching late-night TV ads say, you shouldn't buy life insurance on your child's life (unless his boy band just hit it big and now he's supporting *you*).

  If you do need life insurance, you'll have to figure out roughly how much your spouse and kids would need to live on if you died. Unfortunately, there isn't a simple formula. For instance, if your family is living on a single income because one spouse stays home, you'll need to factor in how much you'd have to pay someone else to cook, clean, and care for the kids until they go off to college. To help you crunch the numbers, use the life insurance calculators at basic.esplanner.com and 360financialliteracy .org/calculators/life-insurance-calculator, a service of the American Institute of CPAs.

  Your best bet is to go with a type of coverage called term life insurance. You can compare prices at LifeInsure.com, SelectQuote.com, and Term4Sale .com. Military veterans can buy life insurance at a relatively low cost through the U.S. Department of Veterans Affairs (benefits.va.gov/insurance). Also, if any family member of yours was in the military, you should check out the rates at USAA (USAA.com). These days, it's tempting to do everything online, but if you have any questions about a policy you're considering, don't hesitate to call an insurance agent or the companies directly.

Be forewarned: There are a slew of other kinds of life insurance products that insurers love to pitch because they are more profitable for them. You'll get compelling-sounding spiels from the so-called experts who'll sing the praises of "tax-deferred" investment returns and savings you get from whole life, universal life, and variable life. Ignore them.

- **Disability insurance.** This type of insurance receives little attention, but the chances of dying at your age are much lower than your chances of getting so sick or seriously hurt in an accident that you're unable to work for a few months. (I'm a barrel of laughs right now, I know.) Unlike workers' compensation, which you get only if you're injured on the job, disability insurance covers you if you can't work, regardless of the reason. Look for a policy that will replace 60% to 70% of your income if you become disabled. See if your employer offers some disability insurance (large companies often do) or allows employees to buy coverage through the company (which can be cheaper than purchasing it on your own). If you do need to buy your own policy, compare quotes from companies that specialize in disability coverage (there aren't that many), such as Northwestern Mutual Life Insurance (NorthwesternMutual .com) and MetLife (MetLife.com). Compare these companies' quotes with those you get at PolicyGenius.com.

Your Estate of Mind

There's no easy way to talk about this. But you need to get your paperwork in place in case the unthinkable happens. Take care of this now and, aside from a ten-minute yearly review, you can go back to thinking happy thoughts. Here is a quick rundown of the documents you'll need.

- **A will.** This document is an absolute *must*, but a shocking number of people with kids don't have one. A will dictates who gets your possessions, designates your executor (the person who will make sure your wishes are followed), and names a guardian for your kids. If you don't have a will and both you and your spouse die, a court will select a guardian for your young children, and their inheritance could be locked in an account that requires court approval for any withdrawal. (Note that wills don't cover certain assets, like retirement accounts, for which you have to name beneficiaries separately.) And pay attention to the names on any joint bank accounts you have that contain money you want to leave to your kids, since the other account holders could swoop in and take all the money when you die, depending on the type of account you have.

- **Durable financial power of attorney.** You can designate a person who is legally able to use your assets to continue to pay your family's bills, file your taxes, and manage your investments if you become incapacitated. Naming someone—like your spouse—to do this is crucial, because otherwise your family won't be able to perform basic financial transactions without going through a complicated and potentially costly legal process. Note: This person is different from the executor named in your will (though you can name the same person to do both things).

- **A living will and durable power of attorney for health care.** A living will lays out your wishes for end-of-life care and spares your family from making major decisions like taking you off life support. A durable power of attorney for health care empowers someone—typically a spouse, relative, or close friend and not necessarily an attorney—to make sure those wishes are followed if you cannot make those decisions.

- **A revocable living trust.** This isn't as necessary as the other documents, but it's something to consider. It lets your heirs avoid probate (the legal process of having your will declared valid), which can be lengthy and costly, and can be a good way to pass on your things to your kids. Get legal advice about whether this could be right for you, since there are creditor and tax issues to consider.

I recommend having a professional help you prepare these documents. For a list of local lawyers specializing in wills, consult the American College of Trust and Estate Counsel (ACTEC.org) or the National Association of Estate Planners & Councils (NAEPC.org). Simple wills generally cost under $1,000, durable powers of attorney can run a few hundred dollars, and a trust can start at around $2,000. (Prices may be higher if you use an attorney who specializes in estate planning, but I think it's worth it.)

You can prepare most of these documents on your own more cheaply, using software like Quicken WillMaker Plus or a site like RocketLawyer.com or Nolo .com. But the downside is that if you download the wrong document template or there's an error in the software or on the website, your family could end up having to spend money to untangle the mess. If you do go the do-it-yourself route, at least ask a lawyer to review the documents.

NO MATTER YOUR GOALS, TAX-FAVORED RETIREMENT ACCOUNTS ARE THE PRIORITY

Although personal finance books bombard you with advice on the many things you should be doing to get your finances into shape, one of the most important is to save as much as you can in retirement accounts. Start immediately if you haven't already, and max it out each year or get as close as you can. Here are your options.

- **401(k).** In this type of account, offered through most large employers, your money grows tax free or tax deferred (depending on the choices your company provides). 401(k)s often offer a matching deal: For instance, for every dollar you put in, your employer will put in a dollar, up to a specific percentage of your salary (often 2% to 6%). That's the equivalent of a 100% return on your money—a deal you shouldn't pass up. As of this writing, the maximum you can put away each year is $18,000, and if you're 50 or older, an IRS "catch-up" provision lets you sock away $6,000 beyond that. If that sounds impossible for now, contribute at least up to the match.

  Chapter 7 talked about 401(k)s, but here's a little refresher: There are two types. The most common is a traditional 401(k), which allows you to delay paying tax on the portion of your paycheck you put into it. Plus, the earnings on traditional 401(k)s are able to grow (without your having to pay taxes) until you withdraw them. This is the best option if you are near or in your peak earning years, because the tax break is probably more valuable now than when you retire and start withdrawing the money. At that point, your income likely will have dropped significantly, and you'll be in a lower tax bracket.

But if you're a young parent who expects to be earning much more in the coming decades than you are today, consider another type of 401(k) offered by many employers: a Roth 401(k). You'll have to pay taxes on the portion of your paycheck that you put in now, but since you're probably in a lower tax bracket now than you will be later, overall it's a better deal for you. Of course, you can't know for sure whether your income will go up or down over the years, so don't sweat it too much. Pick a 401(k) and put in as much as you can.

- **Individual retirement account (IRA).** Again, a quick review: If you don't have access to a 401(k), you need to open an IRA. As with 401(k)s, there are two kinds of IRAs—Roths and traditional—and your choice of which one to contribute to again depends on your income now and your expected income when you retire. Roths tax you now, but your money grows tax free for life. With a traditional IRA, you get to deduct the contribution from your taxes now, and your money grows free from tax until you withdraw it during retirement. For either one, you can contribute as much as $5,500 per year as of 2017. (If you are over 50, the annual cap is $6,500.) To figure out which one is right for you, use the handy Roth vs. traditional IRA calculator on Bankrate.com.

  There are income and other limits on who can invest in an IRA; you can find them at IRS.gov. If your income is too high to qualify for a traditional or Roth IRA, you can still contribute to a nondeductible IRA. While there is no up-front tax break, your money still grows tax deferred. For advice on how to get started investing in an IRA, see p. 147. And if you are investing in a 401(k), you might still want to put additional money in an IRA.

- **SIMPLEs, SEPs, and Solos.** If you're self-employed, you can sock away even more using a SIMPLE IRA, SEP-IRA, or Solo 401(k). As of 2017, these allow you to save as much as $12,500 in a SIMPLE IRA or $54,000 in a SEP-

IRA or Solo 401(k). For more details on these options, see irs.gov/retirement-plans or consult an accountant.

PAY OFF YOUR CREDIT CARDS

The median American household with credit card debt owes $2,300 on the cards. The average interest rate is 15%. Your goal is to get that debt down to zero. Paying it off is equivalent to earning 15% after taxes. There is no investment, other than a 401(k) with matching, that can guarantee that high a return. Put another way, when you don't pay off high-rate debt, you are basically hemorrhaging money. So stop the bleeding immediately by using cash you have to get rid of your debt. (One exception to this rule: Parents need to hold on to a bare-bones emergency saving cushion, which I discuss on p. 213.)

Using cash to pay off your high-rate credit card debt can feel unsatisfying. After you make the payment, you have little to show for it. But here's the thing: For every dollar you put into a savings account, you're actually losing more than you've saved if you're carrying credit card debt. That's because the interest rates on what you *owe* are generally much higher than the interest rates you *earn*.

Say you owe $10,000 on a credit card that charges 15% interest. And you also have $10,000 in a bank savings account earning 1% in interest. In one year, you'll earn $100 in interest from the bank. During that same period, you'll pay out $1,500 in interest to your credit card company. So you're looking at a loss of $1,400. If you use your extra savings to pay off the card instead, you'll earn no interest—but you'll also *pay* no interest. And, to state the obvious, it's better to break even than to lose money. That's why it makes sense to pay off your high-rate debt before starting to save. Otherwise, you might be accumulating dollars, but you are also paying out many more dollars and losing value overall.

To help ease the pain, try to reduce the interest rate you're paying right now. First, call your current card companies and ask if they can lower your rate. (Do this politely, and make sure to say you're looking into other, lower-rate cards.) If that doesn't work, you might be able to transfer your balance to another card with a low teaser rate that lasts for 6 or even 18 months (by which time you should have made a lot of headway even if you haven't paid off your entire balance). Before switching, check the transfer fee (3% or 4% is typical) to make sure you'll end up ahead. Look for low-rate cards on CreditCards.com and CardHub .com, and use the balance transfer calculator on Bankrate.com to help you figure out if the transfer makes sense. But you'll need to keep track of when that teaser rate jumps. If you haven't paid off your debt by then, think about switching to a new card.

SAVE IN AN EASY-TO-ACCESS ACCOUNT FOR EMERGENCIES

It's the unpredictable events—your child breaks an arm, you lose your job, your basement floods—that can scare the bejeezus out of a parent. Before you had kids, maybe you got by with some creative credit card maneuvering or borrowing from your own folks to cover unforeseen problems. But now that you're a parent yourself, you have many more obligations, and you just can't do that.

A survey from not long ago showed that nearly half of all Americans would have trouble scrounging up $2,000 to handle an unexpected situation. What was remarkable about this finding was that the people surveyed weren't simply saying that they didn't have $2,000 in savings. That wouldn't have been much of a shocker. Instead, many were admitting that they didn't have access to credit cards, other lines of credit, or even friends or family members who were flush enough to lend them the money. That so many people can't beg or borrow to cover a sudden financial need is disturbing, particularly if those people have kids. Such a state of financial fragility is tough when you're a parent.

To be prepared for unexpected events, you ideally want to have at least three months' worth of living expenses saved up. Six months' is better. And nine months, better still. The easiest way to establish this cushion is to spend the time to figure out your expenses—including your mortgage or rent, groceries, phone/ Internet, gas/electric, insurance premiums, and every other vital expense that you need to cover each month. Once you have your monthly nut, multiply that by the number of months you'd like to cover.

Don't get discouraged if the number you come up with seems big. It might take a while to save up the full amount, but keep plugging away and stash the money in a supersafe place like an online savings account or a money fund, even if you earn very little interest. Your goal isn't to make that money grow like crazy but to protect it so that it protects *you* when you face the true emergencies life brings.

INVEST IN INDEX FUNDS

Life is complicated enough, so when it comes to investing, go with the simple strategy. The good news is, the simplest is also the smartest. Whether you have a 401(k), an IRA, or both, your best investment choice is the same: low-cost index funds. Same advice goes for investments you make on your own, outside your retirement accounts. Low-cost index funds are your friend.

Here's my quick spiel: No stock investment offers you a guarantee, but in general, having stock in your investment portfolio is important because stocks have historically provided investors with a good way to keep up with inflation over time. Sure, there may be down years, but on average it's more likely you'll come out ahead. The best way to invest in stocks is to spread around your risk and buy a bunch of different ones.

The easiest way to do this is by investing in a stock index mutual fund, which pools the money of lots of investors and puts it into the stocks that make up a particular index. An index is simply a group of stocks that are meant to represent a particular slice of the stock market. So, for example, the S&P 500 index is made up of 500 stocks from many of America's largest companies. Index funds tend to charge much lower fees than other types of mutual funds, and the lower the fees, the more money in your pocket. Another way to invest in stocks is through index exchange-traded funds, known as ETFs, which tend to have even lower fees.

For more on index funds, ETFs, and where to invest, reread Chapter 7 and pick up one of my favorite books, Burton Malkiel's *A Random Walk Down Wall Street: The Time-Tested Strategy for Successful Investing,* which is a deep dive into everything you need to know about investing.

KNOW YOUR CREDIT SCORE, AND GET IT TO 700 OR HIGHER IF IT'S NOT THERE ALREADY

When you're a kid, the most important numbers to learn are your phone number, your home address, and, depending on your priorities, your SAT score or your favorite ballplayer's batting average. As a parent, one of the most important numbers to focus on is your credit score. The type of credit score used by most lenders, known as a FICO score, ranges from 300 to a perfect 850 and is determined by your track record of paying bills on time, how much you owe, and how long you've been using credit, among other factors. The typical score is around 700, and you want yours to be at least that high. (For more on what determines your credit score, see Chapter 4.) Just one late payment can make your score plunge more than 100 points. And generally speaking, the lower the score, the higher the interest rate you'll pay on loans. Lower credit scores can add tens of thousands of dollars to a mortgage, not to mention make it harder to rent an apartment.

To understand your credit score, start by getting a copy of the credit reports on which it's based. There are three major credit bureaus—Equifax, Experian, and TransUnion—and each keeps track of your bill-paying habits in a slightly different way. You can request your credit reports from each of these bureaus once a year for free at AnnualCreditReport.com. If you find mistakes (which, sadly, are more common than you'd think), like a credit card account that mistakenly shows a late payment, you'll need to notify the appropriate bureau. The links for each bureau: equifax.com/dispute, experian.com/dispute, and transunion.com/dispute.

If you sign up at CreditKarma.com, you can get a free credit score. This isn't your FICO score, but it will give you a sense of where you stand. Credit Karma also provides free access to your Equifax and TransUnion credit reports as often as you want. If you're planning to get a loan in the near future, however, shell out $60 to get your official FICO scores (at $20 a pop from each bureau) at myFICO.com.

You can raise your credit score by making sure you pay all of your bills on time—the most important factor. Also, increase your payments by putting more than the minimum toward your credit cards and other loans. (Even $20 more per month helps.) Another tip: Keep old credit accounts open even after you've paid them off. This might sound counterintuitive, but credit bureaus like to see that you have a lot of credit available to you (even if you aren't using it) as well as a long credit history. Also, ideally you shouldn't borrow more than 20% of your available credit. So if you have the potential to charge $10,000 on your credit card, keep your charges below $2,000. Finally, don't cosign a card for your kid or make him an authorized user on your account, because then you'll be on the hook for any wild spending he does. (Which, of course, he wouldn't do because your kid is perfect. I figured I'd mention it anyway.)

SAVE FOR YOUR KID'S COLLEGE— BUT BE SMART ABOUT IT

Few topics have caused parents as much agita as paying for their kids' college education. In Chapter 9, I told you everything you need to know. Here's the abridged version: Once you've put a big chunk of money in your retirement plan, you should start investing in a 529 plan. (See Savingforcollege.com to get started.) These plans allow money earmarked for college to grow in a tax-favored way. Tell your kid that you're saving for his education, because research shows that kids are more apt to go to college when they know that there's money being squirreled away for that purpose. And come college application time, make sure to apply for financial aid even if you think there is only a remote chance you'll get some money. You might be pleasantly surprised.

As I've said before, providing a good education for your kids is perhaps the smartest investment you can make to ensure that they have the best shot at a solid financial future.

Special Acknowledgments

The first thank-you goes to my parents. Educators by both profession and temperament, they taught me the value of a dollar while also imparting the lesson that money isn't everything. Now *that's* genius. Without them, I wouldn't be the person or the parent I am today. I love you both so much. And a big thanks also to my brothers, Perry and Kenneth, who learned the "Kobliner Way" alongside me back in Queens many millions of years ago.

Thanks also to my genius agent, Suzanne Gluck of William Morris Endeavor, who is as tough as she is smart and funny. To my dear friend and Simon & Schuster's fearless leader, Jon Karp: You're still the smartest kid in the class. To my editor, Priscilla Painton, who is a writer's dream and a fierce advocate for this book in addition to being a wonderful person. Also to Millicent Bennett for her encouragement every step of the way. Thanks to the supertalented Emily Oberman at Pentagram, who worked tirelessly to design such a fun—and beautiful—book. Plus, a bonus shout-out to Felix Sockwell, whose amazing line drawings inspired it all. Special thanks to Leslie Schnur, Francine Almash, Charles Ardai, Jessica Ashbrook, Marisa Bardach, Karen Cheney, Ariana Chodosh, Danielle Claro, Max Dickstein, Lynn Goldner, Marjorie Ingall, Jennifer Jaeck, Michael Kantor, Miriam Kobliner, Kathy Landau, Kyle Mehling, Alex O'Neill, Valerie Popp, Zachary Port, Eric Pretsfelder, Kaitlin Puccio, Jeffrey Rotter, Noah Scholnick, Kerry Shaw, Michael Spalter, and Julia Wetherell. Also to Sarah Courteau, a wonderfully talented editor whose astounding work made this book possible.

Extra cheers to Scott DeSimon for his ability to do everything and make it look easy.

Years ago, I asked my cousin Shana Passman how her and her hubby, Don's, four sons all ended up as such super-responsible, wonderful men. Her answer: Each time they faced a challenge as boys, she'd look them in the eye and say, "I know you'll make the right choice." I've tried to remember that advice with our own children because I believe it is true genius.

To Rebecca, who writes beautifully, edits me like no one can, and is ridiculously funny. To Adam, who started asking questions about compound interest (and most everything else) when he was three and these days can answer nearly any question we toss his way. And to Jacob, whose combination of intellectual curiosity and hard work engages and inspires all who meet him.

Finally, to my best friend and partner in life, David. You truly are a genius in just about everything you do. You are also the greatest guy in the world. I love you. Go Blue Jays!

Acknowledgments

As you might imagine, stories from dozens of parents and kids who were willing to tell me about their money experiences fill the pages of this book (though the names and some details have been changed). I thank those people for their candor and their trust. In addition, I drew on the work of hundreds of academics, researchers, and financial experts. I'm grateful to all of them for their inspiration and wisdom. If I have left anyone off this list, I sincerely apologize.

Numerous people contributed their time, opinions, and expertise to make this book what it is. In particular, I'd like to thank Jaison Abel, research officer and head of the Regional Analysis Function at the Federal Reserve Bank of New York; Roland Arteaga, president and CEO of the Defense Credit Union Council; Jerald G. Bachman, senior research scientist at the Institute for Social Research at the University of Michigan; Janie Barrera, founding president and CEO of Liftfund; Sandy Baum, senior fellow at the Income and Benefits Policy Center at the Urban Institute; Ted Beck, president and CEO of the National Endowment for Financial Education; Gary Belsky, author and former *Money* magazine colleague; Lewis Bernstein, former executive vice president of education, research, and outreach at Sesame Workshop; Jeanette Betancourt, senior vice president of community and family engagement at Sesame Workshop; Sherry Salway Black, director, Partnership for Tribal Governance at the National Congress of American Indians; Paul Bloom, author and Brooks and Suzanne Ragen Professor of Psychology at Yale University; Sarah Brown, professor of economics at the University of Sheffield; John Hope Bryant, founder, chairman, and CEO, Operation HOPE; Connie Burton, cofounder of the Speyer Legacy School; Stephanie Carlson, director of research at the Institute of Child Development, University of Minnesota; Kalman Chany, student loan advisor and president of Campus Consultants; Robert P. Chappell, Jr., author of *Child Identity Theft: What Every Parent Needs to Know*; Anna Maria Chávez, former CEO, Girl Scouts of the USA; José Cisneros, treasurer of the City and County of San Francisco; Annette Clearwaters, president of Clarity Investments + Planning LLC; J. Michael Collins, faculty director of the Center for Financial Security at the University of Wisconsin–Madison; Michael L. Corbat, CEO, Citigroup; Gerri Detweiler, author and head of market education at Nav; Ann Diamond, principal at Lighthouse Capital Partners; Kerry N. Doi, president and CEO, Pacific Asian Consortium in Employment; Angela Duckworth, professor of psychology at the University of Pennsylvania; William Elliott III, founding director of the Center on Assets, Education, and Inclusion at the University of Kansas; Roland G. Fryer, Jr., Henry Lee Professor of Economics at Harvard University; Amy Gallo, *Harvard Business Review* contributing editor; Robert J. Glovsky, vice chair and principal, The Colony Group; Ted Gonder, cofounder and CEO, Moneythink; Katherine Griffin, graduate student at the University of California, Los Angeles; Keith Gumbinger, vice president at HSH.com; Julie Heath, director of the Economics Center at the University of Cincinnati; Billy Hensley, director of education for the National Endowment for Financial Education; Tahira K. Hira, senior policy advisor to the president and professor of personal finance and consumer economics at Iowa State University; Jeanne Hogarth, vice president of the Center for Financial Service Innovation and former Federal Reserve Board economist; Karen Holden, professor emeritus of public affairs and consumer science at the Robert M. LaFollette School of Public Affairs at the University of Wisconsin–Madison; Cindy Hounsell, president of the Women's Institute for a Secure Retirement; J. Robert Hunter, director of insurance at the Consumer Federation of America; Samuel T. Jackson, founder, chairman, and CEO, Economic Empowerment Initiative; David Just, professor at the Charles H. Dyson School of Applied Economics and Management at Cornell University; Mark Kantrowitz, financial aid expert; Richard Ketchum, former chairman and CEO of FINRA; Moira S. Laidlaw, attorney with Shamberg

Marwell Hollis Andreycak & Laidlaw, P.C.; Lawrence M. Lehmann, president of the National Association of Estate Planners and Councils; Paul LePore, associate dean for student and academic programs in the College of Liberal Arts and Sciences at Arizona State University; Laura Levine, president and CEO of the Jump$tart Coalition; Martin Lindstrom, branding expert and author; Lillian M. Lowery, president and CEO, FutureReady Columbus; Annamaria Lusardi, Denit Trust Chair of Economics and Accountancy at the George Washington University School of Business; Kay M. Madati, executive vice president and chief digital officer, BET Networks; Lewis Mandell, professor emeritus in the finance department at the University at Buffalo School of Management; Greg McBride, senior vice president and chief financial analyst at Bankrate.com; Walter Mischel, Niven Professor of Humane Letters in Psychology at Columbia University; Rashmita S. Mistry, associate professor of education at the University of California, Los Angeles; Marc Morial, president and CEO, National Urban League; Nan J. Morrison, president and CEO of the Council for Economic Education; Deanna M. Mulligan, president and CEO, Guardian Life Insurance Company of America; Barbara O'Neill, professor and specialist in financial resource management at Rutgers University; Mike Piper, author of the blog *Oblivious Investor*; Carol E. Quillen, president, Davidson College; Addison Barry Rand, former CEO, AARP; John W. Rogers, Jr., chairman, CEO, and chief investment officer, Ariel Investments; Amy Rosen, partner at the Public Private Strategy Group; Mary Rosenkrans, former director of the Pennsylvania Office of Financial Education; Katherina Rosqueta, founding executive director at the Center for High Impact Philanthropy at the University of Pennsylvania; Charles Scharf, former CEO, Visa; Eldar Shafir, Class of 1987 Professor of Behavioral Science and Public Policy at Princeton University; Holly Schiffrin, associate professor of psychology at the University of Mary Washington; Carrie Schwab-Pomerantz, president and chair, Charles Schwab Foundation; Brad D. Smith, chairman and CEO, Intuit; Gene Sperling, former director of the National Economic Council; Michael E. Staten, director of the Take Charge America Institute for Consumer Financial Education and Research at the University of Arizona Norton School of Family and Consumer Sciences; Laurence Steinberg, Distinguished University Professor of Psychology at Temple University; Regina Stanback Stroud, president, Skyline

College; Michael Townsend, director, public relations at the American Bankers Association; Rosemarie Truglio, senior vice president of curriculum and content at Sesame Workshop; John Ulzheimer, credit expert for Credit Sesame; Douglas Van Praet, founder of Unconscious Branding; Kenneth Wade, senior community affairs executive, Bank of America; Senator Elizabeth Warren of Massachusetts; Carol Weisman, author and president of Board Builders; Jordan Weissmann, senior business and economics correspondent at *Slate*; Lisa Wright, director of The Hollingworth Center at Teachers College, Columbia University; and Jason W. Young, cofounder and CEO, MindBlown Labs.

Books for Further Reading

Oh, so much to read and so little time! Still, if you want to dig even deeper into some of the money topics discussed in this book, here is a curated list of some of my favorites.

All Your Worth: The Ultimate Lifetime Money Plan by Elizabeth Warren and Amelia Warren Tyagi (New York: Free Press, 2006). This no-nonsense deep dive into personal finance from Senator Warren and her daughter is a call to action.

The Blessing of a Skinned Knee: Using Jewish Teachings to Raise Self-Reliant Children by Wendy Mogel (New York: Scribner, 2008). This book helps parents of all faiths to instill gratitude and respect in their kids, and to avoid the perils of helicopter parenting.

Filing the FAFSA: The Edvisors Guide to Completing the Free Application for Federal Student Aid by Mark Kantrowitz and David Levy (Las Vegas: Edvisors Network, 2015). A step-by-step guide that demystifies this tricky financial aid form. (Free download available at edvisors.com/fafsa/book/user-info.)

Get a Financial Life: Personal Finance in Your Twenties and Thirties by Beth Kobliner (New York: Touchstone, 2017). My updated guide written for younger adults who need to know how to make their own financial decisions.

Grit: The Power of Passion and Perseverance by Angela Duckworth (New York: Scribner, 2016). The definitive book on a character trait that helps kids (and adults) succeed, by the academic who advanced research in the field.

Happy Money: The Science of Happier Spending by Elizabeth Dunn and Michael Norton (New York: Simon & Schuster, 2014). A collaboration between a psychologist and a Harvard business professor that explores how we can "buy" the most satisfaction in life.

How Children Succeed: Grit, Curiosity, and the Hidden Power of Character by Paul Tough (New York: Mariner Books, 2013). This look into the new science about the traits that help kids thrive is a great read for parents.

The Marshmallow Test: Mastering Self-Control by Walter Mischel (New York: Little, Brown and Co., 2014). A fun-to-read exploration by the professor who created the iconic marshmallow experiment decades ago and pioneered work on the importance of delayed gratification.

Nickel and Dimed: On (Not) Getting By in America by Barbara Ehrenreich (New York: Picador, 2011). A modern classic on the harsh realities of trying to survive on the minimum wage in the United States.

Nudge: Improving Decisions About Health, Wealth, and Happiness by Richard Thaler and Cass R. Sunstein (New York: Penguin, 2009). A fascinating analysis of how small interventions can help you save money, avoid fees, and more, by two distinguished professors.

The Only Investment Guide You'll Ever Need by Andrew Tobias (New York: Mariner, 2016). A completely updated version of this accessible guide to investing. Still one of the very best.

The Opposite of Spoiled: Raising Kids Who Are Grounded, Generous, and Smart About Money by Ron Lieber (New York: Harper Paperbacks, 2016). A *New York Times* financial journalist uses fascinating case studies to shed light on how to avoid raising entitled kids.

Paying for College Without Going Broke by Kalman Chany (New York: The Princeton Review, 2016). A primer on how families can understand and get the most out of the financial aid process.

A Random Walk Down Wall Street: The Time-Tested Strategy for Successful Investing by Burton G. Malkiel (New York: W. W. Norton, 2016). This updated classic is a must-read for anyone who wants to learn more about investing.

Teach Your Children Well: Why Values and Coping Skills Matter More Than Grades, Trophies, or "Fat Envelopes" by Madeline Levine (New York: Harper Perennial, 2013). A clinical psychologist proposes a more balanced definition of parenting "success" in this easily readable guide.

Twisdoms about Paying for College by Mark Kantrowitz (Las Vegas: Edvisors Network, 2015). Pithy advice on scholarships, student loans, and other financial aid subjects.

Why Smart People Make Big Money Mistakes and How to Correct Them: Lessons from the Life-Changing Science of Behavioral Economics by Gary Belsky and Thomas Gilovich (New York: Simon & Schuster, 2010). One of my favorite books on the psychology of how and why we spend money, this is a fun and informative read.

Notes

Introduction

2 *parents are the number one influence on our children's financial behavior.* "7th Annual Parents, Kids & Money Survey," T. Rowe Price, March 2015. Soyeon Shim and Joyce Serido, "Young Adults' Financial Capability: APLUS Arizona Pathways to Life Success for University Students Wave 2," University of Arizona, September 2011.

2 *many of the habits that will help kids manage their money are already set.* David Whitebread and Sue Bingham, "Habit Formation and Learning in Young Children," The Money Advice Service, 2013.

3 *the majority of parents now tell pollsters the opposite . . .* "2015 Next Generation Reality Report," Haven Life and YouGov, August 2015.

3 *the difference between a life of economic stability and one fraught with financial worry.* Shim and Serido, "Young Adults' Financial Capability: APLUS Arizona Pathways to Life Success for University Students Wave 2."

Chapter 1: 14 Rules for Talking to Your Kids About Money

6 *researchers at the University of Wisconsin–Madison report . . .* Karen Holden, Charles Kalish, Laura Scheinholtz, Deanna Dietrich, and Beatriz Novack, "Financial Literacy Programs Targeted on Preschool Children: Development and Evaluation," La Follette School Working Paper no. 2009–009, 2009.

8 *should not go into details with their kids.* Jennifer A. Kam and Ashley V. Middleton, "The Associations Between Parents' References to Their Own Past Sub-

stance Use and Youth's Substance-Use Beliefs and Behaviors: A Comparison of Latino and European American Youth," *Human Communication Research,* vol. 39, no. 2, April 2013, pp. 208–229.

8   *kids mostly don't believe anyway.* "7th Annual Parents, Kids & Money Survey," T. Rowe Price, March 2015.

9   *more likely to owe $500 or more on their credit cards* . . . Adam M. Hancock, Bryce L. Jorgensen, and Melvin S. Swanson, "College Students and Credit Card Use: The Role of Parents, Work Experience, Financial Knowledge, and Credit Card Attitudes," *Journal of Family and Economic Issues,* vol. 34, no. 4, December 2013, pp. 369–381.

9   *One study found that children of divorced parents* . . . Dorit Eldar-Avidan, Muhammad M. Haj-Yahia, and Charles W. Greenbaum, "Money Matters: Young Adults' Perception of the Economic Consequences of Their Parents' Divorce," *Journal of Family and Economic Issues,* vol. 29, no. 1, March 2008, pp. 74–85.

10   *most of the time, kids ask their moms their financial questions.* "5th Annual Parents, Kids & Money Survey," T. Rowe Price, March 2013.

11   *the "math gap" between boys and girls has been well documented* . . . Roland G. Fryer, Jr. and Steven D. Levitt, "An Empirical Analysis of the Gender Gap in Mathematics," National Bureau of Economic Research, NBER Working Paper no. 15430, October 2009.

11   *kids say that Mom and Dad talk to boys more than they talk to girls about money* . . . "6th Annual Parents, Kids & Money Survey," T. Rowe Price, March 2014. "Charles Schwab 2011 Teens & Money Survey Findings," Charles Schwab.

11   *particularly subjects like investing.* Lynsey K. Romo and Anita L. Vangelisti, "Money Matters: Children's Perceptions of Parent-Child Financial Disclosure," *Communication Research Reports,* vol. 31, no. 2, 2014, pp. 197–209.

11   parents *think their sons understand the value of a dollar better than their daughters do.* "6th Annual Parents, Kids & Money Survey," T. Rowe Price.

11   *women still earn less than men* . . . Tanya Somanader, "Chart of the Week: The Persistent Gender Pay Gap," ObamaWhiteHouse.gov, September 19, 2014.

11   *have less money socked away in retirement accounts* . . . "The Pay Gap's Connected to the Retirement Gap," The Women's Institute for a Secure Retirement, WISER Special Report, 2015.

12 *comparing various aspects of our finances with those of our friends makes us less happy overall.* Andrew E. Clark and Claudia Senik, "Who Compares to Whom? The Anatomy of Income Comparisons in Europe," Institute for the Study of Labor, IZA Discussion Paper no. 4414, September 2009.

Chapter 2: Save More

17 *scored a whopping 210 more points, on average, on the SAT.* Walter Mischel, *The Marshmallow Test: Mastering Self-Control* (New York: Little, Brown, and Co., 2014), p. 24.

18 *A study out of the University of Pennsylvania* . . . Angela L. Duckworth, David Weir, Eli Tsukayama, and David Kwok, "Who Does Well in Life? Conscientious Adults Excel in Both Objective and Subjective Success," *Frontiers in Psychology,* vol. 3, Article 356, September 2012.

18 *a third of our ability to save money can be attributed to genetics.* Henrik Cronqvist and Stephan Siegel, "The Origins of Savings Behavior," *Journal of Political Economy,* vol. 123, no. 1, February 2015, pp. 123–169.

19 *inspired by the research of Walter Mischel* . . . Mischel, *The Marshmallow Test.* Brian M. Galla and Angela Duckworth, "More Than Resisting Temptation: Beneficial Habits Mediate the Relationship Between Self-Control and Positive Life Outcomes," *Journal of Personality and Social Psychology,* vol. 109, no. 3, September 2015, pp. 508–525. Catherine Schaefer, "A Different Perspective," *Play by Play: The DSCN Lab Newsletter,* no. 5, Fall 2014, p. 6.

21 *Research shows that even some six-month-olds* . . . Susan D. Calkins, Susan E. Dedmon, Kathryn L. Gill, Laura E. Lomax, and Laura M. Johnson, "Frustration in Infancy: Implications for Emotion Regulation, Physiological Processes, and Temperament," *Infancy,* vol. 3, no. 2, 2002, pp. 175–197.

21 *By the age of three* . . . Mischel, *The Marshmallow Test,* p. 56.

23 *Experiments with babies as young as five months* . . . Paul Bloom, "The Moral Life of Babies," *The New York Times Magazine,* May 5, 2010. Ariel Starr, Melissa E. Libertus, and Elizabeth M. Brannon. "Number Sense in Infancy Predicts Mathematical Abilities in Childhood," *Proceedings of the National Academy of Sciences,* vol. 110, no. 45, November 5, 2013, pp. 18,116–18,120.

23 *A striking study conducted at the University of Rochester* . . . Celeste Kidd, Holly Palmeri, and Richard N. Aslin, "Rational Snacking: Young Chil-

dren's Decision-Making on the Marshmallow Task Is Moderated by Beliefs about Environmental Reliability," *Cognition,* vol. 126, no. 1, January 2013, pp. 109–114.

25 *Research shows that by age seven* . . . Mischel, *The Marshmallow Test,* p. 57.

28 *in one poll, nearly a third of parents* . . . "6th Annual Parents, Kids & Money Survey," T. Rowe Price, March 2014, p. 19.

28 *One Canadian study* . . . Rona Abramovitch, Jonathan L. Freedman, and Patricia Pliner, "Children and Money: Getting an Allowance, Credit vs. Cash, and Knowledge of Pricing," *Journal of Economic Psychology,* vol. 12, no. 1, March 1991, pp. 27–45.

28 *Yet according to research from the United Kingdom* . . . Sarah Brown and Karl Taylor, "Early Influences on Saving Behavior: Analysis of British Panel Data," *Journal of Banking and Finance,* vol. 62, January 2016, pp. 1–14.

30 *Studies show that all of us spend more* . . . Dan Ariely and José Silva, "Payment Method Design: Psychological and Economic Aspects of Payments," Massachusetts Institute of Technology Center for Digital Business Paper 196, 2002. Drazen Prelec and Duncan Simester, "Always Leave Home Without It: A Further Investigation of the Credit-Card Effect on Willingness to Pay," *Marketing Letters,* vol. 12, no. 1, 2001, pp. 5–12.

31 *Research shows that chores are good for kids* . . . Research by Marty Rossmann cited in "Involving Children in Household Tasks: Is It Worth the Effort?" *ResearchWorks,* College of Education and Human Development, University of Minnesota, September 2002.

33 *Research shows that kids whose parents carry the full burden of college costs* . . . Laura T. Hamilton, "More Is More or More Is Less? Parental Financial Investments during College," *American Sociological Review,* vol. 78, no. 1, February 2013, pp. 70–95.

36 *As mentioned earlier, research shows* . . . Hamilton, "More Is More or More Is Less? Parental Financial Investments during College."

39 *a record number of young people are doing just that.* Richard Fry, "For First Time in Modern Era, Living with Parents Edges Out Other Living Arrangements for 18- to 34-Year-Olds," Pew Research Center, May 24, 2016.

Chapter 3: Hard Work Pays

41 *hard work, achieving personal goals, and enjoying the satisfaction that comes with the effort.* Sonja Lyubomirsky, "Happiness at Work," Amazon Exclusive Essay. *The Myths of Happiness* (New York: Penguin Books, 2013).

42 *and are more satisfied with their lives overall.* Angela Duckworth, David Weir, Eli Tsukayama, and David Kwok, "Who Does Well in Life? Conscientious Adults Excel in Both Objective and Subjective Success," *Frontiers in Psychology,* vol. 3, Article 356, September 2012.

42 *Grit matters even more than intelligence . . .* Angela Duckworth and Martin E. P. Seligman, "Self-Discipline Outdoes IQ in Predicting Academic Performance of Adolescents," *Psychological Science,* vol. 16, no. 12, December 2005, pp. 939–944.

42 *It's possible to teach your kids to be gritty.* Angela Duckworth, "Can Perseverance Be Taught?" *Big Questions Online,* August 5, 2013.

43 *research shows, most American kids aren't expected to do much housework.* Wendy Klein, Anthony P. Graesch, Carolina Izquierdo, "Children and Chores: A Mixed-Methods Study of Children's Household Work in Los Angeles Families," *Anthropology of Work Review,* vol. 30, no. 3, 2009, pp. 98–109.

43 *whether they participated in household chores when they were small.* Research by Marty Rossmann cited in "Involving Children in Household Tasks: Is It Worth the Effort?" *ResearchWorks,* College of Education and Human Development, University of Minnesota, September 2002.

44 *plants the idea that one day he will too.* See "The Job Song" video, part of Sesame Street's Tool Kit "For Me, For You, For Later: First Steps to Spending, Sharing, and Saving."

44 *might unwittingly be squelching their work ethic.* David Glenn, "Carol Dweck's Attitude," *The Chronicle of Higher Education,* May 9, 2010. Marina Krakovsky, "The Effort Effect," *Stanford Magazine,* March/April 2007.

51 *about 3 million Americans earn $7.25 an hour or less.* "Characteristics of Minimum Wage Workers, 2014," *BLS Reports,* Report 1054, April 2015.

53 *working a few hours a week might even boost GPA slightly.* John Robert Warren, Paul LePore, and Robert D. Mare, "Employment During High School: Consequences for Students' Grades in Academic Courses," *American Educational Research Journal,* vol. 37, no. 4, Winter 2000, pp. 943–969.

53 *high school students spent less time—49 fewer minutes—doing homework . . .*

Charlene Marie Kalenkoski and Sabrina Wulff Pabilonia, "Time to Work or Time to Play: The Effect of Student Employment on Homework, Sleep, and Screen Time," Bureau of Labor Statistics, Working Paper 450, October 2011, p. 22.

53 *three out of four American 15-year-olds lack the skills to decipher a pay stub.* Beth Kobliner, "Start Early to Raise Money-Savvy Kids," *The Wall Street Journal,* July 27, 2014. "Programme for International Student Assessment (PISA) Results from PISA 2012 Financial Literacy," Organisation for Economic Co-operation and Development, September 2014.

57 *teens are more stressed out in high school than ever before.* J. H. Pryor, S. Hurtado, L. DeAngelo, L. Palucki Blake, and S. Tran, "The American Freshman: National Norms Fall 2010," Higher Education Research Institute at UCLA, January 2011. Taylor Clark, "It's Not the Job Market," Slate.com, January 31, 2011.

57 *your kid's grades will likely start to suffer.* Jerald G. Bachman, Patrick M. O'Malley, Peter Freedman-Doan, and Jeremy Staff, "Adolescent Work Intensity, School Performance, and Substance Use: Links Vary by Race/Ethnicity and Socioeconomic Status," *Developmental Psychology,* vol. 49, no. 11, 2013, pp. 2,125–2,134. Kalenkoski and Wulff Pabilonia, "Time to Work or Time to Play." Jeremy Staff, John E. Schulenberg, and Jerald G. Bachman, "Adolescent Work Intensity, School Performance, and Academic Engagement," *Sociology of Education,* vol. 83, no. 3, July 2010, pp. 183–200.

58 *more likely to drop out of high school.* John Robert Warren and Emily Forrest Cataldi, "A Historical Perspective on High School Students' Paid Employment and Its Association with High School Dropout," *Sociological Forum,* vol. 21, no. 1, March 2006, pp. 113–143. Ralph B. McNeal, Jr., "Labor Market Effects on Dropping Out of High School: Variation by Gender, Race, and Employment Status," *Youth & Society,* vol. 43, no. 1, 2011, pp. 305–332.

58 *has dubbed "premature affluence."* Jerald G. Bachman, "Premature Affluence: Do High School Students Earn Too Much?" *Economic Outlook USA,* vol. 10, no. 3, Summer 1983, pp. 64–67.

59 *Interestingly, this trend didn't hold for students with off-campus jobs.* Gary R. Pike, George D. Kuh, and Ryan Massa-McKinley, "First-Year Students' Employment, Engagement, and Academic Achievement: Untangling the Relationship Between Work and Grades," *NASPA Journal,* vol. 45, no. 4, 2008, pp. 560–582.

59 *feel more invested in their education because they* are *more invested finan-cially.* Laura T. Hamilton, "More Is More or More Is Less? Parental Financial Investments During College," *American Sociological Review,* vol. 78, no. 1, February 2013, pp. 70–95.

59 *might have to settle for an unpaid gig* . . . Phil Gardner, *Recruiting Trends 2014-15,* Collegiate Employment Research Institute, Michigan State University.

60 *nearly 40% of unpaid interns do.* Melissa Schorr, "The Revolt of the Unpaid Intern," *Boston Globe,* January 12, 2014. Phil Gardner, "Reaction on Campus to the Unpaid Internship Controversy," Collegiate Employment Research Institute, Michigan State University, 2012.

60 *the majority of students don't take advantage of them* . . . "Voice of the Graduate," McKinsey & Company, May 2013.

63 *exploited for the free labor they provide.* Tovia Smith, "Unpaid No More: Interns Win Major Court Battle," *All Things Considered,* June 13, 2013.

63 *Negotiate—but do it wisely.* Amy Gallo, "Setting the Record Straight on Negotiating Your Salary," *Harvard Business Review,* March 9, 2015.

63 *recent female college grads earn, on average, 7% less than male peers* . . . Christianne Corbett and Catherine Hill, "Graduating to a Pay Gap: The Earnings of Women and Men One Year After College Graduation," American Association of University Women, 2012. Jenna Johnson, "One Year out of College, Women Already Paid Less Than Men, Report Finds," *The Washington Post,* October 24, 2012.

64 *which are the equivalent of roughly 30% of the average person's salary.* "Employer Costs for Employee Compensation," Bureau of Labor Statistics, June 2016.

64 *roughly 70% of millennials picture themselves working independently at some point.* "Big Demands and High Expectations: The Deloitte Millennial Survey," Deloitte, January 2014.

64 *A full 50% close within five years.* "Entrepreneurship and the U.S. Economy," Bureau of Labor Statistics, April 28, 2016.

64 *before setting out on her own.* Michael Goodwin, "The Myth of the Tech Whiz Who Quits College to Start a Company," *Harvard Business Review,* January 9, 2015.

Chapter 4: Drop Debt

68 *In a recent survey, parents were asked* . . . "5th Annual Parents, Kids & Money Survey," T. Rowe Price, March 2013, p. 18.

69 *Researchers led by Duke University psychologist Terrie Moffitt* . . . Terrie E. Moffitt et al., "A Gradient of Childhood Self-Control Predicts Health, Wealth, and Public Safety," *Proceedings of the National Academy of Sciences*, vol. 108, no. 7, February 15, 2011, pp. 2,693–2,698.

72 *A famous MIT study* . . . Drazen Prelec and Duncan Simester, "Always Leave Home Without It: A Further Investigation of the Credit-Card Effect on Willingness to Pay," *Marketing Letters*, vol. 12, no. 1, 2001, pp. 5–12.

72 *In a nationwide study, kids who paid for lunches with debit cards* . . . David R. Just and Brian Wansink, "School Lunch Debit Card Payment Systems Are Associated with Lower Nutrition and Higher Calories," *Obesity*, vol. 22, no. 1, January 2014, pp. 24–26.

92 *Surveys reveal that this tried-and-true tactic* . . . Michelle Crouch, "Poll: Most Who Ask Get Late Fees Waived, Rates Reduced," CreditCards.com, March 8, 2016. Martin Merzer, "Poll: Asking for Better Credit Card Terms Pays Off," CreditCards.com, September 24, 2014.

Chapter 5: Better, Smarter Spending

98 *to reach our kids well before they can talk or walk.* Brian Braiker, "The Next Great American Consumer," *Adweek*, September 26, 2011. "Marketing to Children Overview," Campaign for a Commercial-Free Childhood.

98 *whereas the characters on adult cereals look straight ahead.* Aviva Musicus, Aner Tal, and Brian Wansink, "Eyes in the Aisles: Why Is Cap'n Crunch Looking Down at My Child?" *Environment and Behavior,* April 2, 2014, pp. 1–19.

98 *small children don't distinguish between ads and TV shows.* "Children, Adolescents, and Advertising," *Pediatrics*, American Academy of Pediatrics policy statement, vol. 118, no. 6, December 2006. Eli A. Rubinstein et al., *Television and Social Behavior: Reports and Papers, Vol. IV:* "Television in Day-to-Day Life: Patterns of Use," Surgeon General's Scientific Advisory Committee on Television and Social Behavior, 1972.

98 *portions of the brain "light up" when they are presented with a shopping spree*

scenario. John Tierney, "The Voices in My Head Say 'Buy It!' Why Argue?" *New York Times,* January 16, 2007.

98 *less happy with what we choose.* Barry Schwartz and Andrew Ward, "Doing Better but Feeling Worse: The Paradox of Choice," in *Positive Psychology in Practice,* eds. P. Alex Linley and Stephen Joseph (John Wiley & Sons: Hoboken, New Jersey, 2004), pp. 86–104.

99 *everything, including mood, memories* . . . Douglas Van Praet, "7 Unconscious Errors We Make When Buying Brands," *Psychology Today* blog, January 13, 2014.

99 *friends* . . . Based on a 2013 survey conducted by the American Institute of CPAs and Ad Council.

99 *and the weather* . . . Kyle B. Murray et al., "The Effect of Weather on Consumer Spending," *Journal of Retailing and Consumer Services,* 2010, pp. 512–520.

99 *tweens alone channel $150 billion of parental dollars annually to the brands they want.* Larissa Faw, "Tween Sensibility, Spending, and Influence," EPM Communications, October 2012.

100 *whether those foods were carrots or chicken nuggets.* Thomas N. Robinson et al., "Effects of Fast Food Branding on Young Children's Taste Preferences," *Archives of Pediatrics and Adolescent Medicine,* vol. 161, no. 8, August 2007, pp. 792–797.

101 *TV used to be the main way that advertisers tried to sell to kids—and it's still a big culprit.* Kristen Harrison et al., "US Preschoolers' Media Exposure and Dietary Habits: The Primacy of Television and the Limits of Parental Mediation," *Journal of Children and Media,* vol. 6, no. 1, 2011, pp. 18–36.

101 *increasingly, it's tablets* . . . Sacha Pfeiffer, "An Ad or a Show? Some Say YouTube Kids Blurs the Line," *Boston Globe,* April 21, 2015.

101 *and smartphones that push ads in front of their shiny little faces* . . . "The Mobile Device Path to Purchase: Parents & Children," Communicus, August 22, 2014.

101 *since they're often disguised as games or include some fun interactive feature.* Anton Troianovski, "Child's Play: Food Makers Hook Kids on Mobile Games," *The Wall Street Journal,* September 17, 2012.

101 *what one marketing study infamously dubbed the "Nag Factor."* Susan Linn, *Consuming Kids: The Hostile Takeover of Childhood* (New York: The New Press, 2004), pp. 33–34.

101   *more likely to hound their mothers to buy stuff that had those characters on the packaging.* Holly K. M. Henry and Dina L. G. Borzekowski, "The Nag Factor," *Journal of Children and Media,* vol. 5, no. 3, August 2011, pp. 298–317.

101   *zero screen time for children younger than two.* American Academy of Pediatrics, policy statement, "Children, Adolescents, and the Media," *Pediatrics,* vol. 132, no. 5, November 2013.

101   *whether the children had TVs in their rooms.* Amy Bleakley, Amy B. Jordan, and Michael Hennessy, "The Relationship Between Parents' and Children's Television Viewing," *Pediatrics,* vol. 132, no. 2, July 2013, pp. 364–371.

105   *Tweens spend more than $43 billion of their own money every year.* Faw, "Tween Sensibility, Spending, and Influence."

108   *participants consistently reported preferring the vino* . . . Hilke Plassman et al., "Marketing Actions Can Modulate Neural Representations of Experienced Pleasantness," *Proceedings of the National Academy of Sciences,* vol. 105, no. 3, January 22, 2008.

109   *and they're willing to pay 10% more for it.* Brian Wansink, James Painter, and Koert van Ittersum, "Do Descriptive Menu Labels Influence Restaurant Sales and Repatronage?" *Cornell Hotel and Restaurant Administration Quarterly,* vol. 42, no. 4, December 2001, pp. 68–72.

109   *order 20% more appetizers and 30% more desserts than people who order in person.* Vanessa Wong, "That Tablet on the Restaurant Table Will Make You Spend More," Bloomberg.com, September 18, 2013.

109   *very little on savings for future education.* Jerald G. Bachman et al., "What Do Teenagers Do with Their Earnings and Does It Matter for Their Academic Achievement and Development?" *Monitoring the Future Occasional Paper Series,* Institute for Social Research at the University of Michigan, Paper 78, 2014.

111   *explain in their book,* Happy Money: The Science of Happier Spending. Elizabeth Dunn and Michael Norton, *Happy Money: The Science of Happier Spending* (New York: Simon & Schuster, 2014), p. 52.

112   *who used cash spent less—sometimes half as much—as those who used credit.* Drazen Prelec and Duncan Simester, "Always Leave Home Without It: A Further Investigation of the Credit-Card Effect on Willingness to Pay," *Marketing Letters,* vol. 12, no. 1, 2001, pp. 5–12.

112 *using a credit card seems to numb that response.* Brian Knutson et al., "Neural Predictors of Purchases," *Neuron,* vol. 53, no. 1, January 4, 2007, pp. 147–156.

113 *Hearing classical music has been shown to make shoppers buy more expensive stuff . . .* Charles S. Areni and David Kim, "The Influence of Background Music on Shopping Behavior: Classical Versus Top Forty in a Wine Store," *Advances in Consumer Research,* vol. 20, 1993, pp. 336–340.

113 *when we see it in the context of a high-priced item.* "Let Them Compare and Contrast," Daily Blog, Program on Negotiation at Harvard Law School, January 25, 2011.

113 *from a National Geographic documentary about the Great Barrier Reef.* Cynthia E. Cryder et al., "Misery Is Not Miserly: Sad and Self-Focused Individuals Spend More," *Psychological Science,* vol. 19, no. 6, June 2008, pp. 525–530.

114 *spending in areas such as dining out and tech gadgets.* Based on a 2013 survey conducted by the American Institute of CPAs and Ad Council.

118 *The average cost of nuptials in the United States . . .* "Wedding Market Summary Report," *The Wedding Report,* 2016.

118 A Consumer Reports *survey found . . .* Tobie Stanger, "Get More Wedding for Your Money," *Consumer Reports,* April 26, 2016.

118 *Many foot the entire wedding bill.* Maggie Seaver, "Here's Who Paid the Most for Weddings in 2015," TheKnot.com.

119 *1.3 times likelier to divorce than were a couple who had paid between $500 and $2,000 . . .* Andrew Francis-Tan and Hugo Mialon, "'A Diamond Is Forever' and Other Fairy Tales: The Relationship between Wedding Expenses and Marriage Duration," *Economic Inquiry,* vol. 53, no. 4, October 2015.

119 *if it was described as a wedding.* "Businesses Hike Prices for Wedding Bookings," which.co.uk, June 16, 2013.

120 *having an over-the-top affair takes the focus off what's most important: the relationship itself.* Francis-Tan and Mialon, "'A Diamond Is Forever' and Other Fairy Tales."

Chapter 6: Get Insured

122 *The reason we need health insurance . . .* Nicole Dussault, Maxim Pinkovskiy, and Basit Zafar, "Is Health Insurance Good for Your Financial Health?" *Liberty Street Economics,* Federal Reserve Bank of New York, June 6, 2016.

127 *adding him to your policy will likely at least double your premiums* . . . Nick DiUlio, "Teen Drivers: Getting Car Insurance for Young Drivers Can Double Your Cost," InsuranceQuotes.com, July 31, 2013.

128 *a half pack a day—the national average for young smokers* . . . Lydia Saad, "U.S. Smoking Rate Still Coming Down," Gallup, 2008.

Chapter 7: The Plain Truth About Investing

142 *A few years ago, the* New York Times *ran a story* . . . Alan Feuer, "Thousands Later, He Sees Lottery's Cruelty Up Close," *New York Times,* August 21, 2008.

146 *A recent North Carolina State University and University of Texas study* . . . Lynsey K. Romo and Anita L. Vangelisti, "Money Matters: Children's Perceptions of Parent-Child Financial Disclosure," *Communication Research Reports,* vol. 31, no. 2, 2014, pp. 197–209.

146 *In a poll of people between the ages of 22 and 35* . . . "Wells Fargo Survey: Majority of Millennials Say They Won't Ever Accumulate $1 Million," Wells Fargo, August 3, 2016.

148 *Research shows that, on average, those funds* . . . Ben Johnson, Thomas Boccellari, Alex Bryan, Michael Rawson, "Morningstar's Active/Passive Barometer: A New Yardstick for an Old Debate," *Morningstar Manager Research,* June 2015.

149 *nearly half of 18- to 29-year-old investors* . . . Michael Cohn, "Madoff Who? Survey Reveals Shocking Ignorance of Bernie," *Accounting Today,* May 15, 2014.

149 *Princeton University professor Burton Malkiel points out shrewdly* . . . Burton Malkiel, *A Random Walk Down Wall Street: The Time-Tested Strategy for Successful Investing* (New York: W. W. Norton, 2016), pp. 258–259.

150 *Recent studies have found that young people* . . . Morley Winograd and Michael Hais, "How Millennials Could Upend Wall Street and Corporate America," Governance Studies at Brookings Institution research paper, May 2014, pp. 5–6.

152 *researchers conducted a study at Stanford demonstrating* . . . Hal E. Hershfield et al., "Increasing Saving Behavior Through Age-Progressed Renderings of the Future Self," *Journal of Marketing Research,* vol. 48, no. SPL, November 2011, pp. S23–S37.

153 *Ryan Cooper, a young business reporter at* The Week . . . "Confessions of a Millennial Who Hasn't Invested a Dime in Stocks," *The Week,* May 19, 2014.

154 *According to a recent National Bureau of Economic Research study* ... Robert L. Clark, Annamaria Lusardi, and Olivia S. Mitchell, "Financial Knowledge and 401(k) Investment Performance," National Bureau of Economic Research, Working Paper no. 20137, May 2014.

155 *Put your money in a stock index fund (Warren Buffett's a big fan of these)* ... Victor Reklaitis, "Warren Buffett's Investing Tip for LeBron James: Stick with an Index Fund," *MarketWatch,* March 2, 2015.

155 *one study found that in a large group of investors* ... Brad M. Barber and Terrance Odean, "The Behavior of Individual Investors," *Social Science Research Network,* September 7, 2011.

158 *two behavioral economists* ... Richard Thaler and Shlomo Benartzi, "Save More Tomorrow: Using Behavioral Economics to Increase Employee Savings," *Journal of Political Economy,* vol. 112, no. 1, 2004, pp. S164–S187.

Chapter 8: Give Back

160 *Research shows that charitable giving* ... Christian Smith and Hilary Davidson, *The Paradox of Generosity: Giving We Receive, Grasping We Lose* (New York: Oxford University Press, 2014).

160 *particularly when it's voluntary rather than mandatory* ... William T. Harbaugh, Ulrich Mayr, and Daniel R. Burghart, "Neural Responses to Taxation and Voluntary Giving Reveal Motives for Charitable Donations," *Science,* vol. 316, no. 5,831, June 15, 2007, pp. 1,622–1,625.

160 *A Harvard Graduate School of Education survey* ... Rick Weissbourd, Stephanie Jones, Trisha Ross Anderson, Jennifer Kahn, and Mark Russell, "The Children We Mean to Raise: The Real Messages Adults Are Sending About Values," Making Caring Common Project, Harvard Graduate School of Education, 2014.

161 *by age four, they are developmentally ready* ... Paul Bloom, *Just Babies: The Origins of Good and Evil* (New York: Crown Publishers, 2013), p. 54.

161 *recommends that parents ask* ... Carol Weisman, *Raising Charitable Children* (St. Louis: F. E. Robbins & Sons Press, 2008), pp. 29–38.

162 *Psychologists at the University of British Columbia found* ... Lara B. Aknin, J. Kiley Hamlin, and Elizabeth W. Dunn, "Giving Leads to Happiness in Young Children," *PLoS ONE,* vol. 7, no. 6, June 14, 2012.

163 *Studies confirm what fund-raisers have long known* ... Dean Karlan and John A. List, "Does Price Matter in Charitable Giving? Evidence from a Large-

Scale Natural Field Experiment," National Bureau of Economic Research, Working Paper no. 12338, June 2006.

167 *That's the surprising finding of a recent study*... "Women Give 2013: New Research on Charitable Giving by Girls and Boys," Women's Philanthropy Institute, Lilly Family School of Philanthropy, Indiana University, and the United Nations Foundation.

168 *One international study led by University of Chicago*... Jean Decety et al., "The Negative Association between Religiousness and Children's Altruism across the World," *Current Biology*, vol. 25, November 16, 2015, pp. 2,951–2,955.

169 *Think about what other people really need.* This discussion on efficient giving draws on the research and expertise of Katherina Rosqueta, founding executive director at the Center for High Impact Philanthropy at the University of Pennsylvania, who gave generously of her time.

170 *a study of nearly 600 Midwestern middle and high school kids*... Constance A. Flanagan, Taehan Kim, Alisa Pykett, Andrea Finlay, Erin Gallay, and Mark Pancer, "Adolescents' Theories about Economic Inequality: Why Are Some People Poor While Others Are Rich?" *Developmental Psychology*, vol. 50, no. 11, November 2014, pp. 2,512–2,525.

171 *According to research, teens who volunteer*... "Volunteering," Child Trends DataBank, December 2015. Edward B. Fiske, "Learning in Deed: The Power of Service-Learning for American Schools," National Commission on Service-Learning, January 2002.

173 *Research shows that schools with mandatory community service requirements*... Sara E. Helms, "Involuntary Volunteering: The Impact of Mandated Service in Public Schools," *Economics of Education Review*, vol. 36, October 2013, pp. 295–310.

176 *People who volunteer have a 27% greater chance*... Christopher Spera, Robin Ghertner, Anthony Nerino, and Adrienne DiTommaso, "Volunteering as a Pathway to Employment: Does Volunteering Increase Odds of Finding a Job for the Out of Work?" Office of Research & Evaluation, Corporation for National and Community Service, June 2013.

Chapter 9: Your Kid's Most Important Financial Decision: College

180 *college graduates earn around* $1 million *more*... Anthony P. Carnevale, Stephen J. Rose, and Ban Cheah, "The College Payoff: Education, Occupations, Lifetime Earnings," Georgetown University Center on Education and the Work-

force, 2011. Mary C. Daly and Leila Bengali, "Is It Still Worth Going to College?" *FRBSF Economic Letter,* Federal Reserve Bank of San Francisco, May 5, 2014.

180   *a degree is* still *worth* . . . Jaison R. Abel and Richard Deitz, "The Value of a College Degree," *Liberty Street Economics,* Federal Reserve Bank of New York, September 2, 2014.

181   *according to research out of the University of Kansas.* William Elliott, Hyun-a Song, and Ilsung Nam, "Small-Dollar Children's Savings Accounts and Children's College Outcomes by Income Level," *Children and Youth Services Review,* vol. 35, no. 3, March 2013, pp. 560–571.

185   *A recent survey found that most people who currently work as executive assistants* . . . "Moving the Goalposts: How Demand for a Bachelor's Degree Is Reshaping the Workforce," Burning Glass Technologies, September 2014.

186   *As I mentioned at the start of this chapter* . . . Carnevale et al., "The College Payoff."

186   *Nearly half of all American parents with kids in school bribe* . . . "AICPA Survey Reveals What Parents Pay Kids for Allowance, Grades," American Institute of Certified Public Accountants, August 22, 2012.

186   *Harvard economist Roland Fryer studied* . . . Bradley M. Allan and Roland G. Fryer, Jr., "The Power and Pitfalls of Education Incentives," The Hamilton Project, Brookings Institution, Discussion Paper 2011–07, September 2011.

187   *A famous psychology experiment* . . . Leon Festinger and James M. Carlsmith, "Cognitive Consequences of Forced Compliance," *Journal of Abnormal and Social Psychology,* vol. 58, no. 2, March 1959, pp. 203–210.

187   *Professor Fryer found that* . . . Allan and Fryer, "The Power and Pitfalls of Education Incentives."

188   *Two terrific studies from economists Alan Krueger and Stacy Dale* . . . "Estimating the Payoff to Attending a More Selective College: An Application of Selection on Observables and Unobservables," National Bureau of Economic Research, Working Paper no. 7322, August 1999. "Estimating the Return to College Selectivity over the Career Using Administrative Earnings Data," National Bureau of Economic Research, Working Paper no. 17159, June 2011.

190   *According to Chany* . . . Kalman Chany, *Paying for College Without Going Broke* (New York: The Princeton Review, 2016), p. 43.

192   *A government study found* . . . "For-Profit Colleges: Undercover Testing Finds Colleges Encouraged Fraud and Engaged in Deceptive and Questionable Marketing Practices," U.S. Government Accountability Office, August 4, 2010.

192   *One study found that 14% of students* . . . David B. Monaghan and Paul Attewell, "The Community College Route to the Bachelor's Degree," *Educational Evaluation and Policy Analysis,* vol. 37, no. 1, March 2015, pp. 70–91.

193   *According to financial aid expert Kalman Chany* . . . Chany, *Paying for College Without Going Broke,* p. xvii.

195   *And as Chany points out* . . . Chany, *Paying for College Without Going Broke,* p. 215.

196   *Recent studies have put the average cost of an extra year of college* . . . "The Four-Year Myth: Make College More Affordable. Restore the Promise of Graduating on Time," Complete College America, December 2014. Jaison R. Abel and Richard Deitz, "Staying in College Longer Than Four Years Costs More Than You Might Think," *Liberty Street Economics*, Federal Reserve Bank of New York, September 3, 2014.

197   *Mark Kantrowitz recommends* . . . Becky Supiano, "How Much Student-Loan Debt Is Too Much?" *The Chronicle of Higher Education,* September 3, 2014.

199   *one survey found that 65% of students* . . . Ethan Senack, "Fixing the Broken Textbook Market: How Students Respond to High Textbook Costs and Demand Alternatives," U.S. PIRG Education Fund and The Student PIRGs, January 2014.

200   *about half of people who get a PhD* . . . David Colander and Daisy Zhuo, "Where Do PhDs in English Get Jobs? An Economist's View of the English PhD Market," *Pedagogy,* vol. 15, no. 1, January 2015, pp. 139–156.

Chapter 10: Financial Advice for You, the Parent

212   *The median American household with credit card debt owes $2,300 on the cards* Jesse Bricker et al., "Changes in U.S. Family Finances from 2010 to 2013: Evidence from the Survey of Consumer Finances," *Federal Reserve Bulletin,* vol. 100, no. 4, September 2014.

213   *they didn't have $2,000 in savings.* Annamaria Lusardi, Daniel Schneider, and Peter Tufano, "Financially Fragile Households: Evidence and Implications," *Brookings Papers on Economic Activity*, The Brookings Institution, Spring 2011.

Index

About the Author

Beth Kobliner is a commentator and journalist, author of the *New York Times* bestseller *Get a Financial Life: Personal Finance in Your Twenties and Thirties,* and one of the nation's leading authorities on personal finance for young people. She has been a columnist for *Money, Glamour,* and *Redbook* magazines and a contributor to the *New York Times,* the *Wall Street Journal, Reader's Digest,* and *O, The Oprah Magazine.* Her writing also appears on *The Huffington Post,* SheKnows.com, and Money .com. Beth has appeared on TV, including NBC's *Today* show, ABC's *Good Morning America,* and CBS's *Early Show,* and on radio shows including National Public Radio's *Morning Edition.* She has been a regular contributor to MSNBC as well as to NPR's *The Takeaway* and *Marketplace.* In 2010 Beth was selected by President Barack Obama to be a member of the President's Advisory Council on Financial Capability, where she created MoneyAsYouGrow.org. The site, offering 20 essential, age-appropriate money lessons for kids, attracted more than 1.4 million visitors before being adopted by the Consumer Financial Protection Bureau in 2016. Beth graduated from Brown University and lives with her family in New York City.